M250 Object-oriented Java programming

Units 1–5
Getting started with objects

This publication forms part of the Open University module M250 *Object-oriented Java programming*. Details of this and other Open University modules can be obtained from Student Recruitment, The Open University, PO Box 197, Milton Keynes MK7 6BJ, United Kingdom (tel. +44 (0)300 303 5303; email general-enquiries@open.ac.uk).

Alternatively, you may visit the Open University website at www.open.ac.uk where you can learn more about the wide range of modules and packs offered at all levels by The Open University.

Alternatively, you may visit the Open University website at www.open.ac.uk where you can learn more about the wide range of modules and packs offered at all levels by The Open University. To purchase a selection of Open University materials visit www.ouw.co.uk, or contact Open University Worldwide, Walton Hall, Milton Keynes MK7 6AA, United Kingdom for a catalogue (tel. +44 (0)1908 858779; fax +44 (0)1908 858787; email ouw-customer-services@open.ac.uk).

The Open University, Walton Hall, Milton Keynes MK7 6AA

First published 2012.

Edited, designed and typeset by The Open University.

Printed in the United Kingdom by Latimer Trend and Company Ltd., Plymouth.

ISBN 978 1 4730 0311 8

2.1

Contents

Unit 1

Introducing objects

Contents

Introduction

Welcome to the first unit of M250 *Object-oriented Java programming*!

As the module title suggests, the emphasis is on object-oriented programming – writing software from an object-oriented perspective. Object-oriented programming is concerned with constructing computer systems out of interacting units of software, called objects. Objects know nothing of how other objects work, but they can interact (when a program is executing) by sending messages to each other. As you will see later, one of the most powerful aspects of object-oriented programming is that the code that produces interacting objects can be reused and interchanged between programs, so increasing programming productivity.

Programming in an object-oriented language requires more than just learning the syntax rules: it requires thinking in terms of the objects that will carry out the required tasks rather than in terms of data structures and algorithms, as might be the case in a non-object-oriented context.

The programming language you will use in M250 is Java. However, the purpose of the module is not to teach you the minutiae of the Java language, but rather to teach you fundamental object-oriented programming concepts and skills that will be transferable to any object-oriented language. Hence, while you will certainly learn quite a lot of Java, and write lots of program code, we will be concentrating on those aspects of the Java language that best demonstrate object-oriented principles and good practice.

The best way to learn any language is to practise using it. Learning a new way of programming is no different, so you will find that this module has many practical programming activities for you to carry out! In working your way through the module and engaging in all the activities you will gain a good understanding of object-oriented principles, and a solid grounding in the use of the Java programming language.

After a brief review of fundamental hardware and software concepts (Section 2), this unit introduces the basic elements of object-oriented software (Section 3) and presents a short history of the Java programming language (Section 4). In Section 5 you will begin to explore objects by engaging in computer-based activities.

Since M250 is an OU level 2 module, we have assumed that you already have some programming experience, such as that gained from previous study or work, and are familiar with common programming constructs such as loops, if statements, assignment statements and variables.

2

Fundamental hardware and software concepts

Before embarking upon the main focus of the module – object-oriented programming – we will review some fundamental hardware and software concepts and then go on to look in more detail at how computers are capable of functioning so flexibly.

2.1 Hardware and software

Hardware consists of the tangible parts of the computer system – the parts that can be touched. Examples of hardware include the electronic circuits inside the casing of your computer such as the central processing unit (CPU) and main memory, and also **peripheral devices** such as a keyboard, a monitor or touch screen, and storage devices such as hard disks and flash drives. Some peripherals, such as hard disks, are usually mounted in the same case as the processor, while others, such as printers, are physically outside the computer and communicate with it via a wired or wireless connection.

Software, on the other hand, is more abstract – it is a general term for all the applications, programs and systems that run on your computer; that is, it covers everything you cannot touch! Software is written using a programming language, and pieces of text in such a language are often called **source code** or just code. This code is then *compiled* (see Subsection 2.3) into a sequence of zeros and ones, that is, **binary digits** or **bits**, which make up the instructions that tell a computer (or rather the hardware) how to perform a particular task. However, it is not generally useful for a programmer to consider software in such low-level terms (that is, they rarely need to explicitly think of binary digits being interpreted by hardware as instructions to the CPU).

There are many synonyms for software (application and program are but two). The term *application* is usually reserved for larger software packages such as word processors, web browsers and email clients. The term **program** is usually used when describing software written by users for their own use – you will be writing programs. However, the difference is typically one of scale and complexity rather than precise definition.

Although software and hardware are very different in nature, they are also inextricably related. Any instruction performed by software can also be built directly into hardware, and instructions executed by hardware can often be simulated in software. So there is a trade-off between flexibility and speed. One could build a computer without any software; it would do just one task – but very quickly. However, we expect computers to help us perform a multitude of tasks such as calculate our tax returns, write a letter, play chess and maybe surf the web. Hence it is usual to get the computer hardware to do a lot of very simple tasks (such as adding or subtracting two binary digits), and write software to combine these simple tasks into various sophisticated applications.

2.2   The operating system

A computer's operating system greatly affects what you experience when you are using the computer. It is the first software that you are aware of when you turn on the computer, and the last software you notice when the computer is shut down. Yet many computer users cannot say with any certainty precisely what it is that the operating system does, so it is worth spending some time getting this clear.

An **operating system (OS)** is the software responsible for the control and management of hardware and basic system operations (such as data input and output), as well as running application software such as word-processing programs and web browsers. Common operating systems include Linux, Mac OS X (for the Apple), iOS (on Apple's mobile devices), Android (used on many other mobile devices) and the various versions of Windows, e.g. Windows XP, Windows Vista and Windows 7.

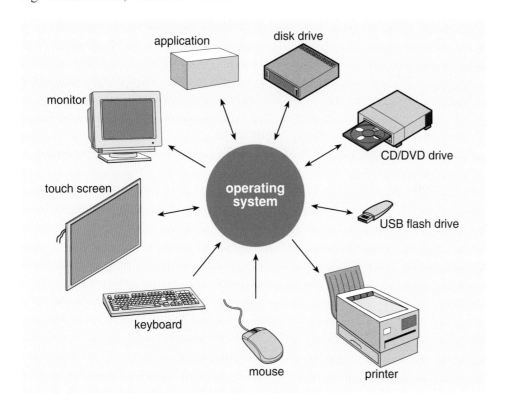

Figure 1 The operating system

In essence an operating system acts as an intermediary between the user (or an application program) and the computer hardware, as shown in Figure 1. It enables the user to carry out a variety of complex tasks on the computer, without the need to know anything about what goes on 'inside the box'.

Not all computers have operating systems. For example, a dedicated computer that controls the fuel-injection system in a car does not need one, since it has just one task to perform and the hardware it controls does not change. The computer is simply constantly running a single program, which can be encoded in read-only memory (ROM).

The next seven short subsections will expand upon the work of the operating system and will explain how it is loaded when your computer is first switched on.

Management of memory

During the execution of a program (or application), data and instructions are stored in the computer's main memory. It is the job of the operating system to allocate an appropriately sized area of memory to each program (or application), and to ensure that program instructions and data do not interfere with each other, or with the data and instructions of other pieces of software.

Coordination and control of peripheral devices

In order to carry out its tasks a computer may need to communicate with one or more peripheral devices. For example, it may wish to receive input data from a keyboard, mouse, or touch screen, read a file from a storage device, send output to a display device, and maintain a connection to a network. The operating system coordinates all these operations, ensuring that data is moved safely and efficiently between the different components of the system.

Scheduling of access to the processor

The operating system manages access to the processor, by prioritising jobs to be run and ensuring that the processor is used efficiently. For example, if the currently running program finishes, or is interrupted in order to wait for data from a hard disk, the operating system will ensure, if possible, that another program is given access to the processor.

Provision of basic utilities

Operating systems also provide basic utilities such as disk formatting facilities, file management systems and software installation wizards.

Provision of an interface between applications/programs and hardware

Another important role of the operating system is to provide a stable, consistent way for software to communicate with the computer's hardware without having to access that hardware directly, or know about the details of the hardware, or the minutiae of the processor's specifications. The operating system provides this through an application programming interface (API), which is a set of high-level instructions (a protocol) through which an application can 'talk' to the operating system to request services such as printing a file or saving a file to disk. So, for example, instead of an application program asking a printer to print a file, it asks the operating system (through the API) to print the file. The operating system then communicates with the printer to carry out the request. This abstraction allows a software developer to write an application on one computer and have a high level of confidence that it will run on another computer with the same operating system even if the amount of memory, and the makes and types of peripheral are different on the two machines.

Provision of a user interface

The user interface is the software that enables you to communicate with your computer. It provides a means of inputting data and instructions, and presents output in an understandable way.

The user interfaces of early operating systems such as CP/M and DOS were text based (termed command-line interfaces), requiring the user to learn a set of commands, which needed to be typed in following precise rules. Output to the screen also consisted entirely of text. Today almost all operating systems provide graphical user interfaces (GUIs), although most also provide (often hidden away from the novice user) a text-based interface.

GUI-based operating systems (of which the various versions of Microsoft Windows are the most common examples) make use of GUI components such as icons, windows, menus, buttons, sliders and other graphical widgets with which the user interacts, usually via a pointing device such as a mouse. Most people find these graphical interfaces more intuitive, quicker to learn and easier to use than sequences of commands.

A further advantage of GUI components is their availability for use by programs other than the core software provided by the operating system. For example, programmers of word processors or spreadsheet packages can make use of these components to avoid 'reinventing the wheel' and writing a brand new GUI. In addition, these graphical libraries provide a consistent way for application programs to communicate with the computer's hardware. This ensures that all applications making use of these GUI components have a consistent 'look and feel', which in turn makes it easier for users to learn how to use applications based on them.

Booting your computer

When you switch on a computer, the first thing it needs to do is to load an operating system (which is usually stored on the hard disk).

To enable it to do this there is a *boot program*, which is stored in the computer's read-only memory (ROM) during manufacture and is often called *firmware*. Firmware consists of programs that provide core functionality to a device that will not disappear when power is lost (hence ROM is termed non-volatile memory). Low-level firmware is permanent and cannot be overwritten, higher-level firmware is sometimes stored on reprogrammable flash memory, and so can be updated later in the life of the computer.

The boot program is executed automatically when the computer is first switched on and it will typically run a test of the computer's main memory and see what peripherals are connected to the system before loading the operating system. The process of using a short program to load a larger program is called bootstrapping, which comes from the metaphor of someone pulling themselves up by their own bootstraps. The use of the boot program for starting up a computer has given rise to the expressions 'booting up' and 'rebooting' a computer.

2.3   How programs execute on a computer

When writing software it is necessary to express a solution to a problem in a programming language resembling a natural language that can be understood – interpreted – by human beings. That solution (as written in a programming language) is called the source code. It must then be translated into a primitive language called *machine code* – the instructions that can be understood and executed by the hardware of a computer. Note that the term 'code' is commonly used without the qualifier 'source' or 'machine', with the context in which the term is used conveying the appropriate meaning. Except for this discussion, we will not be interested in machine code in this module, so mostly we use 'code' to mean 'source code'.

Since the programming language abstracts away from the detail of the machine code language, we call the former a **high-level language** and the latter a **low-level language**.

There are a number of models for this translation process. One such model is depicted in Figure 2.

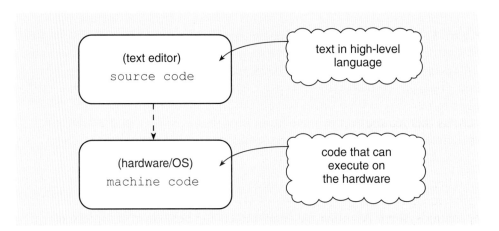

Figure 2 Relationship between source code and machine code

Translation of the high-level language source code to a low-level machine code program is usually carried out by a piece of software called a **compiler**. Translation can also be done by an **interpreter**, which will translate a line of source code into machine code (as opposed to a whole program) as and when it is required.

During compilation a compiler must first check that the source code conforms to the syntax rules of the language; that is, whether it is correctly formed. Only if this check does not show up problems does the compiler proceed to produce the machine code that will be executed.

The major problem with this simple model of compilation is that the compiled code is not portable to other machine architectures, as different machine types employ different machine code languages (see Figure 3).

For example, if Platform A is a PC using an x86-based processor, and Platform B is an ARM-based processor (the precise processor details are not important for this module, it is enough to appreciate that these processors use different machine code instruction sets) then you would have to recompile the high-level language source code with a specific compiler to produce machine code for each architecture.

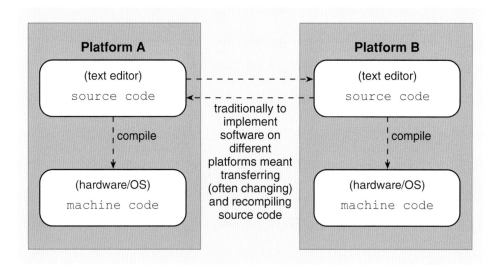

Figure 3 Compiling code for different computer systems

This is one reason why software developers typically provide separate downloads of the same software package for different platforms (although the need to interface with hardware such as sound cards or screens also plays a part, as this requires operating system services, which are also architecture specific). The important point here is that the machine code cannot simply be copied from one platform to another.

Another, more portable, model of compilation makes use of a special layer of software called a **virtual machine (VM)** that resides on top of a real operating system. A virtual machine mimics the behaviour of a piece of hardware and has its own instruction set, just like a real piece of hardware. Furthermore, because it still relies on the operating system layer, a different version of the virtual machine is required for each platform.

In this model of compilation, the high-level language source code is not compiled to a hardware-dependent machine code. Instead, it is compiled to an **intermediate code**, that is, to the machine code of the virtual machine. In Java environments, the intermediate (virtual machine) code is called **bytecode** because each instruction is a byte in size. Using this intermediate code approach allows low-level, essentially executable, code to be moved unchanged between different computer systems (see Figure 4). It should be noted that although this module is focused on Java there are other languages that compile to bytecode.

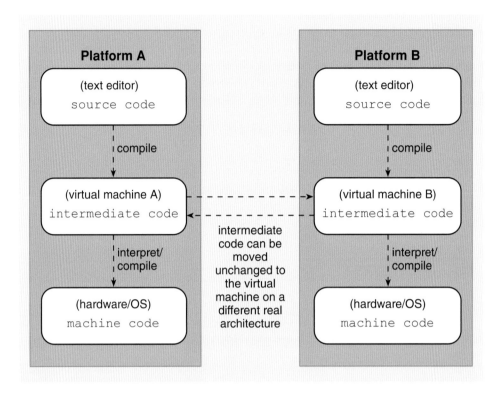

Figure 4 Compiling for a virtual machine

Once the intermediate code has been produced, there are three options for its execution on a real computer.

1   The first is to include an interpreter within the virtual machine software. Every time an application is run, the interpreter takes the intermediate code and translates each VM instruction, one at a time, into the real instructions for the real computer hardware to execute. This is a relatively slow process because so much software is involved in the interpreting, whereas the machine code from a simple compilation can be executed directly by the hardware.

2   The second option is for the virtual machine to include another phase of code generation in which all the intermediate code for a piece of software is translated into real machine code in one go, so that it is ready for the real machine hardware to execute. This is the traditional approach where intermediate code is used; it originates from a time when programs were prepared and tested as a whole rather than in component parts, and has the disadvantage that the programmer must wait for all of the intermediate code to be translated into machine code before the program can be executed and tested (although in programming environments where this option is used, the programmer may never be aware that a second complete translation has taken place).

3   The third option is a combination of the first two and is called **dynamic compilation** (or **just-in-time compilation**). This option is particularly

attractive when software is developed in relatively small chunks – modules that can be separately compiled. This is the option used by the Java Virtual Machine (JVM) in the module software. When a request is made to compile a chunk of code, the programming environment's (in this module's case BlueJ's) built-in compiler produces intermediate code (in our case, bytecode) for that chunk of code. This is then compiled into machine code by the virtual machine software when the code is first executed, and this real machine code is stored for subsequent executions. Therefore subsequent execution of that code has all the speed that results from simple compilation. (Of course, any code that is never executed will never be translated into machine code.)

In summary, the advantage of a compilation model that makes use of virtual machines is that it ensures that the intermediate code, no matter on what machine it was compiled, can be translated for execution on many different computers, so long as each computer has the correct virtual machine.

2.4 The computer as a layered device

In this section we have defined and described the terms hardware and software, the operating system and the Java Virtual Machine (JVM). To bring all these things together it is useful to consider a computer system as a layered device. So, for example, a Java program runs on top of the JVM, which runs on top of the operating system, which itself runs on top of the hardware (Figure 5).

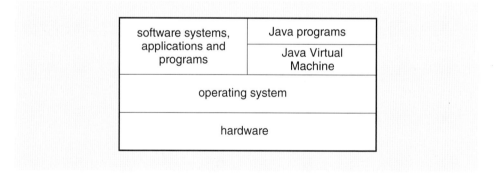

Figure 5 The computer as a layered device

Without the layers of software in modern computers, computer systems would not be as useful and popular as they are today. While the complexity of these underlying layers has increased greatly in recent years, the net effect has been to make computers easier for people to use.

SAQ 1

Why is Java software relatively portable between different platforms?

Answer

Java software is portable because it runs on a virtual machine, and the Java Virtual Machine (JVM) masks inherent differences between the underlying architectures and operating systems on different computer platforms. As long as you have a suitable JVM for a platform, you should be able to run Java software on that platform.

Object technology

Commercial programs are large: very, very large. They typically consist of hundreds of thousands of lines of code, sometimes millions of lines. All such complex systems, whether or not they involve computers, need to be organised in such a way that the human mind can comprehend and deal with them. Comprehension is greatly aided if it is possible to view a complex system as being made up of simpler parts that interact within an overall structure. Throughout the history of software development there has been an active search for useful structuring techniques and for programming languages that support such techniques.

This section describes one structured approach to programming that uses collections of communicating objects to build a more complex whole – object-oriented programming. After briefly looking at the shortcomings of procedural programming, we provide an overview of object-oriented programming and introduce some of the terminology used in the area.

3.1   Procedural programming

To put **object-oriented technology** into context it is useful for us to look at what went before. Before object-orientation the predominant method for structuring programs was procedural programming. **Procedural programming** is so called because the program code gives a step-by-step *procedure* (a set of instructions that accomplish a task i.e. an algorithm) for solving 'the problem'.

When designing a procedural program the programmer will usually break down the problem in a top-down manner (Figure 6). An overall algorithm will be specified which will be successively refined into smaller steps. This design methodology typically yields the structure of a main program, involving a number of calls to smaller procedures or function calls, which can in turn call further functions or procedures (a function is a procedure that returns a value).

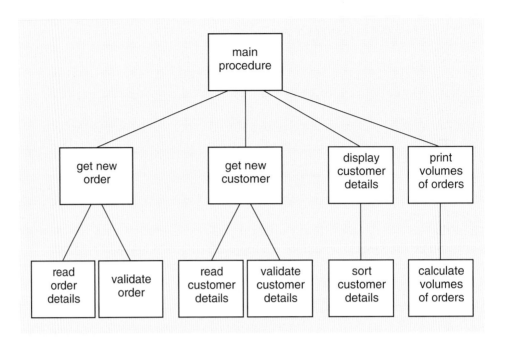

Figure 6 The structure of a procedural program

In such a design, data is placed into separate structures (called data structures). Often this data may be visible to, and able to be accessed by, every function or procedure in the whole program. In such a situation, where the data is said to be 'global', each function/procedure is able to change the data (Figure 7).

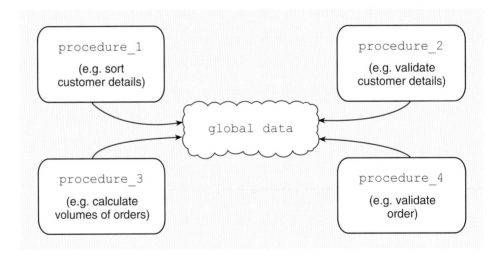

Figure 7 Procedures accessing global data

The ramification of data being global is that if a change is made to its data structure, all the functions and procedures that operate on that data will also have to be modified. Thus one small change could have a knock on effect throughout the program, involving changes to numerous, widely-scattered routines.

3.2 Object-oriented programming

In the object-oriented approach to software design all the processing carried out by software is considered as being done by **objects**. You are already familiar with the concept of objects in the physical world, being surrounded by them every day – cars, people, toasters, DVD players, managers, etc. In **object-oriented programming**, we use *software* objects to **model** real-life ones. The software objects simulate the part of the real world (often called the **application domain** or **problem domain**) with which we are concerned. For example, if we need a system to help manage patients in a hospital (the **domain**), our software will, in some sense, have to construct representations of part of the world of hospital administration. The objects we might need are those that deal with modelling real-world patients, doctors, nurses, wards and so on. Since the system would be a computerised one we would also need objects for the user interface, such as windows, menus and buttons.

In the real world, people, organisations and even machines interact with one another by exchanging requests and passing one another information. In the same way, object-oriented programs consist of code for creating objects that can communicate by sending **messages** to each other and they may get replies back, called **message answers**, from other objects.

Two important aspects of an object are its attributes and its behaviour. An **attribute** is some external property or characteristic of an object, so a patient object might have attributes such as condition, date admitted, medication and so on. The **attribute value** of 'condition' might be 'malaria' and the attribute value of 'date admitted' might be '3/1/2012'. Similarly, a car object may store information about its model name and price.

Each object has a set of messages it understands. The action an object performs in response to a particular message is an example of **behaviour**. We also use the term behaviour to mean the collection of actions an object might carry out in response to all the messages it understands. An object modelling a patient might need to know how to behave in response to messages such as 'take medicine'. The message 'take medicine' might well be sent by a nurse object.

Although as users of a software system we cannot interact directly with software objects, we can communicate with them via a *user interface*. Actions such as clicking the mouse, or pressing a key on the keyboard, will cause messages to be sent to the appropriate objects.

Sometimes, to achieve some end, objects need to collaborate with each other, sometimes they need to delegate work to others – a bit like teamwork. Using the hospital example again, a doctor object may send a message to a nurse object requesting it to give medicine to a number of patient objects. The nurse object would then in turn send 'take medicine' messages to those patient objects.

Figure 8 represents a simple view of what is happening inside an object-oriented program when it is running. The 'microscopic view' in Figure 8 depicts a collection of objects sending or receiving messages. Each object is represented by a square. To get an object to do something, it must be sent a message; messages are depicted as arrows between the objects. When an object sends a message to another object, all it needs to know is what behaviour will result – importantly, it does not need to know how the internal structure of the object receiving the message produces the behaviour. This illustration is limited by the need to show arrows as being fixed: in software that is running, the messages are sent (and received) as required in response to other messages.

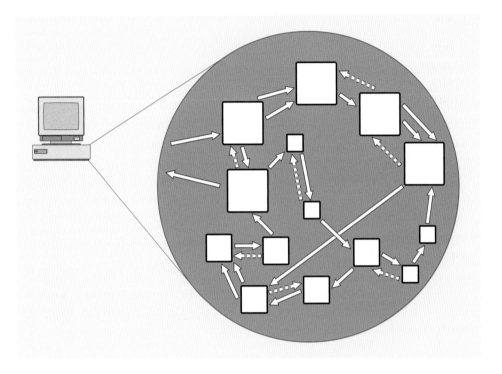

Figure 8 Object-oriented software is a collection of objects sending messages

A simple definition is that an object is an entity that contains both data (in the form of attribute values) and behaviour (the actions it takes on receiving messages). The word *both* is a key difference between object-oriented programming and the more traditional procedural approach. In a well-programmed object nothing outside the object can directly change the values of the object's attributes – indeed the only way to get an object do anything (including, perhaps, changing the values of some of its attributes) is to send it a message. This is one benefit of the object-oriented approach – because an object is responsible for updating its own data, any changes to the structure of that data affect only that type of object. Since it is usual for software to be changed and adapted after it has been built, this is an important benefit. There are further benefits, such as reusability, that will emerge during the module.

Attributes and state

Different kinds of object have different kinds of attribute and keep track of their values. For example, balance and credit limit might be two of the attributes of a bank account object; the attribute 'balance' might have the value 100.00 and the attribute 'credit limit' might have the value 400.00.

When referring to such attributes in code we will have to give them names. For most programming languages it is usual to have to run together multi-word names, or **identifiers** as they are known, such as 'credit limit' into single words. Thus we will prepare you for programming by running together the words `credit` and `limit` to form the identifier `creditLimit`, using a single upper-case letter to mark the start of the second original word. More generally in identifiers we use a single upper-case letter to mark the start of each word after the first, for example: `startOfRace` and `firstPastThePost`.

The values of all an object's attributes together determine the object's **state**. For example, the state of a bank account object, as discussed above, comprises the values of its attributes – the value of `balance` may be `100.00` and the value of `creditLimit` may be `400.00`.

Figure 9 is a simplified representation of a bank account object. The rectangle represents the object. The object has internal structure as represented by the contents of the two sections within the diagram. The object has a 'memory' (the values of its attributes) and it has a list of messages it understands (in Figure 9, the actual message names are omitted).

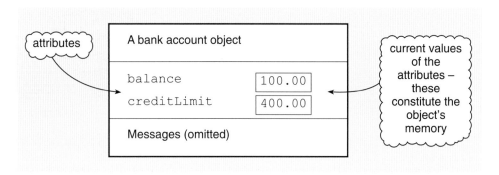

Figure 9 Diagram of a bank account object, showing its attributes and attribute values

SAQ 2

What is the difference between the attributes of an object and the state of an object?

Answer

Attributes describe the kind of information that can be determined about an object. The state of an object is the particular data held by all the attributes at a given time; that is, the attribute values. For example, a bicycle object may have the attributes manufacturer and size; its state is described by the values of these attributes – perhaps Raleigh and 21.

Messages

As mentioned earlier, the only way of getting an object to do something is to send it a message. Thus, to change part of the state of a bank account object (that is, to change the value of one of its attributes) – for example, to increase its balance – a message must be sent to the object. Similarly, to find out the value of an attribute, for example, to find out the balance of a bank account object, a message must be sent to the object. On receipt of a message it understands, the object will perform some action such as changing the value of one of its attributes or returning some information. Sometimes the requested action may involve the object sending messages to other objects. You can picture the object with the messages it understands, as well as the information it holds (as the values of its attributes), as illustrated in Figure 10.

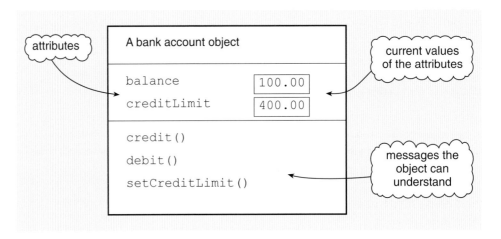

Figure 10 Diagram of a bank account object, with a partial list of the messages it understands

In the above bank account object the message `credit()` would increment the value held by the attribute `balance`, the message `debit()` would decrement the value held by the attribute `balance`, and the message `setCreditLimit()` would set the value held by the attribute `creditLimit`. The behaviour of the `debit()` method would depend on the values of the `balance` and `creditLimit` attributes.

Note the use of a pair of round brackets (parentheses) after the message names – all message names in Java are followed by these brackets. Sometimes additional information (called an argument) needs to be put inside these brackets when a message is sent. For example, to debit 50 pounds from the bank account object you send it the message `debit(50)`. You will learn more about arguments in *Unit 2*.

It is considered good style to give a message a descriptive name. Although the computer would not care if you used an arbitrary name such as `messageF9B()`, human beings who want to understand the program find meaningful names extremely helpful! The message names `credit()` or `debit()`, for example, are descriptive of what they cause a receiving object to do. Just as you saw with the names of attributes, in Java the name of a message must be a single word and therefore `set credit limit` would not be allowed. So, to preserve the meaning of the phrase, while obeying the rules of Java, we run the words together and use a capital letter to show where a new word would have begun.

3.3   Object-oriented technology in context

The idea of viewing software (and, indeed, of designing and writing software) in terms of objects is not a new one. The idea started in the mid-1960s with the language Simula, a language designed for performing simulations (for example, using computer graphics). However, the value of the object-oriented approach only really became evident in the next two decades with the development of languages such as Smalltalk, Eiffel, Objective C and C++.

By the 1990s C++ had emerged as the market leader in object-oriented languages. Its popularity was due in part to the familiarity of its syntax to the large existing base of C language programmers. C is used extensively on computers that run the Unix operating system and its derivatives, such as Linux, and indeed is still frequently used today.

Although C++ created many converts to object-oriented ideas it does have a major drawback. It is what is termed a hybrid language, a procedural language that has had the capabilities for object-oriented programming bolted on. The ramifications of this are that it is possible for a programmer to write in an object-oriented style, or a procedural style, or a mixture of both! This can (and does) result in complicated, hard to follow code that is difficult to maintain.

In the next section you will learn about the development of Java, a programming language that was built from the ground up with object-orientation in mind. While its syntax superficially resembles C, it is a fully-fledged object-oriented language owing more to the spirit of Smalltalk than to C. Java has done much to increase the spread of object-oriented programming and today object-oriented programming (delivered via languages such as Java, Ruby and C#) is the dominant form of software development, especially for software with graphical user interfaces.

4   The origins of Java

In this section we look at the history of the Java language and try to answer the question as to why Java is such a popular language today. In short, the answer to this is one of convergent technologies, good design and serendipity.

4.1   The Oak programming language

In 1990, Patrick Naughton, a disgruntled software engineer working for Sun Microsystems (the company was acquired and merged into the Oracle Corporation in 2010), was considering leaving Sun Microsystems for a rival company and detailed in a letter to Sun Microsystems' management, the shortcomings of Sun's software division. Shaken by Naughton's perceptive assessment of the problems their software division faced, Sun Microsystems's management persuaded Naughton, Bill Joy, James Gosling and three others to form a research group to create something new and exciting that would allow them to catch the next wave of computing.

In early 1991 the group met and decided to look at the application of computers to consumer electronics. At this early stage the team were considering such household items as video cassette recorders, fridges, microwave ovens and washing machines, and thinking about the possibilities of developing, say, a central control unit (possibly handheld) for all the units in the system. In this way the group evolved the concept of a network of different types of device (kitchen equipment, entertainment units, etc.) that could all pass information between each other as necessary. A crucial part of the project was to decide on the best programming language to achieve the team's objectives. This task fell to James Gosling who initially looked at C++. However, further investigation led to the conclusion that the difficulties encountered with C++ were best addressed by creating an entirely new language.

Given the application, the language needed to have the following characteristics.

- *Familiarity* – the C and C++ languages were widely used in consumer electronics, so basing the syntax of the new language on these existing ones would aid acceptance and hence use.

- *Platform independence* – the concept was to have a range of devices from different manufacturers communicating with each other, and thus the language would need to be able to perform on a variety of processors. This characteristic meant the language would have to be an interpreted language that could be run on virtual machines located on each device. Under this scheme, bytecode containing the appropriate instructions could be produced on one device (for example, the central control unit), then sent around the home network for execution on the virtual machine residing on the device requiring control (see Subsection 2.3 if you need to remind yourself how an interpreted language is used).

- *Robustness* – for consumer acceptance the new technology would need to run without failure. Thus the underlying language technology should omit various error-prone features of C and C++, and incorporate strong syntax checks.

- *Security* – as the various devices would be exchanging information within their network, the language would need to prevent intrusion by unauthorised code getting behind the scenes and introducing viruses or invading the file system.

- *Object-orientation* – as the architecture of object-oriented languages fits so well with the architecture of client–server systems running over a network, the language should be designed to be object oriented from the ground up. In a client–server system, software is split between server tasks and client tasks. A client sends requests to a server asking for information or action, and the server responds. This is similar to the way that objects send messages to each other and get replies (message answers) back.

The design and architecture decisions were drawn from a variety of languages including Eiffel, Smalltalk, Objective C and Cedar/Mesa, and Gosling completed an interpreter for the language by August 1991. He named the language 'Oak', apparently after the tree that grew outside the window of his office (although other stories abound). Despite great expectations, no commercial applications were found for 'Oak' and in 1993 the project was cancelled by Sun.

4.2   The world wide web

In the meantime, since 1991, Tim Berners-Lee's brainchild, the world wide web (WWW), had gone from strength to strength because Berners-Lee had made the source code public. However, at this point the web was still the preserve of mainly scientists and academics. There were only about 50–100 websites, they were complex to use, and interaction was limited by slow internet connections. Early browsers could not display images, video and text on the same web page; websites mainly consisted of hypertext (text containing links to other mainly text documents), and users (concentrated in academia and government) still relied heavily on command-line based tools (such as telnet and ftp). Finding resources was also not straightforward as there were no user friendly search engines. Few people had email addresses. In all, it was a hugely more limited experience than the situation today – thus the web was not of much interest to the general public.

A major step forward occurred in early 1993 after a graduate student at the University of Illinois' NCSA (National Center for Supercomputing Applications), called Marc Andreessen, together with a team of colleagues, released the first version of a new Unix-based browser. The browser – NCSA Mosaic for the X Window system – was especially interesting as it offered the user a straightforward graphical user interface. Andreessen and co-workers continued their programming and, later that year, a real landmark in the history of the world wide web was reached when they released free versions of the Mosaic browser for the Macintosh and Windows operating systems. Not only could the browser display text, graphics and video clips on the same page (and play audio), but, crucially, the browser was relatively easy to use and available for three popular operating systems. The world wide web had become multimedia and the online community liked it. No longer was the web an environment for dry scientific documents; it now became a virtual world full of colour and moving images. Subsequently Andreessen and most of his team left NCSA to form the Mosaic Communications Corp., which later developed the Netscape browser, catching the wave of public interest at just the right moment to make them all millionaires.

Until that point, the web had been totally overlooked by large corporations such as Sun Microsystems and Microsoft. However, public reaction to Mosaic convinced a few key members of the original Sun Microsystems team that Oak could play a part in the web explosion. After all, Oak was platform independent, ran on a virtual machine and was designed to run over a network – albeit a network of toasters, fridges and televisions. However, if a browser were written that incorporated an Oak virtual machine, any Oak program residing on a web server could be executed on a browser that incorporated an interpreter. Such applications could make the web experience far more interactive and, more importantly, lead to commercial exploitation of the web. An Oak program running within a web browser would be able to query a database, take customer details, and take online payments. A eureka moment had been reached.

In September 1994, Patrick Naughton wrote a prototype browser called WebRunner that incorporated an Oak virtual machine. The idea that a browser could support Oak applications (called applets) excited many and WebRunner was the perfect platform from which to demonstrate the power of the language. Unfortunately a patent search revealed that Oak was already a trademark and, so the story goes, the team came up with the replacement name – Java – during a trip to a coffee shop. Thus Oak was renamed Java and WebRunner renamed HotJava.

The first public release of Java and the HotJava web browser came on 23 May 1995, at the SunWorld conference. The announcement was made by John Gage, the Director of Science for Sun Microsystems. His announcement was accompanied by a surprise announcement by Marc Andreessen, Executive Vice President of Netscape, that Netscape would be including Java support in its browsers. As Netscape was, at the time, the world's most popular browser, such support gave the Java language a major boost and significant credibility – so much so that Microsoft soon followed suit and implemented Java support in Internet Explorer. From then on Java's popularity as a programming language grew meteorically and it has now grown into a full-scale development system, capable of being used for developing large applications that exist outside the web environment. More recently, although the importance of Java for web browsing has been reduced by the advent of web development technologies such as Adobe Flash and AJAX, Java continues to be widely used for producing desktop, mobile (handheld) and commercial-scale applications.

4.3   Versions and editions of Java

Java has undergone some significant changes since its first release, so it is important to have some appreciation of the different flavours of Java in use.

Java's initial success was as a programming language for the web, but in 1999 it was recognised that the concept that one standard Java language package could apply to all sorts of computing platform was not really feasible. So the concept of **Java editions** was introduced, to cater for the different needs of, say, large international business systems running on extensive networks with many servers as opposed to software running on mobile phones with very limited hardware resources.

The three main editions are:

- Java™ Platform, Standard Edition (Java SE) – the original edition, targeting desktop environments;
- Java™ Platform, Micro Edition (Java ME) – targeting environments with limited resources such as mobile phones;
- Java™ Platform, Enterprise Edition (Java EE) – targeting large distributed enterprise or internet environments.

The core language in these editions is the same; the editions differ in what libraries (APIs) are provided and what the JVM can do on the targeted hardware.

Java editions are available in a variety of **Java versions**. Differences between versions tend to be minor, but later versions are not generally compatible with earlier ones. For example, the first publicly available version of the Standard Edition language was Java 1.0. This was followed by Java 1.1, Java 1.2, Java 1.3 and Java 1.4.

Java 1.2 was also called Java 2 and saw the adoption of a framework for graphical interfaces called Swing, as well as 'collection classes' that you will meet later in this module.

Further significant changes occurred in Java 5 in 2004 and the naming convention for the versions of the language changed from dot notation (1.2, 1.3 and so on) to version numbers (5, 6, 7 and so on), although you will still see the earlier dot notation in some contexts.

Each version has introduced improvements and expanded the API set, and within each major release there have also been many minor releases that have fixed bugs.

In this module we will be using Java Platform, Standard Edition (Java SE), in particular Java SE 7.

SAQ 3

What are the main reasons for Java's popularity as a programming language?

Answer

Some of the main reasons for Java's popularity are:
- familiarity of style to existing programmers
- platform independence (portability) – Java runs on a wide range of hardware platforms
- robustness – Java avoids many error-prone features of some other languages
- security - by design, Java allows the coding of relatively secure applications
- object-orientation – Java was designed with object-oriented programming in mind, and so provides all the benefits of this programming approach.

Exploring objects in a microworld

We now begin some practical explorations of object behaviour by sending messages to objects and look in more depth at the state of an object as given by the values of its attributes. We will see that an object is an instance of a class of objects that share the ability to understand a common set of messages, called a protocol.

We will also introduce to you an application, developed specifically for the module, called Amphibian Worlds. This application contains a series of **microworlds** – computer-based simulations that allow you to practice sending messages to objects and to observe the messages' effects. Amphibian Worlds contains (unsurprisingly) amphibian objects, which will help you to explore object-oriented ideas. In this section you will be investigating the microworld 'Two Frogs' – study of other microworlds forms part of *Unit 2*.

The activities start with the investigation of sending messages to objects. From this exploration you will discover what attributes an object may have and how to use the software to inspect the state of an object at any given time.

You will also write your first piece of Java code so that you can manipulate objects via code, rather than via a button in a user interface. You will then begin your journey into **object technology** by considering classes.

To access the microworld used in this section, launch the Amphibian Worlds application by double-clicking the shortcut that has been installed on your desktop and then, from the Microworld *menu, select* Two Frogs.

5.1   Sending messages to objects

The microworld Two Frogs (Figure 11) has a user interface that allows you to send messages to two frog objects, either by clicking named message buttons, or by entering Java code into a code pane and clicking the Execute button. The frog objects also have **graphical representations** so that you can observe the effects of sending messages to them – these graphical representations are displayed in the graphics pane at the top of the microworld. In the Two Frogs microworld two frog objects are shown sitting on stones in a pond.

The Inspect button in the microworld will enable you to 'look inside' an object to find out its state – the values of its attributes.

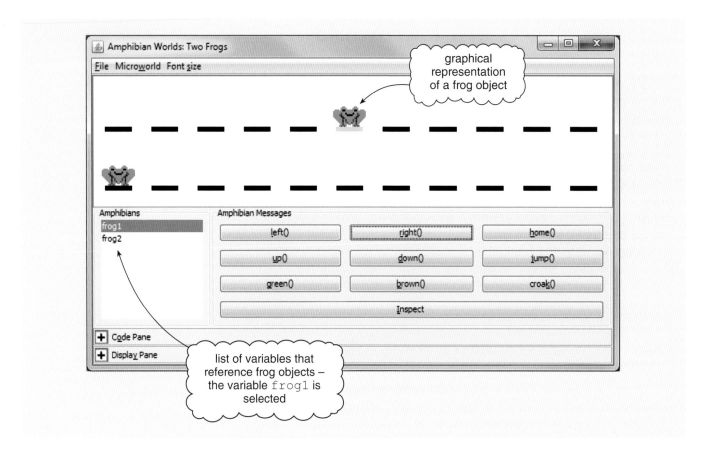

Figure 11 The microworld Two Frogs

In order to send messages to these objects you need some way of referring to them; for this variables are used. A **variable** is a named block of computer memory into which data can be stored (variables are discussed in more detail in *Unit 3*). In the case of the microworld Two Frogs there are two variables, frog1 and frog2. These variables are listed in the list pane labelled Amphibians, on the left below the graphics pane. These two variables *could* have been given any names we pleased; for example, x and y, or aObject and bObject. However, using frog1 and frog2 is a better choice because the names remind you what sort of object is involved.

The buttons labelled left(), right(), home(); up(), down(), jump(); green(), brown() and croak() to the right of the list of variables (in the pane labelled Amphibian Messages) allow you to send messages to the two frog objects and observe their behaviour in the graphics pane. However, before sending a message it is necessary to choose the frog object you wish to send the message to in the microworld. To select a particular frog object, you will need to highlight its variable in the list pane by clicking once on it. Once you have selected a variable the graphics pane will identify the graphical representation of the corresponding frog object by turning the stone from black to yellow. You will then be able to send the selected frog object a message by selecting (clicking once on) a message button.

Variable terminology

At this point it is useful to clarify some terminology associated with variables. We may use informal shorthand phrases such as 'send a message to the object `frog1`', or 'as before, `frog1` behaved as expected'. However, since a variable is just a label on a block of memory, to be technically precise the phrases should be 'send a message to the object *referenced by the variable* `frog1`' and 'as before, the object *referenced by the variable* `frog1` behaved as expected'. Most programmers would be perfectly happy using the shorthand style in casual speech, but you should always be prepared to use the more precise terminology when required and bear in mind that the variable that references an object is not the object itself.

Activity 1

Launch the application Amphibian Worlds and then select the microworld `Two Frogs` from the `Microworld` menu.

We want you to explore the behaviour of the two frog objects in this microworld – a few suggestions and questions for working systematically are listed below. You may find it useful to record the behaviours of the frog objects in response to each message. To send the message `right()` to the object referenced by `frog1`, highlight the variable `frog1` in the Amphibians list pane and then click once on the button labelled `right()`. The representation of the object in the graphics pane will then move one position to the right (to a new stone).

Remember that the icons of frogs you see in the microworld are *graphical representations* of the frog objects that exist within the microworld; they are not the objects themselves, which you cannot, of course, see.

1 What are the colour and position of each frog object when you first open the microworld `Two Frogs`?

2 Select one of the frog objects (highlight a variable in the list pane) and send it each message in turn (by clicking once on a message button), noting the response. An error report will appear in the window labelled `Display Pane` when you send some of the messages. Read the text and then press the `Clear` button in the `Display Pane` to remove the error report. List the messages the frog object understands, and record the response each such message invokes in the frog object.

3 Does the other frog object respond in the same way to each message?

4 With a frog object sitting on the rightmost black stone, send it the message `right()` two or three times in succession – you will see a blue arrow. What is the blue arrow indicating? Try to reposition the frog object on the rightmost stone by sending `left()` messages to the frog object.

With a frog object sitting on the leftmost black stone, send it the message `left()` a few times – you will see a red arrow. What is the red arrow indicating? Try to reposition the frog object on the leftmost stone by sending it `right()` messages.

5   What happens when the message `up()` is sent to a frog object? What happens when the message `down()` is sent to a frog object?

6   Following from your explorations of the messages to which the frog objects respond and their resultant behaviour, what information do you think each frog object is storing? Can you make any guesses about the attributes of these frog objects and the state a particular frog object may have?

Discussion

1   When the microworld `Two Frogs` is opened, each frog object is green and is on the leftmost stone (position 1).

2   Whichever frog object you select, it responds to the following messages with the following behaviours:

     `left()` – moves one position to the left
     `right()` – moves one position to the right
     `home()` – moves to (or remains on) the leftmost black stone
     `jump()` – jumps, and lands again in the same position
     `green()` – turns green (unless already green)
     `brown()` – turns brown (unless already brown)
     `croak()` – croaks audibly (and displays a red !).

3   The two frog objects behave in exactly the same way when the same message is sent to them. For example, both objects move one position to the right when sent the message `right()`.

4   If a frog object on the rightmost black stone is sent the message `right()`, the graphics pane shows a blue arrow pointing to the right to indicate that the frog object has disappeared from view. If a frog object on the leftmost black stone is sent the message `left()` the graphics pane shows a red arrow pointing to the left to indicate that the frog object has disappeared from view.

If either a blue or a red arrow appears, then a horizontal scrollbar will appear underneath the graphics pane, allowing you to scroll the graphics pane left or right to view the frog object that has gone out of sight. Alternatively, a message to the frog object to move in the opposite direction will cause it to reappear. The frog object can also be repositioned onto the leftmost black stone (position 1) by selecting the variable that references the frog object in the list pane and pressing the `home()` button.

5   When the message `up()` or `down()` is sent to a frog object, a pane – the `Display Pane` – opens up at the bottom of the Amphibian Worlds window, and a message in the pane appears to inform you that an error has occurred. This is because you are *not allowed to* send `up()` and `down()` to ordinary frog objects, which are not capable of acting on these messages. However, these messages *can* be sent to a more versatile kind of frog that you will investigate in *Unit 2*! To close the `Display Pane` click on the – sign next to the words `Display Pane`.

6   The messages `left()`, `right()` and `home()` are intended to alter the position of a frog object. (You see the icon representing the frog object

move to – or remain on – a particular stone.) The object must therefore hold information on its position, so it is likely to have an attribute with a name like `position`. In fact, the attribute `position` holds a number, reflected in the graphics pane by mentally numbering the stones from left to right, with the frog object appearing on the leftmost black stone when the attribute's value is `1` and the frog object appearing on the rightmost black stone when the attribute's value is `11`.

As you have seen in the previous activity, frog objects can move to positions outside the range of the window they are displayed in. When this happens a red or blue arrow appears in the graphics pane to indicate that the frog has moved out of sight, but you can scroll the graphics pane to bring the frog back into view. Stones representing positions less than 1 are coloured light red, and stones representing positions greater than 11 are coloured light blue.

A frog object's colour can be changed by sending it the message `green()` or `brown()` (the icon changes colour). You might guess that information on colour must therefore be part of the object's state and that there is an attribute with a name like `colour`. This attribute must be able to specify the colour of the frog object – including the colours green and brown.

Activity 2

In the previous activity you made a guess at the attributes and attribute values of frog objects. Now you are going to 'look inside' each object to see what attributes each has been given by the programmer. A more precise way of saying 'look inside' is *inspect the state of an object*. The microworld provides an **inspector** tool for finding out an object's attributes and for inspecting an object's state (the current values of the attributes). Figure 12 shows an example of the inspector tool displaying the attributes and attribute values of a frog object.

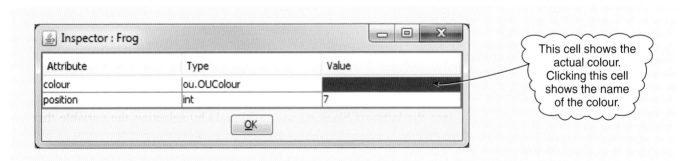

Figure 12 An inspector on a frog object

1   Highlight the variable `frog1` in the list of variables and click the button labelled **Inspect**. An inspector will open on the object referenced by the variable `frog1`, enabling you to 'look inside' the object – that is, to ascertain the attributes of the object referenced by `frog1` and its current state.

What attributes has the object referenced by `frog1`? How would you describe the current state of the object referenced by `frog1`?

Close the `Inspector` window before proceeding.

2   Now inspect the attributes of the object referenced by `frog2`, following the approach given above for `frog1`. Do the two frog objects have the same attributes? Do the frog objects currently have the same state?

How can the state of a frog object (or, in general, of any object) be changed?

Close the `Inspector` window before proceeding.

Discussion

The left-hand column of the `Inspector` window gives the attributes of the object being inspected and the right-hand column gives the attribute values – its state.

1   You can see that `frog1` has two attributes – `colour` and `position`. If the frog object is in its default position (the leftmost black stone) and in its original colour (green) then the inspector will show the state of `frog1` to be `position 1` and `colour GREEN`. Note that when you click on the value of the `colour` attribute the text name for the colour will be shown rather than the colour itself.

2   Both frog objects have the same attributes. They may or may not have the same attribute values; this will depend on what messages have been sent to them. If `frog1` has `position` set to `1` and `colour` set to `GREEN`, and `frog2` has `position` set to `2` and `colour` set to `BROWN`, the states of the two frog objects are not the same.

The state of an object can be changed by sending it a message.

An inspector shows a snapshot of the state of an object, not a live report. If you leave an inspector open on, say, `frog1`, and send a message to `frog1` that changes its state, and then return to the open `Inspector` window, this inspector does not reflect the new state. To see the new state of `frog1`, it is necessary to open another inspector. The new state of the object referenced by `frog1` is then displayed in the new inspector.

Activity 3

The microworld `Two Frogs` includes a `Code Pane`. Instead of clicking the various named message buttons to send messages to frog objects, you can use the `Code Pane` to write Java code that will send messages to these frog objects once you click on the `Execute` button.

To try this out, firstly click on the + sign next to the words `Code Pane` (just above the `Display Pane`) to open the pane, then place the cursor in the `Code Pane`, type the name of a variable that references a frog object, and then the message you wish to send. *Take care to place a full stop between the variable and the name of the message because, in the syntax of Java, a full stop is how you indicate that a message is to be sent.* Make sure that you copy the capitalisation (upper or lower case) of each letter exactly, and complete your message with a semicolon. An example line of code is:

```
frog1.brown();
```

If you make a typing mistake you may see error messages from the Java compiler such as 'cannot find symbol' (which indicates that a receiver or message name you typed is not recognised), 'Missing;' (which means you did not terminate the statement correctly with a semicolon), or 'not a statement', which means that the text you typed is not a well-formed Java statement.

You can correct your mistakes much as in a word processor. Once you are happy with what you have typed, click the Execute button. The effect of your message will be shown in the graphics pane.

If you send a message with a typing mistake in it, an error report will appear in the Display Pane. If the advice does not help, try typing the message again, making sure you have deleted everything you don't want before retyping. Pay particular attention to spaces (you do not need any), capitalisation (use of upper and lower case) and spelling, as these are the most common typing errors. Highlight and delete your message line each time before typing the next.

Try typing a variety of messages to each frog object, including the messages up() and down().

Discussion

Sending messages to objects using the Code Pane produces the same results in the graphical display as sending the same messages by selecting a variable in the list pane and clicking a button.

In your work in the microworld Two Frogs you learnt that you need a way of referring to an object – a variable – before it can be sent a message. You then sent messages to the two frog objects and observed the results of those messages – the behaviour of the frogs in response to the messages. You did this in two ways.

- First, by selecting a variable in the Amphibians list pane and then clicking an appropriate message button to send a message to the frog object referenced by that variable.

- Secondly, by typing Java code into the Code Pane and then clicking the Execute button. When you did this you had to ensure that you spelled the name of the variable and the message correctly, and used the correct syntax. Using the Code Pane acted as your first exposure to the Java programming language.

In both cases you observed the results of sending the messages in the graphics pane of the microworld that displayed graphical representations of the frog objects. You also checked the state of the frog objects, by first selecting an appropriate variable from the Amphibians list pane and then clicking the Inspect button to open an inspector that displayed the attributes and attribute values of the object referenced by that variable.

We call the object that is sent a message the **receiver** of the message, as shown in Figure 13.

```
        receiver
         ⌢
         ⎨
    frog1.left()
         ⎬
        message
```

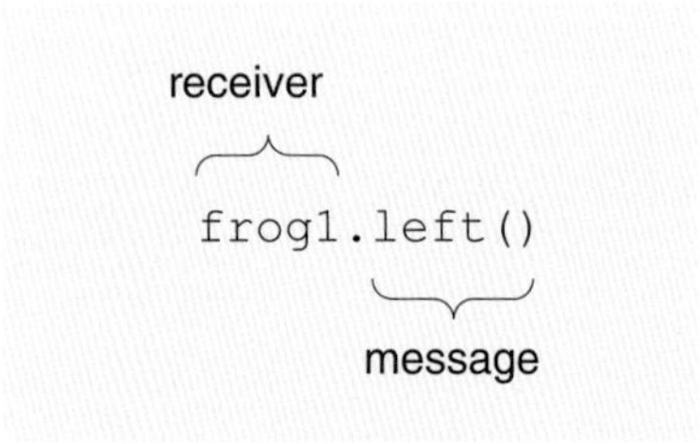

Figure 13 The message `left()` being sent to the receiver `frog1`

The code that is made up of a variable name, followed by a full stop and then a message (as shown in Figure 13) is called a **message-send**.

SAQ 4

In the following code, indicate the message and the object receiving the message.

```
frog2.brown()
```

Answer

The message `brown()` is sent to the object referenced by the variable `frog2` – this object is the receiver.

5.2   Grouping objects into classes

You have discovered that the variables `frog1` and `frog2` refer to very similar objects. In fact, these objects understand exactly the same set of messages, have the same attributes, and behave in exactly the same way in response to the same message.

These similarities occur because the objects referenced by `frog1` and `frog2` belong to the same class. You can see this in the microworld when using an inspector to 'look inside' a frog object, as both `Inspector` windows have the title `Inspector: Frog`.

The two frog objects in the microworld have been created as instances of the `Frog` class. A **class** is like a blueprint or template for the creation of objects and ensures that all its **instances** have the same attributes, and are able to respond to the same set of messages in an identical manner. So two different objects that belong to the same class and are referenced by the variables `frog1` and `frog2`:

- understand the same messages
- respond in the same way to each message (depending on their current state)

- have the same attributes.

On creation, the objects referenced by the variables `frog1` and `frog2` each have their own set of attributes and their states are the same, i.e. they both have the attribute `position` with value `1`, and the attribute `colour` with value `GREEN`. Each object has its own independent *copy* of these attributes, so that it can remember its own individual state because, although all new `Frog` objects are created with identical state, the state of any particular frog will get altered during its lifetime when it is sent messages such as `right()` or `brown()`. For example, at a later time, `frog1` may still have a value of `1` for its attribute `position`, whereas `frog2` may have this attribute set to `3`.

Note that when talking about objects and classes, as well as saying that the 'object referenced by x belongs to class A', it is also acceptable to use the synonymous phrase 'x refers to an instance of class A'.

SAQ 5

'Instances of a given class have the same attributes.' Explain this statement.

Answer

A class defines what attributes each instance of the class will have. For example, `frog1` and `frog2` are instances of class `Frog` and have the attributes `colour` and `position`. However, each instance has its own set of attribute values: if the message `green()` is sent to `frog1` and the message `brown()` is sent to `frog2`, the value of the attribute `colour` is different for each object.

5.3   Grouping messages into a protocol

The list of messages any instance of the class `Frog` can understand is called its **protocol**. The protocol of a `Frog` object, as we know it so far, is `left()`, `right()`, `home()`, `jump()`, `green()`, `brown()` and `croak()`.

SAQ 6

Use the terms 'class' and 'protocol' to explain why a `Frog` object does not understand the messages `up()` and `down()`.

Answer

The class defines the set of messages (the protocol) an instance of the class understands. `Frog` objects are instances of class `Frog` and the protocol for this class does not include the messages `up()` and `down()`.

5.4   Attributes of `Frog` objects

The only attributes a `Frog` object has in the microworld you have been exploring are `colour` and `position`. In our example, the values to which these attributes are set are shown in Figure 14 and these values constitute the state of a `Frog` object.

We now introduce a more complete **object diagram**, a standard way of summarising information about objects. The object is represented by a rectangle, with three sections:

- the top section shows the class of the object;
- the middle section shows any attributes of the object and their values;
- the bottom section shows the protocol of the object – the list of messages it understands.

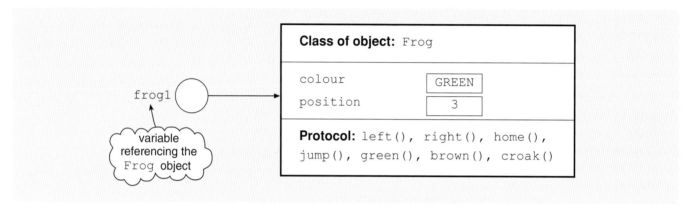

Figure 14 Diagrammatic representation of a variable referencing a `Frog` object

Figure 14 shows a variable named `frog1` referencing an object of class `Frog`. Notice that the variable `frog1` is shown next to a circle and the reference to the `Frog` object is shown by an arrow going from the variable `frog1` to the object diagram rectangle.

The top part of the object diagram states that the object is of class `Frog`. The middle part lists the attributes of `Frog` objects, `colour` and `position`, and tells us that in this case the attribute values are `GREEN` and 3. The bottom portion of the object diagram shows the protocol for `Frog` objects (consisting of the seven messages in the protocol of `Frog`).

The only way that the state of a `Frog` object can be changed is by sending it a message. The value of the attribute `colour` can be set to `GREEN` or `BROWN`. The value of the attribute `position` can only be a number. (This number is reflected in the graphics pane of the microworld Two Frogs as the stone on which the `Frog` object icon sits, with 1 being the leftmost black stone and 11 the rightmost black stone.)

SAQ 7

What is the state of the `Frog` object depicted in Figure 14?

Answer

The state of the `Frog` object is `position` set to 3 and `colour` set to `GREEN`. More colloquially you might say something like 'It's in position 3 and its colour is green'.

SAQ 8

Frog objects have the attributes colour and position. If the Frog object referenced by frog1 is shown in the graphics pane to be on stone 1 and is sent the message brown(), what is its state after responding to the message?

Answer

The state of the Frog object referenced by frog1 comprises the values of its attributes. After it has responded to the message brown(), the value of its attribute position is 1 and the value of its attribute colour is BROWN.

5.5   Messages that do not alter an object's state

Most of the messages you have experimented with so far alter some aspect of an object's state – either its colour or position. However, it is quite common to come across messages that do not cause any state change. As an example, we have included the message jump() in the protocol of Frog objects. Sending the message jump() to a Frog object makes it send another message to the microworld to tell it to display it graphically jumping, but leaves its state unaltered. You can tell that the state is still the same, because the only attributes Frog objects have are colour and position, and neither is affected by the message jump().

Later, in *Unit 2*, we discuss messages that query an object's state and reply with the value of a particular attribute. Such messages do not usually change the state of the receiver.

6 Classes as software components

Now that you have had a chance to discover some of the characteristics of objects, it is a good time to consider why object technology has become so important to the software industry.

When forming a new product in traditional industries, such as car manufacturing, the designer no longer designs a unique, handcrafted artefact, down to individual nuts and bolts. The designer can take advantage of ready-made sub-assemblies (components): for example, a gearbox from Honda, an engine from Mazda, a fuel injection system from Bosch, suspension from Lotus and a body shell from Pininfarina. All these companies will have ensured that the fixing brackets for their products are of a standard size and that they have holes pre-drilled to accept standard sized nuts and bolts.

Until the early 1990s, although the software industry employed libraries containing standard software routines (such as numerical algorithms libraries), such libraries had limited, specialised uses and many parts of an application or system would be designed from scratch. More recently, standard **software components** have been produced in a similar fashion to car components, with the aim of reuse. The same reliable, reusable software components can be incorporated into many completely new systems, thus saving the considerable time and effort it can take to generate new software. These possibilities have been brought about by object technology.

A growing part of the software industry is now focused on the production of generally useful software components (and at the other end of the scale, highly specialised software components) that can then be bought by other software developers to speed the development of their own applications (by avoiding reinventing the wheel!). For example, if a company were to write a system for an online shop, it is very unlikely that they would write all the code from scratch. It is more likely they would buy a database component from one vendor (to hold descriptive details and stock levels of the items for sale) and a component for secure payment transactions from another vendor.

The reason why this is now possible is that objects are relatively self-contained units of software that can be tested and proved to be robust and reliable. In the context of object-oriented programming, a software component is a class, or, more likely, a closely related group of classes. (Note that the **component** is the class, not the object; what you 'buy' as a component is the code for constructing and using instances of a class, not the instances themselves.)

The concept of software components has led to the possibility of replaceable parts for systems – not just for replacing faulty components with correct versions, but for replacing limited components with more flexible ones. For example, imagine a photo image processing package. If the relevant component were to accept only JPEG format files, but you wanted to process TIFF format files, it would be helpful to replace the original limited component with one that accepted that format (and maybe others). This is entirely possible so long as the classes in the new component defined objects with the same protocol, just as your garage can simply replace the tyres on your car with other brands if the fittings are compatible.

SAQ 9

Why are the components of a domestic electrical system (such as plugs and light bulbs) a suitable analogy for the ideal software industry?

Answer

It is a suitable analogy because the domestic electrical system depends on standard parts; you can exchange different makes of each component, such as a plug or a bulb (at least within one country), and the system will still work. As long as each component works as intended, its make is irrelevant.

7   Summary

After studying this unit you should understand the following ideas.

- Ultimately software executes on hardware; software delivers instructions to hardware.

- An operating system (OS) is the software responsible for the control and management of hardware and the basic computer system operations.

- Source code must be translated by a compiler into a low-level language, called machine code, in order to run on your computer's hardware.

- The translation of source code to machine code can be a two-stage process. In a two-stage process source code is first compiled to bytecode, which is the machine code of a virtual machine. This virtual machine will then, in a second stage, interpret the bytecode into machine code when the code is run.

- The advantage of a compilation model that makes use of a virtual machine is that it ensures that the bytecode, no matter on what machine it was compiled, can be translated for execution on many different computers, so long as each computer system has the correct virtual machine installed.

- In object-oriented software all the processing that is carried out by a program is done by 'objects'.

- An object can be thought of as a self-contained unit of software that holds data and knows how to process that data.

- The only way to get an object do anything is to send it a message.

- All messages ask an object to perform some action – these actions constitute what is termed the behaviour of the object.

- The set of messages an object understands is called its protocol.

- An object has attributes; the values of these attributes at any one time constitute the state of the object.

- A message may change the state of an object.

- A message may make an object do something without altering its state.

- Objects are instances of classes and create simple software components. A class defines the attributes and behaviour of its instances. Therefore, objects belonging to the same class (instances of the class) have the same set of attributes and understand the same set of messages, responding to each message in an identical manner.

- Object technology has advanced the concept of software components, which are produced with the aim of reuse. The same reliable, reusable software components can be incorporated into many completely new systems, thus saving considerable time and effort in producing new software. Objects of different classes can work together to create more powerful components.

Learning outcomes

After studying this unit you should be able to:

- describe the role of the operating system;
- explain various methods for translating source code into machine code;
- describe the role of a Java Virtual Machine;
- describe factors contributing to the success of Java;
- explain what is meant by Java versions and editions;
- appreciate and describe what characterises object-oriented software;
- appreciate and describe how procedural software differs from object-oriented software;
- explain and make appropriate use of the terms attribute, attribute value, state, behaviour, message and protocol as they apply to objects;
- reason about what attributes a particular object might have and what values those attributes might have at a given time;
- describe how objects are organised into classes, which determine what attributes an object has and which messages they can understand;
- explain how object technology has made possible the building of software systems out of components.

Unit 2

Object concepts

Contents

Introduction

This unit builds upon the object concepts introduced in *Unit 1*.

Here we will look at messages in more detail and discuss:

- how every object has an initial state when it is created
- how an object's behaviour when it receives a message may depend on its state
- how some messages need extra information in the form of arguments
- how some messages change the state of the receiver, while others simply return a message answer – often the value of one of the receiver's attributes
- object collaboration – how, once an object is sent a message, that object may then need to send messages to one or more other objects to help it carry out the behaviour associated with that message.

We also introduce the superclass and subclass relationships between classes, whereby an object of a subclass inherits the protocol and attributes of its superclass but then the subclass may define additional attributes and behaviour for its instances. This relationship is central to object-oriented programming and results in robust and economical code.

Much of your work in this unit will involve practical activities and you will be using a variety of microworlds from the Amphibian Worlds application introduced in *Unit 1*. However, in addition to `Frog` objects, these microworlds are also inhabited by `HoverFrog` and `Toad` objects.

In Section 6 you will also use a simple programming tool, called Accounts World, which has been developed specifically for this unit and allows you to experiment with objects within a different context.

All the concepts introduced in this unit will be revisited and explored from different points of view in subsequent units.

SAQ 1

Based on *Unit 1*, how would you describe an object?

Answer

Unit 1 describes an object as a self-contained unit of software that holds data and understands a set of messages that may cause it to perform behaviours such as changing state. Each object is able to communicate with other objects via messages.

2

Classes and protocols

This section explores further the ideas of *class* and *protocol*, which were introduced in *Unit 1*. We will also look at the *initialisation* of an object.

In *Unit 1* you looked at a simple microworld called Two Frogs. In this unit you will explore a whole series of similar worlds, all involving various kinds of amphibian. The different microworlds contain additional features designed to gradually introduce and illustrate important ideas in object-oriented programming. This may give the impression that the classes concerned are changing; however, it is simply that the full protocol of the class is only being revealed in stages.

2.1   Frogs and toads

For the next activity you will be using the Two Frogs and Toad microworld in the Amphibian Worlds application. This has a new species – toad – represented by instances of a new class, Toad. In the microworld, the icons you see are, of course, graphical representations of Frog and Toad objects. The visual representation of a Toad object in the graphics pane is slightly different from that of a Frog object; this simply reflects the way that the application designer has chosen to portray these objects in the user interface to help the viewer. (In a different graphical interface the appearance of the two amphibians may differ in another way.)

Activity 1

In this activity you will be comparing the behaviours and attributes of Toad objects and Frog objects. In Amphibian Worlds you may assume that when an object understands a message, if that message changes the object's state it is reflected in the microworld in some way.

To start, launch the Amphibian Worlds application and choose Two Frogs and Toad from the Microworld menu.

1   You will see three objects, referenced by the variables frog3, frog4 and toad1. For each object, what are the initial values of the attributes position and colour? (Another way of phrasing this is to ask how each object has been **initialised**.)

2   Remember that the protocol of instances of a class is the set of messages these instances (objects) understand. To investigate the protocol of Toad objects, see if the object referenced by toad1 responds to the message jump() in the same way as the Frog objects referenced by frog3 and frog4. To do this select toad1 and send it the jump() message, either by clicking the message button or writing Java code in the **Code Pane**. Send the same message to each of the Frog objects.

3   Now determine as much of the rest of the protocol of Toad objects as you can by sending each of the other messages, in turn, to the object referenced by toad1 using the buttons in the microworld. In each case

record your observations. How does this compare with the protocol of
Frog objects? Are the behaviours of the Toad and Frog objects the same?

4 Select toad1 in the scrollable pane and click on the **Inspect** button. An
Inspector window will open on toad1. What attributes has the Toad
object referenced by toad1, and how do these compare with those of the
Frog objects?

Discussion

1 When the microworld is first opened, toad1 is brown and is in
position 11, whereas both frog3 and frog4 are green and in position 1.
In other words, these Frog objects have been initialised with position
and colour having the values 1 and GREEN respectively, but the object
toad1 has been initialised with position having a value of 11 and
colour having a value of BROWN.

2 On receiving the message jump() the objects referenced by frog3 and
frog4 behave identically (as you saw in *Unit 1*, this is because these
objects are instances of the same class, Frog). If you select toad1 and
press the **jump()** button, you see the error message 'message jump()
not understood by class 'Toad''. If you type toad1.jump(); in
the **Code Pane** and press the **Execute** button you see a compiler error
message saying 'cannot find symbol - method jump()'. These are
different ways of describing the same error.

3 When you select toad1 and send it each of the other messages, in turn,
you should observe the following:

left() – moves *two* positions to the left
right() – moves *two* positions to the right
home() – moves to (or remains on) the rightmost black stone
green() – turns green (unless already green)
brown() – turns brown (unless already brown)
croak() – croaks audibly (and displays a red !)

When the messages up() or down() are sent to the Toad object
referenced by toad1, an error report appears in the **Display Pane**
indicating that the object cannot understand the message.

Thus, from the messages we know about, the protocol for the Toad object
includes the messages left(), right(), home(), green(), brown()
and croak(). The messages up(), down() and jump() are *not* in the
protocol of Toad objects.

Toad objects behave differently from Frog objects in response to left(),
right() and home() messages (jump() features only in the protocol of
Frog objects).

In response to the messages left() and right(), Frog objects move
position by one unit, whereas the object referenced by toad1 moves
position by two units. In response to the message home() Frog objects
move to (or remain on) the leftmost black stone, whereas the object
referenced by toad1 moves to (or remains on) the rightmost black stone.

It should also be noted that Toad objects behave identically to Frog
objects in response to the messages green(), brown() and croak().

4   The information displayed in the **Inspector** window shows that `toad1` has the same attributes as the `Frog` objects – `position` and `colour`.

Note that, although both kinds of objects have a `colour` and a `position`, there is no attribute that records what icon should be used to represent either. Any icon shown in the graphics pane is part of the state of the graphics pane and not part of the state of the object it is representing. However, the overall colour and position of an icon is *derived* from the state of the object it is representing.

When the microworld **Two Frogs and Toad** was opened, it created one `Toad` and two `Frog` objects, each with an initial state; that is each object had some initial attribute values. You saw in the graphics pane that the `Toad` object icon was a different colour and in a different initial position from the `Frog` object icons – and each icon reflected the state of the corresponding software object. We say that the `Toad` and `Frog` objects are initialised differently, that is their states are different when they are newly created.

You also saw that, although `Frog` and `Toad` objects have the same attributes, they have different yet overlapping protocols, and behave in a different way in response to some of the same messages. These observable differences, by themselves, are not conclusive evidence that these objects belong to different classes, but, as we said, the object referenced by `toad1` belongs to the `Toad` class, whereas the objects referenced by `frog3` and `frog4` belong to the `Frog` class and in fact the differences you see in their behaviour are due to their different classes.

This is a general feature of classes in object-oriented programming: instances of different classes may understand different sets of messages, and may respond to the same messages in different ways.

Classes of objects are quite flexible in terms of their attributes and behaviour, but, thus far, we have said very little about why the idea of a class of objects is important. We will now rectify that situation by further clarifying the advantages of using classes in software.

2.2   Classes and writing software

One of the goals of software development is to avoid having the same chunk of code replicated in different parts of a program. This is because making a simple change can mean having to make that change in lots of different places in a program. This is inherently error prone. Adopting the idea of classes can avoid such code duplication and save the programmer work. This is because code is written just once, in a class that then acts as a blueprint or template from which individual objects can be created time and time again.

When building object-oriented software, the programmer may have to specify the behaviour of many objects that must collaborate to make some system or program work (for example, the graphical objects in a drawing application).

In particular, it will be necessary to specify somehow the attributes that each object will have and the messages each object will understand.

It would be perfectly possible to build every object afresh from the ground up, by providing all the code necessary to specify its attributes and behaviour; however, when a program can involve thousands of objects, this would be unbearably tedious. Moreover, many errors would probably be made and every individual object would need to be tested separately to make sure it was correct. So it's useful to look for a way to save effort by writing code only once and reusing it, and this is where classes can help. In any given program very often there is a group of objects that are essentially the same. For example, in a payroll program you would expect to find many objects representing employees, and in a drawing program there might be many objects that represent rectangles. When writing a program, whenever you identify that a set of objects all belong to a common classification, with the same attributes and behaviour, you can define a class for this kind of object. The attributes and behaviour will need to be specified just once, in the class definition, and then you can use the class, as a template, to generate an object of that particular kind whenever you like.

However many instances of a class are created, each will automatically have the same attributes and protocol, with no additional work on the part of the programmer.

Moreover, once you have tested your code and know it is correct you can rely on all the objects belonging to that class working as intended; you do not need to test them individually.

Of course, different instances of the same class may acquire different states (for example, `frog1` may have its `colour` attribute set to GREEN, while `frog2` has the value of this attribute as BROWN).

If the attributes or any part of the protocol of an object needs to be changed, the change need be made only once – to the class. The change will automatically apply to all instances of the class.

The concept of classes is a key part of object-oriented software development. Identifying classes of objects at the planning stage enables programs to be written in a concise and economical way.

SAQ 2

In your own words, what does it mean to say that an instance of a class is *initialised*?

Answer

Instances of a class have attributes. It is usual for a newly created object to have its attributes initialised to some initial values. For example, the instances of the class `Frog` have the attributes `colour` and `position`. The instances of the class `Frog` are initialised so that the value of `colour` is GREEN and the value of `position` is 1.

3 Classes and subclasses

We will now explore the concept of classes that are related to one another through relationships that are described by the terms *subclass* and *superclass*. We will also see that an object's response to a message sometimes depends on its state when the message is received; this *state-dependent behaviour* is illustrated in Activity 3.

3.1 Hoverfrogs

In this section you will meet a new species of amphibian – the hoverfrog.

Activity 2

In this activity you will explore the behaviour of hoverfrogs.

Launch the Amphibian Worlds application and then choose **HoverFrogs** from the **Microworld** menu.

In this microworld there are two `HoverFrog` objects, referenced by the variables `hoverFrog1` and `hoverFrog2`. (You will see a rotor blade on the head of the graphical representation of each `HoverFrog` object.)

You will now explore the messages `HoverFrog` objects understand, and how they behave in response to these messages. The results you obtain will help you to decide how `HoverFrog` objects are related to `Frog` objects.

1   Do `HoverFrog` objects understand the same messages and behave in the same way in response to those messages as `Frog` or `Toad` objects? To find out, send some messages to the `HoverFrog` objects and observe the effects.

2   What is the protocol of the `HoverFrog` objects (as shown in this microworld)? Describe the resulting behaviour for each message in the protocol.

Discussion

1   A `HoverFrog` object understands the same messages as `Frog` and `Toad` objects, and it responds to all of these messages in the same way as a `Frog` object. In *addition*, a `HoverFrog` object can understand two messages a `Frog` object cannot, namely `up()` and `down()`.

2   The protocol for the `HoverFrog` objects as shown in the microworld **HoverFrogs** is `left()`, `right()`, `home()`, `up()`, `down()`, `jump()`, `green()`, `brown()` and `croak()`. The usual behaviour of the `HoverFrog` objects in response to each of these messages is shown below.

> `left()` – moves one position to the left
> `right()` – moves one position to the right
> `home()` – moves to (or remains on) the leftmost black stone (which then turns yellow)
> `up()` – moves up by one step on the six steps above the stone
> `down()` – moves down by one step on the six steps above the stone

```
jump() – jumps and lands again on the same stone
green() – turns green (unless already green)
brown() – turns brown (unless already brown)
croak() – croaks audibly (and displays a red !)
```

In the discussion of Activity 2, the descriptions of the behaviour of a `HoverFrog` object in response to the messages `up()`, `down()` and `jump()` are incomplete. The discussion takes no account of the fact that the response to these messages varies according to the state of the `HoverFrog` object when it receives the message. Exploration of state-dependent behaviour forms the basis of the next activity.

Activity 3

This activity explores how the behaviour of an object sometimes varies according to the state it has when it receives a message.

1   Launch the Amphibian Worlds application and then open the microworld **HoverFrogs**. Experiment with the `up()` and `down()` messages in succession using the same object and note the object's behaviour. Write more detailed descriptions than those given in the discussion of Activity 2 for the behaviour of a `HoverFrog` object in response to these messages. Take into account the way that this behaviour depends on the message receiver's state.

In the same way, give an improved description of the behaviour of a `HoverFrog` object in response to the message `jump()` that takes account of its dependency on the receiver's state.

2   Without using an inspector, deduce an attribute which `HoverFrog` objects possess that `Frog` and `Toad` objects do not. Try to deduce what values such an attribute might take.

Select a variable that references a `HoverFrog` object and press the **Inspect** button to check your answer – what are the attributes of a `HoverFrog` object?

3   Send the `up()` and `down()` messages to a `HoverFrog` object, inspecting its state after each message. What sort of values can be held by the attribute that is changing in response to these messages? Is a `HoverFrog` object initialised identically to a `Frog` object?

Discussion

1   What is missing in the discussion of Activity 2 is an account of the behaviour of a `HoverFrog` object when it is at its minimum height (on a stone) and the message `down()` is sent to it, and when it is at its maximum height and the message `up()` is sent to it. In both cases no visible action results. Also, when a `HoverFrog` object is not at its minimum height the message `jump()` has no visible effect. a more complete description for these messages is as follows.

up() – moves up by one step on the six steps above the stone (unless already at maximum height)

down() – moves down by one step on the six steps above the stone (unless already at minimum height)

jump() – jumps and lands again on the same stone (provided the hoverfrog is at minimum height)

2   HoverFrog objects have the attributes colour, position and height. Frog and Toad objects do not have a height attribute.

3   If you experiment with a HoverFrog object and use the inspector you should discover that the attribute height only ever holds integer values of 0 to 6.

In the graphics pane, HoverFrog objects appear to be initialised identically to Frog objects. However, this is not strictly correct, as the additional attribute, height, that HoverFrog objects have is initialised to 0.

State-dependent behaviour

You have seen that the way that an object behaves in response to a message may depend on its state as well as its class. In other words, the behaviour of an object in response to a message may be state-dependent. This can be illustrated by sending the message up() or down() to a HoverFrog object. In the microworld, a HoverFrog object icon in the graphics pane does not reflect a response to any message requesting it to go higher than step 6 or lower than step 0. This is because the messages that affect the attribute height can give it only integer values from 0 to 6. So any up() or down() message to a HoverFrog object that attempts to set the value of height beyond these limits leaves the value unchanged.

As you continue to learn more about objects you will discover that state-dependent behaviour is very common.

3.2   Subclasses

In Activity 2 we saw that whilst there are differences between Frog objects and HoverFrog objects in our particular Amphibian Worlds, there is also quite a lot in common between them. A HoverFrog object can understand *all* the messages that a Frog object can understand, and it apparently behaves in exactly the same way as a Frog object in response to these messages. However, it can *also* understand extra messages that a Frog object cannot, namely up() and down(). A HoverFrog also has an extra attribute: height.

In fact, behind the scenes there is a relationship between HoverFrog objects and Frog objects. The programmer took the Frog class as a basis and added the extra attribute and protocol required to define the HoverFrog class. The relationship between two such classes is described by saying that the HoverFrog class is a **subclass** of the Frog class, and the Frog class is the **superclass** of the HoverFrog class. The fact that the HoverFrog class is a subclass of the `Frog` class does not mean that a `HoverFrog` object is 'less' than a `Frog` object. The term 'subclass' indicates that the subclass is derived from the superclass. A `HoverFrog` object has *at least* the attributes and protocol of a `Frog` object.

The relationship between the `Frog` and `HoverFrog` classes can be summarised as follows.

(a) The protocol of `HoverFrog` objects includes that of `Frog` objects.

(b) `HoverFrog` and `Frog` objects respond in the same way to the messages common to their protocols.

(c) Instances of the `HoverFrog` class have the attributes of instances of the `Frog` class.

(d) `HoverFrog` objects have an additional attribute.

(e) There are messages in the protocol of `HoverFrog` objects that are not in the protocol of `Frog` objects.

(f) The common attributes of the instances of both classes are initialised in the same way.

When the programmer was developing the code for the `Frog` and `HoverFrog` classes, they had these relationships in mind and recognised that this was a typical case for using the subclass and superclass relationship. Using this relationship, the subclass can make use of attributes and behaviour developed for the superclass and add other attributes and behaviour to them. This relationship is illustrated in Figure 1.

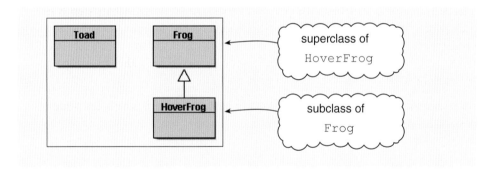

Figure 1 Relationship between the `Frog`, `HoverFrog` and `Toad` classes

The subclass/superclass relationship is often expressed using the words *is a*, as in the phrase 'a hoverfrog is a kind of frog'. This expresses that hoverfrogs are kinds of frogs, and so share some behaviours and attributes with frogs (but may have others). You can think of many such relationships in real life, for example, we might say 'a poodle is a kind of dog', or 'a hatchback is a kind of car'.

Figure 1 also includes the `Toad` class we have already encountered; in Activity 2 we saw that there were some similarities and several differences in the protocol and behaviour of `Frog` objects as compared to `Toad` objects. For example, `Frog` objects understand the message `jump()`, but `Toad` objects do not, and frogs and toads do not behave in the same way in response to some of the messages they both understand.

So could the `Frog` class be a superclass of the `Toad` class? The answer to that is no – the `Frog` class cannot be a superclass of the `Toad` class, because instances of `Toad` do not understand the `jump()` message, and if `Toad` were a subclass we would expect `Toad` objects to be able to jump.

Conversely, could the `Toad` class be a superclass of the `Frog` class? Possibly, but this would be undesirable – we would not normally say in common conversation that a frog *is a* toad. The programmer recognised this and so did not use the subclass and superclass relationship between these classes. Our use of subclasses should reflect our usual views of the way objects relate to one another.

The importance of relationships

The superclass/subclass relationship is important because `Frog` objects and `HoverFrog` objects have aspects of their protocol and attributes in common. As you will see in the next subsection, you need to define these common aspects just once – for the superclass (`Frog`). Then, the fact that `HoverFrog` is a subclass of `Frog` automatically ensures that `HoverFrog` objects also have these attributes and behaviours.

In later units you will see that it is possible to program a subclass so that its attributes are initialised differently from the corresponding ones in the superclass. (In this particular case `HoverFrog` objects have an additional attribute that has to be given an initial value, but the attributes they have in common with `Frog` objects happen to have the same initial values).

You will also see that instances of a subclass *may* respond to a message differently from the way instances of the superclass would respond to that message.

You will learn more about how to design classes using these object-oriented relationships in *Unit 6*. Because the superclass/subclass relationship is actually very common in real life, it is one of the central features of object-oriented programming. This relationship helps us to model the world in a natural way, reflecting the ways in which classes of things are related to one another.

3.3   Programming and subclasses

Beyond helping us to model the real world in software in a natural way, using subclasses when building programs enables programming effort to be saved. When building object-oriented software, the programmer has to specify somehow what the objects of each class will be able to do. But sometimes it turns out that the objects of some prospective class (the `HoverFrog` objects in our example) need to be able to do everything that objects of some existing class can already do (the `Frog` objects). In addition, objects of the prospective class may need to be able to understand some extra messages (`up()` and `down()`), and may have extra attributes (`height`). In such a case there is a simple way to save work: the programmer can declare the new class to be a subclass of the existing class.

Simplistically (this topic will be covered in more depth in *Unit 6*), this is what happened when HoverFrog was implemented as a subclass of Frog. Objects of the class HoverFrog have, *as a minimum*, the same attributes and protocol as objects of the existing class Frog. This will happen automatically as a consequence of declaring the new class HoverFrog to be a subclass of the existing class Frog. The subclass HoverFrog is said to **inherit** these attributes and this protocol from the superclass Frog. All the programmer needs to do subsequently is to determine any additional attributes and messages for the subclass.

SAQ 3

Which word or phrase best fits in the following sentence?

The protocol of a HoverFrog object … the protocol of a Frog object.

(a) is part of

(b) is similar to

(c) includes

Answer

The missing word is *includes*. (HoverFrog is a subclass of the class Frog. The protocol of HoverFrog includes the protocol of Frog. As you have seen, HoverFrog objects understand a few more messages than Frog objects.)

SAQ 4

What criteria do you think the programmer has applied in deciding to create the class HoverFrog as a subclass of the class Frog?

Answer

The programmer required the instances of the class HoverFrog to have all the attributes of the class Frog, to understand all the messages that instances of the class Frog understand, and to behave in an identical way in response to most of these messages.

4   Message arguments

This section introduces the idea of *message arguments*, which allow the message sender to include information in messages.

4.1   Messages and arguments

Messages become a much more powerful mechanism when you allow them to include extra information. For example, previously there were separate messages for turning an object green or brown. A message that sets the colour of an object and allows you to state the colour required allows a much more general approach.

When a message requires extra information for it to make sense, each required piece of information is called an **argument** of the message. (Note that some books call an argument a **parameter**).

In our microworlds we have made it possible for you to send messages with arguments through the use of menus. In this context, when more information is required from the user after a button is pressed, a menu will be presented – you must choose an item from the menu before the message triggered by the button can be sent. In Activity 4 you will meet the setColour() button that presents a menu of colours from which one is chosen as the message argument. The use of an argument makes a wider choice of colours available.

Activity 4

In this activity you will explore the use of messages that use arguments.

From the Amphibian Worlds application open the microworld Frog & HoverFrog. This microworld contains three new buttons: setColour(), upBy() and downBy(). These buttons are *menu buttons* – in each case a menu will be displayed when the button is pressed and you will need to make a choice from the menu before a message is sent. (Remember to highlight a variable referencing a frog or hoverfrog before sending a message.)

1   Explore the setColour() button by using it to send messages to the Frog and HoverFrog objects.

   Do objects of both classes understand the setColour() message? Which colours are available?

2   Send messages using the upBy() and downBy() buttons.

   Do both kinds of object respond to a press of these buttons? What information do you have to supply before an object will hover?

3   The buttons in this microworld reveal more of the protocol of the Frog objects. What is the name of the additional message that has been revealed in this activity? What is the protocol of Frog objects, as revealed in this and previous activities?

Discussion

1   Both the `HoverFrog` and `Frog` objects understand the message sent by pressing the `setColour()` button. Before you can send a message using the `setColour()` menu buttons, you have to provide some information.

The menu for the `setColour()` button offers a choice of colours: `OUColour.BLUE`, `OUColour.BROWN`, `OUColour.GREEN`, `OUColour.PURPLE`, `OUColour.RED` and `OUColour.YELLOW`.

2   Only `HoverFrog` objects respond to a press of the `upBy()` or `downBy()` buttons. Again further information is needed before one of these messages can be sent.

The menus for the `upBy()` and `downBy()` buttons offer a choice of 1, 2, …, 6. These determine how many steps up or down you want a `HoverFrog` object to move.

3   You can now see that the message name `setColour()` is in the protocol of `Frog` objects. The protocol of `Frog` objects as revealed in this and previous activities is `left()`, `right()`, `home()`, `jump()`, `green()`, `brown()`, `croak()` and `setColour()`. `Frog` objects do not understand messages for hovering.

The equivalent in Java of selecting the button `setColour()` and choosing `OUColour.RED` is executing the code `setColour(OUColour.RED)`. Note that when a message has an argument you must always supply it between the parentheses to form the message.

You may have been wondering what arguments such as `OUColour.GREEN` and `OUColour.RED` are exactly. Well, we have created a set of `OUColour` objects for you to use. These objects are held by the `OUColour` class as 'class variables' (you will learn about class variables in *Unit 7*). All you need to know at this point is that to get hold of one of these ready-made colours, you just type the name of the class, followed by a full stop and then the colour you want (in capitals), for example, `OUColour.YELLOW`.

4.2   Message names

We have said that when a message requires an argument, the message is incomplete until an argument is chosen. Thus `left()` is a message, whereas `setColour()` is not a message until an argument is provided. That means that it is not accurate to talk about 'the message `setColour()`', since this will not be a message until you pick a particular argument. But what if you want to talk about the entire family of messages represented by `setColour()`, irrespective of the choice of a particular argument? It would be helpful to have words to make this distinction.

The term **message name**, is used for this purpose. For example, the message name for the message `setColour(OUColour.RED)` is `setColour()`.

The phrase 'message name' is also used with a message that does not take an argument. In this case, the distinction between message and message name is less obviously useful, but the distinction still exists. So, for example, you might say either of the following.

'`Frog` objects understand the message `left()`.'

'I sent a message to a `Frog` object using the message name `left()`.'

Thus the message name for the message `setColour(OUColour.PURPLE)` is `setColour()` and the message name for the message `left()` is `left()`.

In summary, a message is something you send, but a message name is the name of a message or family of messages. So, when we give the protocol of `HoverFrog` as `left()`, `right()`, `home()`, `up()`, `down()`, `jump()`, `green()`, `brown()`, `croak()`, `setColour()`, `upBy()` and `downBy()`, we are giving the protocol in terms of message names.

SAQ 5

What is the message name in each of the following?
(a) `setColour(OUColour.YELLOW)`
(b) `jump()`
(c) `frog1.setColour(OUColour.BROWN)`
(d) `hoverFrog2.green()`

Answer

(a) `setColour()`
(b) `jump()`
(c) `setColour()`
(d) `green()`

Activity 5

In this activity you will use the **Code Pane** to explore messages that require arguments.

Open the microworld **Frog & HoverFrog** (if it's not already open).

In the Java programming language, where a message requires an argument, you write the argument within the message name's parentheses. For example:

`setColour(OUColour.RED)`

In the **Code Pane** to send a message to change the colour of an object, it is necessary first to type the name of the variable referencing the receiver, then a dot, and then the message name with the argument in parentheses, followed by a semicolon. For example:

`frog5.setColour(OUColour.RED);`

To send the message press the **Execute** button.

Try sending some colour-changing messages to both `frog5` and `hoverFrog3` using the **Code Pane**.

If you make a mistake and obtain an error report in the `Display Pane`, clear it by pressing the `Clear` button and then check the spelling, spacing and capital letters in your typing. (Colour objects have names in upper-case letters and must be preceded by `OUColour`.)

Type `frog5.setColour();` – with the argument omitted – and press the `Execute` button. You will see that an error report appears in the `Display Pane`.

Discussion

The objects referenced by `frog5` and `hoverFrog3` should have changed colour in accordance with the messages you sent.

Activity 6

In this activity you will continue to explore sending messages that use arguments.

To make `hoverFrog3` hover using the message `upBy()`, an argument has to be supplied; the argument here is a number chosen from the integers `1` to `6`. Hence the following is typed in the `Code Pane` to form a message asking `hoverFrog3` to move up two steps, i.e. by two units:

```
hoverFrog3.upBy(2);
```

Send this message. Check that your typing matches the above exactly, taking particular care with the spacing, semicolon and capitalisation, before pressing the `Execute` button.

Try sending several versions of the same message with other arguments, and also try sending some messages using `downBy()`.

What is the protocol of `HoverFrog` objects, as revealed in this and previous activities?

Discussion

The protocol of `HoverFrog` objects as revealed in this and previous activities is `left()`, `right()`, `home()`, `up()`, `down()`, `jump()`, `brown()`, `green()`, `croak()`, `setColour()`, `upBy()` and `downBy()`.

SAQ 6

In general, what is the difference between a message and a message name? What is the difference between a message and a message name when the message has no arguments?

Answer

A message name is the textual form of a message except that any arguments it takes are not shown. If a message takes no arguments the message and its name will be indistinguishable.

SAQ 7

What is the message name in each of the following?
(a) `oldBicycle.remove(bell)`
(b) `oldBicycle.install(bell, newBicycle)`

Answer

(a) `remove()`
(b) `install()`

Message answers and collaborating objects

We start this section with two activities that look at answers generated in response to some messages. We then distinguish between a message that modifies the state of an object and a message that interrogates an object's state. We conclude this section by discussing collaborating objects and sequence diagrams.

5.1 Message answers

In the following activities you will explore messages that request information from the receiver. These activities show that message answers can be used by objects that need to collaborate (typically to share information).

Activity 7

In this activity you will explore methods to get and set a frog's colour.

From the Amphibian Worlds application open the **Three Frogs** microworld. The graphics pane in this microworld shows representations of three `Frog` objects – `frog6`, `frog7` and `frog8` – and has two new buttons (for two new messages in the protocol of frogs), labelled **getColour()** and **sameColourAs()**. In this activity you will see that some messages result in a message answer, but some do not.

Select a `Frog` object and send it the message `getColour()` by pressing the button labelled **getColour()**. Look at the text in the **Display Pane** and make a note of what you read.

Now send the same object the message `setColour(OUColour.RED)` using the button labelled **setColour()** and look at the **Display Pane**: has any text been added?

Use the **Code Pane** to type and execute some similar examples. Look in the **Display Pane** after each line has been executed.

What are the differences in the behaviour of the `Frog` objects in response to messages with names `getColour()` and `setColour()`?

Discussion

When the **getColour()** button is pressed, some text describing the colour of the selected `Frog` object, for example, **OUColour.GREEN**, appears in the **Display Pane**. The message `getColour()` seems to be asking the receiver frog 'What is the value of your `colour` attribute?' and the message is answered. Similarly, if you execute `frog6.getColour();` in the **Code Pane**, the **Display Pane** shows the text `OUColour.GREEN`.

What you see in the **Display Pane** is a textual – as opposed to a graphical – representation of the message answer returned in reply to the message. Hence, for example, you will see the text `OUColour.GREEN` rather than a patch of greenish hue.

When a `Frog` object is sent the message `setColour(OUColour.RED)` it responds by changing its `colour` attribute to `OUColour.RED`, and nothing appears in the `Display Pane`. A `setColour()` message does not return an answer.

In contrast, the message `getColour()` does not visibly change the state of the receiver; it returns as the message answer the value of the attribute `colour`.

Activity 8

We will now ask you to use the `sameColourAs()` button and the message named `sameColourAs()` in the microworld **Three Frogs**.

The `sameColourAs()` button is used to send a `sameColourAs()` message to a `Frog` object requesting it to change its colour to the same colour as another `Frog`, `Toad` or `HoverFrog` object. The argument specifies the object from which you want the receiver to take its new colour.

1   Select the variable `frog6` and press the button labelled **green()**.
    Select the variable `frog7` and press the button labelled **brown()**.

2   Select the variable `frog6`, press the button labelled **sameColourAs()** and select the variable `frog7` from the menu. This sends the message `sameColourAs(frog7)` to the selected receiver `frog6`. You can use the button labelled **setColour()** to send messages to the three `Frog` objects so that each is a different colour again. Practise sending similar messages.

3   Now use the **Code Pane** to send messages to the three `Frog` objects so that each is a different colour. For example, the following lines, on execution, will change the colour of `frog6` to purple and `frog7` to brown.

```
frog6.setColour(OUColour.PURPLE);
frog7.brown();
```

Now type a line in the **Code Pane** similar to the one below and execute it.

```
frog6.sameColourAs(frog7);
```

4   Send other messages using the `sameColourAs()` message name.

Discussion

In part 2 the receiver changed colour to that of the `Frog` object specified as the argument to the message – `frog6` was initially green, and changed from green to brown in response to the `sameColourAs(frog7)` message. In part 3 you used the **Code Pane** to send `setColour()` and `sameColourAs()` messages.

When one object (`frog7`, for example) is used as an argument in a message to another object (`frog6`, for example) we say that the argument object and the receiver are *collaborating*.

5.2   Setter and getter messages

The message `getColour()` has a different purpose from the previous messages you have seen. In sending the message `getColour()`, you are not interested in changing the state of the receiver object. Instead you are interested in obtaining information about its state.

When the message `getColour()` is sent to a `Frog` object, the object replies with information about its colour. The requested information is returned as the message answer (sometimes called a *message reply*). In sending this message, you ask the `Frog` object for the value of its `colour` attribute. It is usual to say that the message `getColour()` *returns* the colour of the receiver.

In sending the message `setColour(OUColour.RED)` to a `Frog` object, you request the receiver to set its attribute `colour` to `OUColour.RED`. Note that you are not requesting an answer, and no answer is given.

It is common for the protocol of an object to include such pairs of messages: each pair consisting of a message that gets the value of an attribute of the receiver object and one that allows that attribute to be set. A message that gets an attribute value is also called a **getter message** or an **accessor message**, because it allows you to access information about an object. The corresponding **setter message** is also called a **mutator message**, because it is intended to change the state of an object. In our example we have `getColour()` and `setColour()`, where `getColour()` is the getter message name and `setColour()` the setter message name.

SAQ 8

What, if anything, is returned as the message answer when you send the following messages to a `Frog` object that is brown and is on the leftmost stone?
(a) `getColour()`
(b) `setColour(OUColour.RED)`

Answer

(a) `OUColour.BROWN`
(b) No answer is returned.

5.3   Collaborating objects

The message `right()` when sent to a `Frog` object does not involve any other objects. Often, however, before an object can act on a message it has to collect some information from another object or objects; it does this by sending them messages. The required information comes back as answers to the messages sent, enabling the object to deal fully with the initial message. In such cases, several objects are *collaborating* by sending messages to each other. (This is not the only form of collaboration; some objects might collaborate by taking responsibility for particular bits of required behaviour.)

Message answers can also provide information that is to be used with a later message. Sometimes the information is the value of a particular attribute of an object. For example, if a `Frog` object needs to know the colour of another `Frog` object, it would have to send the other `Frog` object a message and the information would be returned as the message answer. There is no reason why message answers should not be used as message arguments in subsequent messages.

Two `Frog` objects collaborate when `frog1.sameColourAs(frog2)` is executed, as described below.

The message named `sameColourAs()` when sent to a `Frog` object requests it to change its colour to be the same as another `Frog` object. The argument for `sameColourAs()` specifies the `Frog` object from which the receiver takes its new colour. There is nothing new about asking a `Frog` object to change its colour, but in all previous cases the message indicated explicitly what the new colour should be – as in the message `setColour(OUColour.RED)`. However, in using the message named `sameColourAs()`, an argument specifies another `Frog` object that has the required information (as the value of its attribute `colour`).

A technique that is often used to follow a sequence of messages between collaborating objects is to put yourself in the place of the receiver of the message. To follow the sequence of messages when the message `sameColourAs(frog2)` is sent to `frog1`, this technique requires you to put yourself in the place of `frog1`. You are asked to use this important technique in Exercise 1.

Exercise 1

Imagine that you are the object `frog1`. If you, as `frog1`, are sent the message `sameColourAs(frog2)`, describe informally the messages you would have to send and the answers you would use in order to satisfy this request.

Note that the solution to this exercise involves an object sending a message to itself. This is in line with the rules by which objects communicate – it is often the simplest (and sometimes the only) way for an object to get something done.

The interaction between the objects when the statement

```
frog1.sameColourAs(frog2);
```

is typed into the **Code Pane** and executed by a user can be seen in diagrammatic form in Figure 2 as, what is sometimes known as, a **sequence diagram**. The user originates the chain of messages, and will see an effect in the form of a change to the visible `frog1` icon. It is the collaborations between the software objects, rather than between the user and user interface, that are important here.

In Figure 2, vertical lines, called timelines, represent the objects named above them, solid arrows represent messages from sender to receiver, and dashed arrows represent message answers. The time elapsed increases from the top of the diagram running vertically downwards. (It is assumed that the attribute colour of frog2 has the value OUColour.GREEN.)

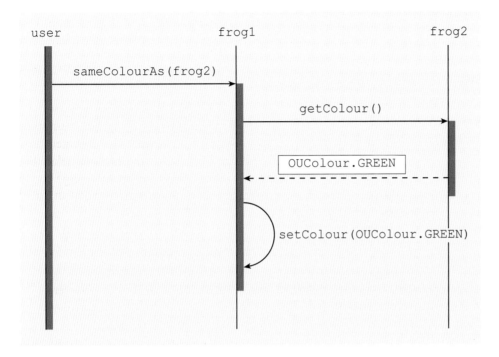

Figure 2 A sequence diagram

In Figure 2, the messages sent from one object to another are shown ordered from top to bottom reading down the page. The sequence is as follows.

(a) The user sends the message sameColourAs(frog2) to frog1.

(b) frog1 sends the message getColour() to frog2.

(c) frog2 returns as the message answer the value of its attribute colour (OUColour.GREEN) to frog1.

(d) Finally, frog1 sends itself the message setColour(OUColour.GREEN), where the argument OUColour.GREEN is the message answer from the previous message. This results in it sending itself a further message, update(), but to keep things simple, we've not shown this in the diagram. You will learn about the update() message in Unit 4.

In the above example, the user did not directly specify the new colour for frog1; rather the user indirectly caused a Frog object to send a message to another Frog object: frog1 had to ask frog2 for the colour information. Then frog1 changed its own colour (by sending a message to itself). The two Frog objects worked together in order to do something you (the user) requested. This is an example of collaborating objects.

5.4   A summary of `Frog` class features

Before proceeding to another scenario, we will summarise the key features of a class in terms of the `Frog` class.

A class describes a group of objects that the programmer considers to be similar. Instances of the same class understand the same set of messages (their protocol), have the same attributes and behave in the same way in response to each message.

All instances of the class `Frog` are created with the same attributes `colour` and `position`, but each `Frog` object is an 'individual' in that the values of its attributes belong to itself. So `frog1` may have `position` as `1` and `colour` as `OUColour.BROWN`, whereas the attributes of `frog2` may have the values `2` and `OUColour.BLUE`.

The protocol for the `Frog` objects is defined in the class `Frog`, so all instances understand the messages `left()`, `right()`, `home()`, `jump()`, `brown()`, `green()`, `croak()`, `getColour()`, `setColour()` and `sameColourAs()`, and behave in the same way in response to each message. The initialisation of each instance is also defined in the class `Frog` so that each `Frog` object is initialised with the value of `position` as `1` and the value of `colour` as `OUColour.GREEN`.

A bank account class

In this section we reinforce the notions of object, message and message answer by using them in an everyday situation.

We will describe a particular application, a simple banking system, which is designed to handle very basic bank accounts. The only information the accounts will store will be the name of the account holder, the account number and the current balance. These accounts will be modelled using Account objects; one object for each customer. An Account object will have the following attributes: holder, number and balance. Figure 3 shows how such an Account object can be represented by an object diagram.

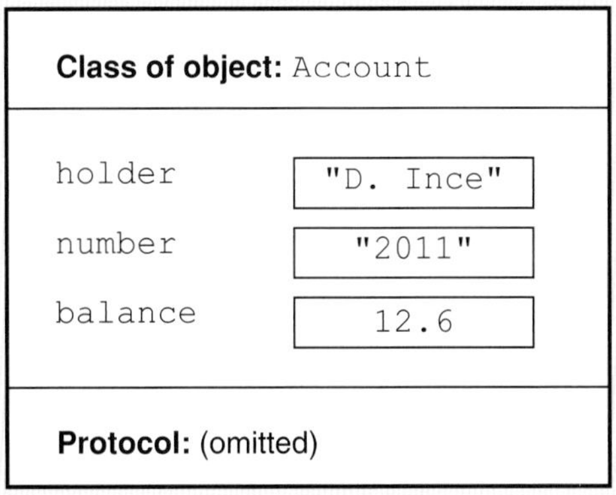

```
Class of object: Account

   holder          "D. Ince"

   number           "2011"

   balance           12.6

Protocol: (omitted)
```

Figure 3 An object diagram of an Account object

The object shown in Figure 3 has the attributes holder, number and balance, and each currently has a value – "D. Ince", "2011" and 12.6 respectively. Note that account numbers are treated as textual rather than as numeric quantities.

The diagram reflects the fact that this object belongs to a class called Account. There is space in the diagram for the protocol of the object i.e. a listing of the messages that class Account objects understand. The space for the protocol is blank for now; later in this unit you will discover what messages an Account object can understand.

A banking system can be modelled (in part) as a set of Account objects, each of which corresponds to someone's account with the bank. Some means of referring to each Account object is required. A solution would be to have suitably named variables, each referencing an account object, just as was done earlier with Frog objects. The Account object represented by Figure 3 can be referenced by a variable called e.g. myAccount (note the use of a capital A in the middle of the variable name, which is consistent with the **convention** for variable naming). Figure 4 represents the myAccount variable as a circle, labelled myAccount. It shows that myAccount references a particular object by means of an arrow pointing to the object from the circle representing `myAccount`.

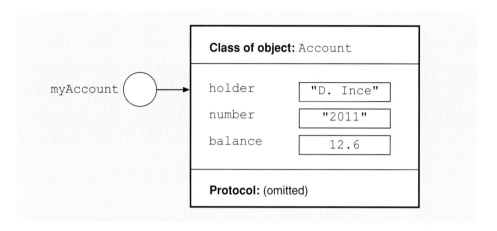

Figure 4 A named `Account` object

You will carry out the activities in this section using a simple programming tool for `Account` objects called Accounts World, which allows you to create new `Account` objects, and to send messages to them.

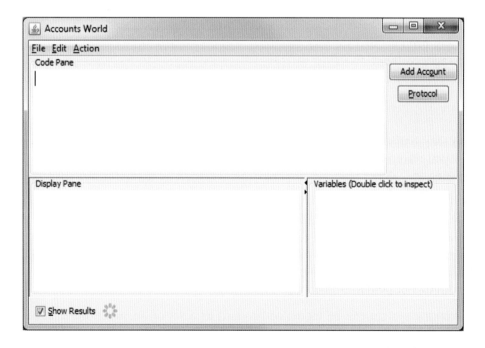

Figure 5 The Accounts World programming tool

The Accounts World (Figure 5) has three panes. The top pane in the Accounts World is called the **Code Pane**. This is where you type statements that you want to be executed. Statements are not executed until they have been highlighted (selected) and their execution requested by choosing **Execute Selected** from the **Action** menu. To the right of the **Code Pane** are two buttons. The button labelled **Add Account** is used to create `Account` objects (you will be prompted for a variable name when you click this button). The other button, labelled `Protocol`, is used to open another window, which you can use to get information on the protocol of `Account` objects.

Below the `Code Pane` there are two further panes. On the left there is the `Display Pane`. This has two functions. First, it is where the Java compiler will write any error messages if you make a mistake in any statement(s) you are testing in the `Code Pane`. The second function of the `Display Pane` is to display the value of the last expression evaluated in a statement (or series of statements). This will occur only if you check the `Show Results` check box.

To the right of the `Display Pane` is the `Variables` pane. This pane will display any variables declared in the `Code Pane`.

Remember that when you close the Accounts World any objects you created will be lost.

6.1   Creating and inspecting Account objects

Most of your study time in this subsection will be taken up with practical activities.

These activities are intended to give you a flavour of how objects and messages can be used to represent an everyday situation: the use of bank accounts. In the Amphibian microworlds you worked with objects that had already been created for you; here you will create new objects and send messages to them. In doing so, you will be introduced to terminology about Java code that will be very important later in the module.

Typing and dealing with errors

You may find that unexpected problems arise when you try to execute code that you have typed. This is often the result of incorrect typing. To help avoid these errors, please read the following advice.

Error messages may result from Java not understanding what you have typed when you try to execute the code, or from a typing error causing you apparently to ask Java to send a strange message to a strange object. The error messages displayed in the `Display Pane` may not always make much sense, but do not worry – in the majority of cases, the solution can be found among the following points, which you should read carefully before you start.

1   Check spelling, capitalisation (or its absence), spaces and punctuation. All of these can alter the meaning of a variable name or message. Always take care with capitals when typing, since Java distinguishes between upper-case and lower-case letters (i.e. it is case sensitive).

2   Make sure you are selecting the desired text, the whole of the desired text and nothing but the desired text when you execute it.

3   By convention, all message names begin with lower-case letters, but message names may include upper-case letters (e.g. `getNumber()`).

4   When you are creating a new `Account` object, you are asked to supply a name for a variable to reference it. Make sure that the name contains no spaces.

5   Use the `Variables` pane to check you are using the name of the variable referencing the `Account` object exactly as you declared it when you created it. You may have typed it in differently from the way it appears in this text. In particular, check spelling and capitalisation.

6   Use the protocol for the `Account` class to check you are spelling message names correctly.

7   Later, you will meet messages with multiple arguments. There should be commas separating multiple arguments. Java does not require a space after such a comma and before the following argument, but please include one for clarity.

Activity 9

Here you are going to create a new `Account` object, referenced by a variable called `myAccount`. In Accounts World click on the **Add Account** button. In the window that opens you will need to give the name for a variable to reference the new object. Use the name `myAccount` (be careful about capitalisation) and then press the **OK** button.

You have now created an `Account` object referenced by `myAccount`, but you do not know yet what state it is currently in. To examine the state of the object referenced by `myAccount`, double-click its variable name in the `Variables` pane. An inspector will be opened on the newly created `Account` object. Use the **Inspector** window to answer the following two questions.

1   What is the initial state of the object referenced by `myAccount`?

2   Has the name of the variable `myAccount` had any effect on the value of the `holder` attribute of the object?

When you have finished, close the **Inspector** window.

Keep the Accounts World open, as the `Account` object will be used in the next activity.

Discussion

When you created your new `Account` object you should have seen the name of the variable you created appear in the `Variables` pane.

1   The `holder` and `number` attributes of the new `Account` object are given as `""`, which is called a **string**. The `balance` is given as `0.0`. When an `Account` object is created, its attributes are always initialised in this way.

2   As the inspector shows, the name of the variable referencing an `Account` object and its `holder` have no connection – they are entirely different things.

Activity 10

You have created an `Account` object, but to change its state, or get it to do anything else, you will need to send it messages. In our banking system, an account belongs to someone (represented by the `holder` attribute of an `Account` object) and the account has an account number and current balance. To make a start, you are going to make the holder of the account be someone named `"Grendel Barty"` with an account number of `"1234"`, and you are going to credit the account with a sum of `100`.

Return to Accounts World, and send the message `setHolder("Grendel Barty")` to `myAccount` (taking care not to forget the quotes). You will need to type into the **Code Pane** the following statement, which, as usual, must be terminated using a semicolon.

```
myAccount.setHolder("Grendel Barty");
```

To execute the message, select it and right-click, and choose the menu item **Execute Selected**.

Recall, from *Unit 1*, that this is known as a **message-send** and consists of a receiver (the object being sent a message), followed by a full stop and then a message. The receiver is the object referenced by `myAccount` and the message is `setHolder("Grendel Barty")`.

Then type in and execute the message-send

```
myAccount.setNumber("1234");
```

and then

```
myAccount.credit(100);
```

Inspect `myAccount` and note what you see.

Discussion

As a result of your messages the inspector should report that the `holder` is `"Grendel Barty"`, the `number` is `"1234"` and the `balance` is `100.0`.

Activity 11

In the Accounts World, create two more `Account` objects:

- an `Account` object referenced by a variable called `hisAccount` (for the holder `"Everest Grundy"`, who has an account number of `"2468"`) and credit it with `200`;

- an `Account` object referenced by a variable called `herAccount` (for the holder `"Lucy Nijholt"`, who has an account number of `"1111"`) and credit it with `300`.

After you have created these objects and initialised them using appropriate messages, inspect them to check that their states are what you expect.

Keep the Accounts World open, as the `Account` objects will be used in the next activity.

Discussion

Creating the new accounts in the Accounts World is just a matter of clicking on the **Add Account** button, and providing a variable named `hisAccount` (or `herAccount`) for the `Account` object you want to create. When you have clicked on OK, the `Account` object is created. You should then see the variable name `hisAccount` (or `herAccount`) appear in the `Variables` pane.

Once you have created the accounts, the statements you should have executed are given below.

```
hisAccount.setHolder("Everest Grundy");
hisAccount.setNumber("2468");
hisAccount.credit(200);
herAccount.setHolder("Lucy Nijholt");
herAccount.setNumber("1111");
herAccount.credit(300);
```

Inspecting your newly created objects should confirm that the object referenced by the variable `hisAccount` is held by "Everest Grundy", with a `number` of "2468" and a `balance` of 200.0; and that the object referenced by the variable `herAccount` is held by "Lucy Nijholt", with a `number` of "1111" and a `balance` of 300.0.

Exercise 2

In Activity 9, step 1, you managed to use an inspector to find out the state of an object referenced by the variable `myAccount` immediately after it was created, without apparently sending any message to `myAccount`. Using what you know about objects, can you think of a straightforward explanation of what happened when you used an inspector to find out the state of `myAccount`?

Exercise 3

For each of the message-sends `myAccount.setNumber("1234")` and `myAccount.credit(100)`, identify the receiver, message name, argument and message.

SAQ 9

What is the connection between the name of the variable used to reference an `Account` object and the account's `holder` attribute?

Answer

There is no connection. An `Account` object referenced by the variable `thisAcc` might have a `holder` named "J. Bloggs". Furthermore, you could reference this object using `thisAcc` and send a message to change the `holder` to "Mary Brown" or any other value.

6.2   Exploring the protocol of Account objects

Now that you have three Account objects this is a good time to explore some more of the Account protocol. As in the previous subsection, most of your work here will consist of activities.

Activity 12

Return to Accounts World and explore the protocol for the Account class. To do this, click on the **Protocol** button – this will open a window displaying information about the credit() message. On the left-hand side of the window are a set of buttons labelled with the names of the messages in the protocol of Account objects; clicking one of these buttons will then display the information (documentation) for that message – what it does, what arguments it takes and what value (if any) it returns.

You can now turn your attention to changing the state of an Account object, namely that referenced by the variable herAccount. (If you had previously closed the Accounts World then you will need to create an Account object referenced by the variable herAccount then set the holder to "Lucy Nijholt", the account number to "1111" and the balance of the account to 300.)

Using the documentation as a guide, send messages to perform the actions listed below, in the order given, by entering the relevant code in the **Code Pane**. After sending each message, look in the **Display Pane** and note the textual representation of any message answer that is produced.

1   Use the message getHolder() to check that the holder of the account referenced by the variable herAccount is "Lucy Nijholt".
2   Debit 100 from Lucy's account.
3   Use the message getBalance() to check the resulting balance.
4   Set the number of Lucy's account to "2000".
5   Send a message to check the account number of Lucy's account.
6   Debit 3000 from Lucy's account.
7   Use the message getBalance() to check the resulting balance of Lucy's account.

Draw an object diagram to depict the object referenced by herAccount and its current state. Add the names of the messages you have used so far to the Protocol section of the diagram.

Discussion

The corresponding Java statements and message answers are as follows.

1 `herAccount.getHolder();`
   (the textual representation of the message answer is `Lucy Nijholt`).

2 `herAccount.debit(100);`
   (the textual representation of the message answer is `true`).

3 `herAccount.getBalance();`
   (the textual representation of the message answer is `200.0`).

4 `herAccount.setNumber("2000");`
   (there is no message answer).

5 `herAccount.getNumber();`
   (the textual representation of the message answer is `2000`).

6 `herAccount.debit(3000);`
   (the textual representation of the message answer is `false`).

7 `herAccount.getBalance();`
   (the textual representation of the message answer is `200.0`).

A `debit()` message returns the answer `true` if the transaction has been actioned (which happens if the `balance` is large enough) and `false` if it has not been actioned (because there are insufficient funds). Figure 6 shows the object diagram. Only the part of the protocol you have used is shown.

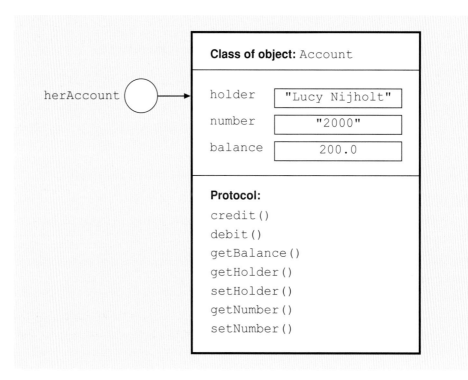

Figure 6 Object diagram for `herAccount`

Note that, as in the Amphibian Worlds, the message used to find the value of an attribute has a name consisting of the name of the attribute preceded by the word `get`. This is a common convention in Java programming. Similarly, a message used to set the value of an attribute has a name based on the name of the attribute, but preceded by the word `set`.

SAQ 10

Will Java treat `MyAccount` and `myAccount` as the same name?

Answer

They are not the same: spelling and capitalisation are significant in names of variables (and in names of messages and classes).

6.3   Collaborating `Account` objects

In this subsection you will be using the Accounts World to explore how objects in the `Account` class can collaborate.

There are some messages in the protocol of the `Account` class that you have not yet tried to send. One of these is the message used to transfer money directly from one `Account` object to another. The name for this message is `transfer()`. In Activity 13 you will use this message to transfer 300 from the account referenced by `myAccount` to that referenced by `herAccount`.

The `transfer()` message requires two arguments. In Java, when a message requires more than one argument, the arguments are listed between the parentheses of the message and are separated by commas. In the case of the `transfer()` message, the first argument is the `Account` object to which the money is to be transferred and the second argument is the amount to be transferred. For example, to transfer 300 from the receiving object to account `herAccount` you would use the message `transfer(herAccount, 300)`.

Activity 13

In Accounts World, make sure you have two `Account` objects referenced by the variables `myAccount` and `herAccount`; if you do not have them, create them. Next, send a message to credit `myAccount` with 500.

Before you start, make sure you know the current balances in `myAccount` and `herAccount`. Now, try using `transfer()` to transfer 300 from `myAccount` to `herAccount`. Then inspect the two `Account` objects, referenced by `myAccount` and `herAccount`, to see if they have changed state in the way you would expect from the sense of the message.

Discussion

To transfer 300 between the accounts you use the statement

```
myAccount.transfer(herAccount, 300);
```

The money has been transferred in the way you would expect. The answer from this message is `true` – the transfer was successful.

Exercise 4

The purpose of this exercise is for you to think about how the receiver of a `transfer()` message will carry out its responsibility to respond to this message, in the case where there are sufficient funds in the receiver account for the transfer to be actioned. (Strictly speaking, `transfer()` is not a message, it is only a message name. But most programmers say things like this for simplicity. This habit is fine provided that you make sure you understand the difference.)

Imagine now that you are the object referenced by `myAccount`, in a state with a `balance` of `800`. Imagine that a user of the system sends you the message `transfer(herAccount, 400)`, which requests you to transfer `400` to the account referenced by `herAccount`.

Imagine that you must respond to this message. To achieve your goal, you can send any messages you like (except `transfer()`) to any `Account` object. To solve the problem, try to break it up into stages. What would a person do to carry out the same responsibility step by step? Try to find a message to help you carry out each stage. Fill in a table like the following one to show in turn each receiver, each message including any arguments, and message answers, if relevant, of any messages you need to send to satisfy your responsibility.

Receiver	Message	Message answer

Hint: you may need to send a message to yourself (`myAccount`) as a necessary step in discharging your responsibility.

Activity 14

In the Accounts World, make sure you have two `Account` objects referenced by the variables `myAccount` and `herAccount`; if you do not have them, create them. Ensure that `myAccount` has a `balance` of at least `400`. Then execute the following two statements one at a time in the **Code Pane**, and then inspect the objects to look at the resulting state of affairs.

```
myAccount.debit(400);
herAccount.credit(400);
```

Discussion

The effect on the final state of the objects is exactly the same as sending a single message `transfer(herAccount, 400)` to the object referenced by `myAccount`, requesting it to take responsibility for the whole transfer. We studied this example in Exercise 4.

Whilst Exercise 4 may seem a little like a game, it is in fact an accurate description of how an `Account` object discharges its responsibility of responding to a `transfer()` message when there are sufficient funds for the transfer.

The receipt of the `transfer()` message results in the `Account` object, which is the receiver, sending two messages (without any human intervention).

1   The receiver sends a `debit()` message to itself. The argument to `debit()` is the amount specified as the second argument of the `transfer()` message.

2   The receiver sends a `credit()` message to the `Account` object that is specified in the first argument of the `transfer()` message. The argument to `credit()` is the same amount that was specified in the second argument in the original `transfer()` message and used in the `debit()` of step 1.

This is an example of an object discharging its responsibility by collaborating with other objects by sending them messages.

Exercise 5

You have now seen two sequence diagrams, one in Subsection 5.3 and one in the solution to Exercise 4. Looking at these diagrams, what interesting similarities and differences can you see between the way the following two lines of code are carried out?

```
frog1.sameColourAs(frog2);
myAccount.transfer(herAccount,400);
```

6.4 Recap of terminology

At this point it is useful to review some of the message related terminology you have encountered.

- The receiver is the object to which a message will be sent.
- A message must be in the protocol of the receiver, otherwise a statement attempting to send such a message cannot be executed.
- The arguments are the pieces of information required by the message: some messages require no further information, and some require one or more pieces of information.
- A message answer is some information returned by a message-send.

So, for example, in the case of the message-send

```
myAccount.debit(7)
```

myAccount is the receiver, debit() is the message name, 7 is the argument and the message answer will be either true or false.

SAQ 11

A message may:
(a) change the state of an object
(b) make an object do something without changing its state
(c) get back some useful information from an object
(d) cause an object to send a message to another object
(e) cause an object to send a message to itself.

For each item in the list above, give an example of a message or a message-send from this unit that meets that description.

Answer

	Effect	Example
(a)	change the state of an object	left()
(b)	make an object do something without changing its state	jump()
(c)	get back some useful information from an object	getColour()
(d)	cause an object to send a message to another object	frog1.sameColourAs(frog2) – the receiver sends getColour() to frog2
(e)	cause an object to send a message to itself	in response to frog1.sameColourAs (frog2) the receiver frog1 changes its own colour. The name of the message sent is setColour().

Exercise 6

Fill in the following table for the message-send

```
herAccount.transfer(myAccount, 200)
```

Receiver	
Message	
Message name	
Argument(s)	
Message-send	

Exercise 7

Decide whether each of the following statements is true or false. If false, say why.

(a) All messages consist of a *name* and an *argument*.

(b) An object is associated with a particular *class*.

(c) A message is an instance of a class.

7 Summary

After studying this unit you should understand the following ideas.

- The values of an object's attributes constitute its state.

- An object's behaviour is determined by how it responds to the messages it understands (its protocol).

- The behaviour of an object in response to a message may be dependent on its state. An example of such state-dependent behaviour is the behaviour exhibited by `HoverFrog` objects when sent the `upBy()` message.

- Objects are organised into classes. Objects belonging to the same class (instances of the class) have the same set of attributes and understand the same set of messages, responding to each message in an identical (but often state-dependent) manner. Classes can be thought of as templates (blueprints) for creating objects.

- When an object is created it has an initial state (its attributes have initial values).

- A class may have subclasses. An instance of a subclass has all the attributes and protocol of the parent class (the superclass), but the subclass may add to them.

- A subclass may modify the response to a particular inherited message so that an instance of the subclass will respond to that message in a different way to an instance of the superclass.

- It is common for instances of unrelated classes to have the same message in their protocol and instances of those classes may or may not respond differently to that message.

- Messages may return a message answer, and/or change the state of a receiver, or do neither. For example, the message `getColour()` merely returns the colour of the receiver whereas `setColour()` changes the value of the `colour` attribute. In the protocol of `Frog` objects `jump()` neither changes the object's state nor returns a message answer.

- Some messages require arguments – extra information that is required for the message to make sense. For example, the `setPosition()` message requires an integer argument specifying what position the receiver should move to, as in the following message-send: `frog1.setPosition(5)`.

- It is common for the protocol of an object to include pairs of messages to provide access to each of its attributes. For example, in the protocol of `Frog` objects the message `getColour()` returns the value of the receiver's `colour` attribute, and `setColour()` sets (changes) the receiver's `colour` attribute.

- A message may cause the receiver to send a message to another object to help it carry out the behaviour required. For example, the message-send

      frog1.sameColourAs(frog2)

  results in `frog1` sending `frog2` a `getColour()` message in order to determine the colour of `frog2`. This behaviour is termed collaboration.

- A message may cause the receiver to send a message to itself; for example, the message-send

      frog1.sameColourAs(frog2)

  indirectly results in `frog1` sending itself the `setColour()` message.

Learning outcomes

After studying this unit you should be able to:

- use appropriately the terms: object, message, protocol, state, attribute, argument, class, instance, receiver, message-send, message answer, message name, getter message, setter message, subclass, superclass, initialisation;
- use the microworlds in the Amphibian Worlds application to send messages to `Frog`, `HoverFrog` and `Toad` objects, including messages that require arguments;
- use the Accounts World programming tool to create and send messages to `Account` objects, including messages that require arguments;
- inspect the state of objects;
- draw an object diagram to depict an object and its current state;
- describe and explain the superclass/subclass relationship between the `Frog` and `HoverFrog` classes;
- describe the role of setter and getter messages in an object's protocol;
- discuss how two or more objects can collaborate to perform a task;
- interpret a sequence diagram to understand the interactions between the objects in the form of messages and message answers.

Unit 3

Data types and variables

Contents

Introduction

In *Unit 2* you did a lot of practical work in self-contained microworlds, sending messages to different objects in order to investigate their behaviour and to see that they have state, a protocol (the messages that they understand) and that they are organised into classes.

In this unit we begin to 'lift the lid' on how the behaviour and state of objects might be implemented. You will learn that there are two categories of data types in Java – *primitive data types* and *reference data types*.

Values of primitive types include numbers (`1234` or `564.33`), Boolean values like `true` and `false`, and characters like `'?'`, `'G'` and `'b'`. The primitive types are built into the language and so are available to a programmer for use in constructing more complex data types. In particular, primitive types are used when creating classes of objects and in their underlying (machine level) representation.

Reference data types are defined by classes and are used in relation to objects.

This unit will also introduce you to the concept of *expressions*, chunks of program code that evaluate to a single value, and to how values can be assigned to variables so that a program can remember them for future use.

You will also be introduced to BlueJ, which is an example of an IDE – an **integrated development environment**. Later on in the module you will use this IDE to modify classes of objects and to create entirely new classes. In this unit, however, you will be using BlueJ to access the OUWorkspace, a programming tool that the M250 module team have integrated into BlueJ. This tool is designed to enable you to get used to the syntax of Java and to write and test snippets of Java code in a quick and convenient way.

Data types and variables

All computer programs deal with data. Data comes in all shapes and sizes. For example, it could be simple numbers such as temperature readings, or strings of characters such as the names of account holders, or information related to complex objects such as bank accounts or frogs. If a program running on a computer is going to be able to make use of this data, the data needs to be stored in the computer's memory, and in order to access the stored data, the program needs some way of keeping track of where the data is stored – this is where variables come in.

You can think of a variable as a named 'chunk' or block of the computer's memory where data is stored (although you do not have to worry about where data is stored in the computer's hardware). By using the name of a variable in program code you are able to access the data stored in the corresponding block of memory and also to change what is stored there. It is because the value that is stored in a memory location can change that the term 'variable' is used for these named memory locations. For example, as you will see in the next unit, the position of a `Frog` object is stored in a variable called `position`. The value that is stored in `position` changes every time the frog moves to the right or the left. In other words the value of `position` varies; `position` is a variable.

In this section we will explain how Java distinguishes between two sorts of data: values of primitive data types and instances of classes (objects). Numbers such as `5` and `56.35` are examples of values of primitive data types. The frogs, hoverfrogs and toads you interacted with in the microworlds in *Unit 2* are objects – instances of the `Frog`, `HoverFrog` and `Toad` classes.

In this unit you will see that a *primitive type variable* is used to store a value of a primitive type, such as the values `5` and `56.2`. A different kind of variable, called a *reference type variable*, is used to store an object reference, which allows us to send messages to an object. The variables you used in the **Variables** pane in the Amphibian Worlds and Accounts World, such as `frog1` and `myAccount`, were examples of reference type variables.

2.1   Primitive data types

A **primitive data type** is defined as a set of values together with operations that can be performed on them. Such types are called *primitive* because they are built-in constructs within the language. (Classes also define types, and they are defined using built-in constructs, but they are not part of the language itself.)

There are four categories of primitive data type in Java:

- integer types that represent integers within various ranges
- floating-point types that represent non-integer numbers (ones that have a decimal point)
- a character type, which is used for representing individual characters
- a Boolean type, which is used for dealing with logical values.

Here we will concentrate on the aspects of primitive data types encountered most commonly during M250; more detailed information is contained in Appendix 1, which you may wish to consult at a later stage.

Integer types

There are four integer types: `byte`, `short`, `int` and `long`. The values of each of these types are positive and negative whole numbers and zero. The differences between these types are in the range of values they can represent and the amount of memory each requires. The smallest is the `byte` type, which requires only 8 bits of memory, but can only store an integer in the range -128 to 127. The size and range of the integer data types are summarised in Table 1.

Table 1   The integer types

Type	Size	Range
byte	8 bits	-128 to 127
short	16 bits	-32768 to 32767
int	32 bits	-2147483648 to 2147483647
long	64 bits	-9223372036854775808 to 9223372036854775807

In Java all numeric types (including floating-point types – see below) are implicitly *signed*. What this means is that each of them can have a positive or negative value, or the value zero. (Java uses the leftmost bit of the number expressed in binary to hold the 'sign'; 0 indicates a positive number, 1 indicates a negative number.)

When choosing a numeric data type for a variable in a program, the programmer must pick a type that allows for any of the values their variable might need to store. As there may be several types that are suitable it is usual to pick the one with the smallest size. However, for convenience, in this module we will mainly use the `int` data type for integer values.

Floating-point types

In order to store numbers that use a decimal point, such as 17.34, **floating-point types** are used. There are two of these types in Java – `float` and `double`. A value of the `float` type takes up 32 bits of memory while one of the `double` type requires 64 bits. The `double` type not only covers a wider range of numbers, but, more importantly, has greater accuracy (more significant figures of the number are stored).

Floating-point variables cannot store all floating-point values exactly. Sometimes you just get the best approximation available.

Operations and numeric literal values

We said above that a primitive data type is a set of values together with operations that can be performed on them. The operations on numbers include the familiar ones of addition, subtraction, multiplication and division: we will look at these and the other operations available on primitive types in more detail in Section 3.

In order to represent particular values of any primitive type in a program *literals* are used. A **literal** is just a textual representation of a particular value of some type – the symbol defines itself. For example, 17 is the literal that represents the `int` value 17 and `1.7` represents the `double` floating-point number 1.7. There are other ways of representing literals for primitive types such as `float` that you can read about in Appendix 1.

In M250, for numeric types we will generally restrict ourselves to `double` and `int`, since their literal representations are simple.

Character type

For characters Java has just one primitive data type, `char`, and it requires 16 bits. The literal values of the type `char` can be represented by characters in single quotation marks, including both printable (e.g. `'A'`, `'B'`, `'x'` and `'%'`) and non-printable characters, such as tabs or line breaks (sometimes called control characters).

You have already encountered values of type `char` as the individual letters in strings; for example, the string `"Java"` is made up of the characters `'J'`, `'a'`, `'v'` and `'a'`.

Boolean type

Finally, Java has the primitive data type `boolean` for Boolean data. (Booleans are named after English mathematician George Boole, hence the capitalisation.) There are only two values of this type, represented by the literals `true` and `false`. The amount of space occupied by variables of the `boolean` type depends on the Java virtual machine you are using, but it can be as little as one bit.

2.2   Primitive type variables

Now that we have introduced the primitive data types we need to consider how Java uses variables to hold values of these types in a program. Recall that a variable is like a named block of memory. Before you use a variable in a Java program you need to *declare* it; this will ensure that the variable is allocated a chunk of memory of a suitable size to store the required type of value. After declaration we usually **assign** a value to a variable to ensure that it has some useful information in it.

Primitive variable declaration

To declare a variable in Java you simply give the type of the variable and its name in a **statement** as shown in Figure 1. Note that a semicolon (;) must be used to terminate the statement.

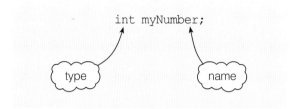

Figure 1 A variable declaration

Figure 1 shows a variable **declaration** statement, that is, a statement that reserves memory for a variable of some type.

The declaration is:

```
int myNumber;
```

The type is written first, and should be chosen to be suitable for the kind of data we want to store. After the type comes the variable identifier (i.e. variable name), in this case myNumber. Note that the name used *must* conform to the language rules for valid identifier names.

In Java, variables declared to hold values of some primitive data type are called **primitive type variables** (they may also be referred to simply as *primitive variables*, and in some languages a primitive variable is referred to as a *value type variable*).

When a declaration statement is executed it reserves enough memory for the type of variable that has been declared, in this case enough to store an int value (32 bits), and records the identifier as a way of accessing that block of memory.

This is illustrated in Figure 2, where an empty rectangle represents a 'blank' block of memory and the adjacent text, myNumber, indicates that, in this case, myNumber is the name for the block of memory. This is, of course, just a visual representation of what has happened as a result of the declaration of the variable myNumber; however, it is significant that we left the rectangle blank, because the variable does not yet have a value. In this situation it is said that we have not yet assigned a value to the variable, or that we have not initialised it.

Figure 2 The result of variable declaration

Note that, in general, it is sensible to assume that when a variable is first declared its value is undefined. However, you will learn later that there are some contexts in which variables are automatically provided with a default value of their type.

Assigning a value to a primitive variable

To assign a value to a variable you use the **assignment operator** =. The values that can be assigned to primitive variables are collectively referred to as **primitive values**.

For example, after the variable `myNumber` has been declared as above you can assign the literal value `17` to it by executing the statement:

```
myNumber = 17;
```

This type of statement is called an **assignment statement**, and this example will cause the value `17` to be stored in the variable `myNumber`. We can illustrate this as in Figure 3.

Figure 3 The result of an assignment statement

Note that, in practice, the assigned number is stored in the actual named block of memory.

When a variable is first assigned a value in this way the process is called *initialisation*.

You can only assign a value of a compatible type to a variable. For example, you could not have assigned the literal `1.2` to `myNumber` because `1.2` is a floating-point number, and floating-point literals have the type `double` – the type of the variable `myNumber` is `int`, hence it cannot store a value of type `double`. The Java language enforces rules about how you can use different types with each other, for example, when assigning values. This is a programming language feature called **strong typing**. These rules make it impossible to accidentally use incompatible types, which, if allowed, might later lead to errors in your programs. As such the Java language is said to be *strongly typed*.

In the text above we have used one statement to declare the variable and another to assign a value to it; however, you can also declare and initialise a variable in a single statement. For example, `myNumber` could have been declared and initialised as follows:

```
int myNumber = 17;
```

In some cases there are good reasons to split up the declaration and initialisation, as you will see in *Unit 4* when we discuss **object initialisation** in more detail.

Exercise 1

With pencil and paper, write two Java statements, one which will declare a character variable called `letter` and then another that will assign the character `'D'` to the variable.

You can have more or less as many variables as you like, provided they have distinct identifiers. Each variable can independently store a value. You will explore using simple variables in the next section.

2.3 BlueJ and the OUWorkspace

Now that you have a little bit of Java under your belt, you are ready to experiment with some code using BlueJ and the OUWorkspace.

BlueJ is a Java teaching environment that encompasses a *programming language*, a *library of classes* and a *development environment*. All commercial programming systems contain these three parts, with the major variation being in the development environment. For M250 the module team have enhanced BlueJ by adding a general-purpose programming tool called the *OUWorkspace* to the standard BlueJ installation. The OUWorkspace is a tool that enables Java statements to be written and tested in a quick and convenient way. Indeed, for now you will confine your work to this tool as you explore how simple statements work.

Once you have launched BlueJ, you can open the OUWorkspace by selecting `OUWorkspace` from the `Tools` menu.

Activity 1

Launch BlueJ using the BlueJ icon on your computer desktop. If a project is already open, close it by selecting `Close` from the `Project` menu. Then select `OUWorkspace` from the BlueJ `Tools` menu (Figure 4).

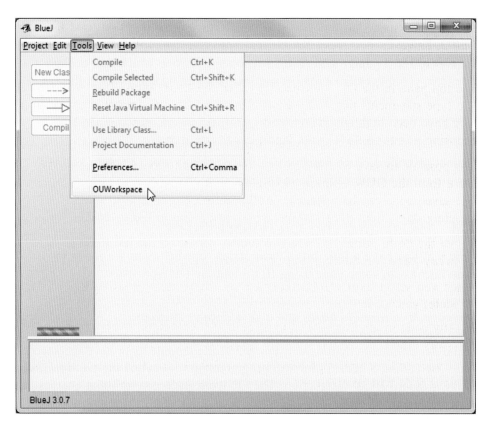

Figure 4 Opening the OUWorkspace

After selecting `OUWorkspace` from the `Tools` menu, the window shown in Figure 5 should open.

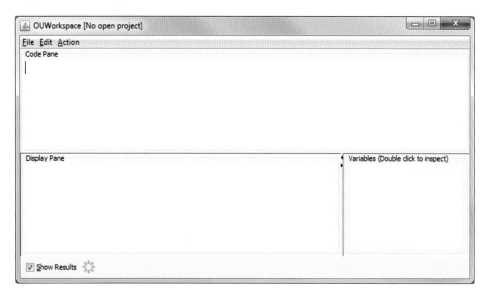

Figure 5 The OUWorkspace

The OUWorkspace has many similarities to the Accounts World used in *Unit 2*; however, it is more flexible and powerful, and will be used throughout the rest of the module.

The top pane in the OUWorkspace is called the `Code Pane`. This is where you type statements that you want executed. Statements are not executed until they have been highlighted (selected) and their execution requested by choosing `Execute Selected` from the `Action` menu.

It is possible to save code typed into the `Code Pane` to a file by selecting `Save` from the OUWorkspace `File` menu and giving the file a sensible name. The saved code can be reloaded into the `Code Pane` at a later point by selecting `Open` from the `File` menu and navigating to the saved file.

Below the `Code Pane` there are two further panes: on the left there is the `Display Pane`, on the right the `Variables` pane.

When you select `Executed Selected`, the OUWorkspace will attempt to run (execute) your code:

1   Any code in the `Code Pane` must be compiled before it can be run. Any errors found by the compiler will be shown in the `Display Pane`.

2   If your code compiles successfully it will then be run and any output from your code will be displayed in the `Display Pane`. In addition, the OUWorkspace has a feature that automatically displays the value of the last expression evaluated in the code you selected, as long as the `Show Results` checkbox is selected.

Any errors detected while your code is running are also displayed in the `Display Pane`.

The `Variables` pane displays any variables created as a result of executing your code.

Now try the following.

1   Type the following code into the `Code Pane` (remembering the semicolons).

```
int myNumber;
myNumber = 17;
```

Ensure that the `Show Results` checkbox is checked.

Now highlight *both* lines of code and execute them by selecting `Execute Selected` from the `Action` menu.

What do you see in the `Display Pane` (bottom left) and in the `Variables` pane (bottom right)?

What happens when you double-click the variable name in the `Variables` pane?

2   Close the inspector window and type in the following statement.

```
myNumber = 45;
```

Select and execute the statement. Inspect the variable `myNumber`.

3   Clear the `Code Pane` and the `Display Pane` by choosing the appropriate items from the `Action` menu. (You will be asked if you want to save the code in the `Code Pane`. You can answer 'No' to this.)

Now enter the following statement into the `Code Pane`, highlight it and then execute it.

```
yourNumber = 34;
```

What happens? Try to explain it.

4   Enter and execute the following statement.

```
int yourNumber;
```

Describe what happens. What happens when you double-click the variable name in the `Variables` pane?

5   Enter and execute a pair of statements that will declare a character variable called `choice` and give it the value `'Q'`.

Discussion

1   After executing the code

```
int myNumber;
myNumber = 17;
```

the `Variables` pane displays the name of the variable you have just declared (`myNumber`) and the `Display Pane` shows the number 17 – the result of executing `myNumber = 17;`. This is shown in Figure 6.

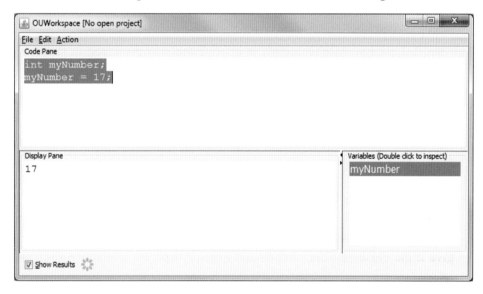

Figure 6   Executing code in the OUWorkspace

When you double-click `myNumber` in the `Variables` pane, an `Inspector` window opens, as shown in Figure 7.

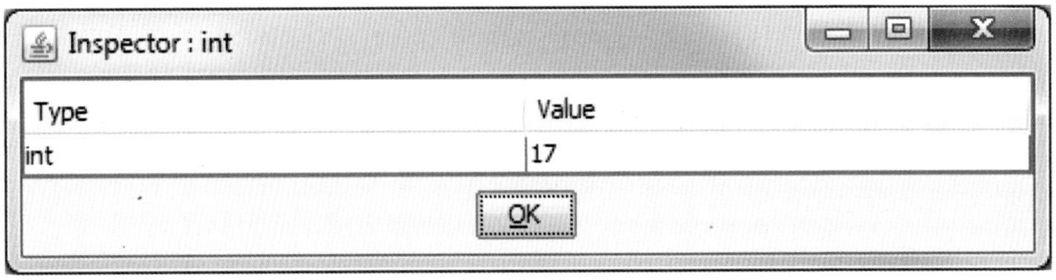

Figure 7 An **Inspector** window showing the value of the variable myNumber

2   The **Display Pane** should show the result 45 and the inspector should also show that myNumber has the value 45. Both of these confirm that the value of the variable myNumber has changed from its previous value of 17.

3   Executing the code

```
yourNumber = 34;
```

results in the **Display Pane** showing an error message similar to the following:

```
Compilation failed (24/11/2012 11:44:54)
Error: line 1 - cannot find symbol - variable yourNumber
```

This is a compilation error message (including a date and a time stamp) informing you that the code you attempted to execute was not valid Java code. In this case it was because the variable yourNumber had not yet been declared, and therefore you could not assign a value to it.

Note that the line numbering in the error message depends on the number of lines of code you selected for execution rather than the complete contents of the **Code Pane**.

4   When you execute the statement

```
int yourNumber;
```

yourNumber appears in the **Variables** pane. Inspecting its value results in a message saying 'yourNumber has never been assigned a value' because this variable has not yet been assigned a value. If you now assign a value to yourNumber (by, for example, executing the code presented in step 3), you will be able to see its value in the inspector.

5   The statements you need to declare a character variable called choice and give it the value 'Q' are:

```
char choice;
choice = 'Q';
```

2.4 Reference type variables and objects

We noted in Subsection 2.2 that variables declared to hold values of some primitive data type are termed primitive type variables (or simply primitive variables). In this section we will introduce you to the other broad category of variable type in Java, the **reference type variable** (often abbreviated to the simpler *reference variable*) which is used with objects.

Reference variables, like primitive variables, are named memory locations in which you can store some information. They typically occupy 32 or 64 bits of memory, depending on the underlying computer hardware.

A reference variable holds a reference value, but we will normally just say 'a reference variable holds a reference'. A reference is a software mechanism for locating an object in computer memory and you can think of the reference value as representing the address of an object in memory. Often we will talk about a (reference) variable *referencing an object* and sometimes we even talk about the reference as if it *is* the object. You never actually need to know where exactly in memory the object you are referencing is stored, but as long as you have a reference to it, you can communicate with it by sending messages. So, as you become more familiar with references and objects, you will start naturally to blur the distinction between the two.

A reference variable may reference only one object at a time, just as a primitive variable can hold only one value at a time.

Reference variable declaration

We have not yet explained how you declare a reference type variable. For that, we need a reference type. As you saw in *Unit 2*, objects are instances of classes. Each class in fact defines a reference type.

Reference variable declaration is just like primitive variable declaration: you write down the type of the variable and then an identifier for it.

For example, the class Frog defines a reference type called Frog. To declare a reference variable of type Frog, you simply choose a name for your variable, and write it after the type in a statement:

```
Frog myFrog;
```

In terms of its **syntax** this is just the same as any other variable declaration, but because the type of myFrog is Frog, the variable will be able to hold a reference to an object of class Frog. More surprisingly, you can also assign to myFrog a reference to an instance of a class that is a *subclass* of Frog. We will discuss more about this in Section 4.

In diagrams in M250 we use a circle rather than a rectangle to represent a reference variable. So we could represent the situation after the above declaration of myFrog as in Figure 8.

Figure 8 A reference variable, named `myFrog`, of type `Frog` that has not been initialised

The identifier `myFrog` is written next to an empty circle to show that the reference variable has not yet been assigned a value. Below the circle the text `(Frog)` indicates the type of the reference.

The `null` value

Once you have a reference variable you will normally want to assign a value to it.

There is a built-in literal value that you can assign to a reference variable, which is the value `null`. The value `null` represents a reference that does not refer to any object, and it can be used with any reference type. So, a valid assignment statement to initialise the reference variable `myFrog` is:

```
myFrog = null;
```

The situation after this **assignment** has been performed is illustrated in Figure 9, which shows the circle representing the `myFrog` reference variable containing the value `null`.

Figure 9 A reference variable, named `myFrog`, of type `Frog` containing the value `null`.

The value `null` is of limited use, however. More typically, a reference variable will be used to hold a reference that actually represents the memory address at which an object is stored.

Objects compared to primitive values

Before we show you how to initialise `myFrog` to reference a `Frog` object, it is worth drawing out further some of the differences between objects and primitive values.

Whereas the primitive types (and their possible values) in a language are fixed, classes (and their instances, objects) are much more flexible – in fact a programmer can invent new classes of object (you will find out how to make new classes in *Unit 4*). This is useful because it gives you power to model the real world in software. If your programming problem seems to call for a `Fish` class, you can invent one. If it needs a `Shoal`, you can invent that too.

You can create as many different instances (objects) of a class as you want. For example, there is no real limit to the number of `Frog` objects that you can create.

Objects usually take up much more memory than values of primitive data types. This is because an object will normally have a number of attributes. For example, a `Frog` object has two attributes: `position`, which is a value of the primitive type `int`, and `colour`, which is an `OUColour` object.

The space needed to store a given object in memory also turns out to be unpredictable a lot of the time, even though the space needed to store an object reference is the same for all objects in a particular JVM.

The main point to take away from this discussion is that a reference type variable does *not* hold an object; instead a reference variable contains a *reference* to where an object is stored in memory.

2.5   An amphibian example

As we have seen, reference variables are declared in the same way as primitive variables. First you give the name of the type of variable (which is the class name) and then the name you have chosen for the variable. Thus

```
Frog kermit;
```

declares a reference variable called `kermit` that can be used to reference instances (objects) of the class `Frog`.

In order to give the variable `kermit` a useful value, you can create a `Frog` object for it to reference. You do this by using the keyword `new` together with something called a constructor. As its name suggests, `new` is used for creating new objects. A **constructor** is a piece of code, associated with a class, for giving an object an initial state (initialising it).

To use the constructor for the `Frog` class we write `Frog()` in conjunction with the keyword `new` as follows.

```
new Frog()
```

When this code is executed, the keyword `new` first creates a new `Frog` object. It knows that it has to create a `Frog` object because the name of the constructor always follows the word `new` and the constructor name is always the same as the name of the class whose objects it initialises. The code of the constructor `Frog()` sets the attributes of the new `Frog` object to their initial values, which were determined by the programmer when the constructor was written.

However, if you want to use this new `Frog` object in a program you need to have some way of keeping track of its reference. You store the reference in a reference variable by assigning your new object to your reference variable when the object is created. To assign the new `Frog` object to the variable `kermit` (which is of type `Frog`) you need to execute the following statement:

```
kermit = new Frog();
```

At this point we can say that we have initialised the variable `kermit` to reference an object. Note that if we simply created a `Frog` object, but did not store its reference somewhere, we would not be able to send the frog object any messages.

It is important to note that references are *not* like primitive values. For example, Java references cannot be converted to or from numerical values and you cannot do arithmetic with them, so you should not think of a reference value in Java as being similar to a primitive value. A reference is simply used to communicate with an object (but it is not the object itself).

Variable reference diagrams

When dealing with objects and references it is useful to be able to represent the situation graphically. A common way of doing this is by using a **variable reference diagram**. In such diagrams, small rectangles (which may contain a value) represent primitive variables and small circles represent reference variables. The name of the variable is written next to the circle or rectangle. In these diagrams we also usually show some or all of the objects' state. In *Units 1* and *2* you learnt that an object's state is dependent on the values of its attributes.

In Java, an object's attributes are usually implemented by special variables called **instance variables** that are defined in the object's class. Instance variables can be either primitive or reference type variables. For example, the `Frog` class implements the position attribute with an instance variable `position` which is a primitive variable (an `int`) and the colour attribute with an instance variable `colour` which is a reference variable (of type `OUColour`). We will explain more about the relationship between attributes and instance variables in *Unit 4*.

When a new object is constructed, any reference type instance variables that have not been assigned a value will automatically be given the special value `null`, which indicates that no object is referenced by the variable. The value `null` is the only value we ever write in a circle in a variable reference diagram. A non-null reference is shown using an arrow that starts at a reference variable circle and ends at an object.

Figure 10 shows a reference variable `gribbit` referencing a particular instance of the class `Frog`. The diagram shows that the variable `gribbit` holds a reference by having an arrow coming from the circle, pointing to a representation of the `Frog` object (the large rectangle). While the `position` instance variable of the `Frog` object holds the `int` value 5, the `colour` instance variable references an `OUColour` object (which in this case represents the colour brown).

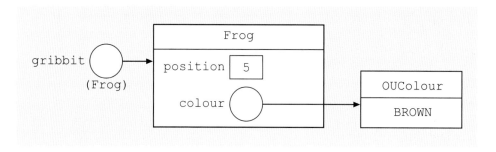

Figure 10 A variable reference diagram

The end result of executing the two statements:

```
Frog kermit;
kermit = new Frog();
```

is to produce the situation illustrated in Figure 11.

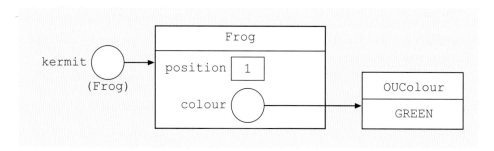

Figure 11 A variable reference diagram showing a new Frog object, referenced by the variable kermit

SAQ 1

Describe the three steps that take place when the statement

```
kermit = new Frog();
```

is executed.

Answer

First, the keyword new causes a new instance of Frog to be created.

Second, the constructor Frog() causes the new instance of Frog to have its position instance variable initialised to 1 and its colour instance variable initialised to OUColour.GREEN.

Finally, the assignment operator = causes a reference to the new, initialised, instance of Frog to be assigned to the reference variable kermit.

After these steps we can also more simply say that kermit references a Frog object.

Activity 2

Launch BlueJ and select Open Project from the Project menu (if you already have BlueJ running with an open OUWorkspace window, close the OUWorkspace before continuing). Navigate to the folder called Activities and then to Unit3, and then the project named Unit3_Project_1. Opening the project displays a number of icons in the main BlueJ window: one document icon and three rectangular class icons labelled HoverFrog, Frog and Toad. The subclass relationship between the HoverFrog and Frog classes is indicated by an arrow with an open arrowhead going from HoverFrog to Frog (see Figure 12).

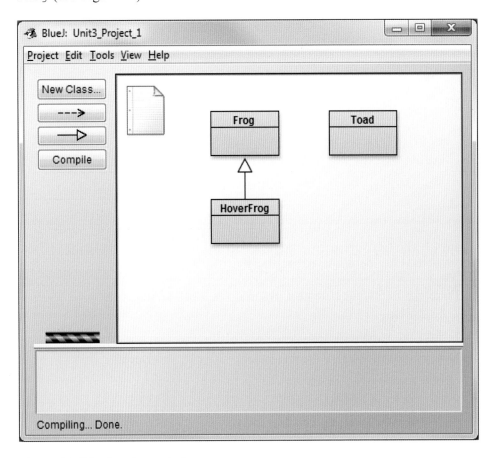

Figure 12 BlueJ project window

The rectangular class icons indicate that in this project the classes HoverFrog, Frog and Toad are available and that you will be able to create instances of them in the OUWorkspace.

The document icon gives access to the README.TXT file associated with the project. This text file can be used for writing informal notes, or documenting your work on that project. In some projects the README.TXT file will have been edited by the module team so that it contains code associated with an activity (or possibly two or more activities since a BlueJ project may be used for more than one activity). To save time, you can copy and paste code from this file into the Code Pane of the OUWorkspace. Alternatively, you can open the README.TXT file directly into the Code Pane by selecting Open from the OUWorkspace's File menu. If you do edit the contents of the README.TXT file while working in the Code Pane, it is up to you whether or not you save the changes.

From BlueJ's Tools menu select OUWorkspace. The OUWorkspace window that opens has a menu bar with (in comparison to that shown earlier) an extra menu: Graphical Display (Figure 13).

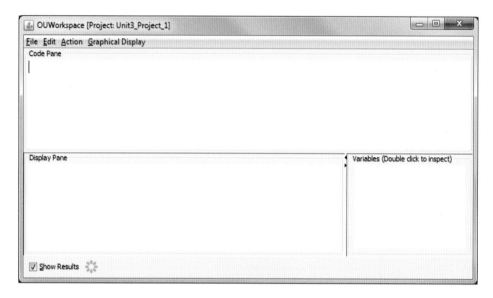

Figure 13 The OUWorkspace window associated with projects containing classes whose objects can be displayed graphically

1 Enter the following statement in the Code Pane and execute it:

```
Frog kermit = null;
```

Inspect the variable kermit.

2 Now enter and execute the statement:

```
kermit = new Frog();
```

Inspect the variable kermit.

3 Now enter and execute the statements:

```
kermit.right();
kermit.right();
kermit.setColour(OUColour.BROWN);
```

Inspect kermit.

4 Next enter and execute the statement:

```
kermit = new Frog();
```

and inspect kermit once again.

5 From the `Graphical Display` menu of the OUWorkspace choose `Open`. Once you have done this, a new window labelled `Amphibians` should appear behind the OUWorkspace.

What can you see in this window?

Arrange the windows conveniently, then, using the OUWorkspace, try sending some messages to `kermit` by typing and executing them in the `Code Pane`. Try, things like:

```
kermit.right();
kermit.setColour(OUColour.PURPLE);
kermit.left();
```

What do you observe in the `Amphibians` graphics window?

6 In the OUWorkspace declare a variable called `gribbit` and assign to it a new `Frog` object. What do you see in the graphical display?

Discussion

1 The variable `kermit` appears in the `Variables` pane of the OUWorkspace. Inspecting `kermit` shows that its value is `null`.

2 Inspecting `kermit` now shows that it references an instance of the `Frog` class, and indicates that `position` has the value `1`, and `colour` has the value `OUColour.GREEN`. You cannot see the reference value held by `colour` (knowing its value is not useful to us; what matters is the object it references). Instead, the value of `colour` has been displayed in the inspector using the colour green.

Note that although the inspector uses the more general word 'attribute' rather than 'instance variable', `position` and `colour` are instance variables of `Frog`.

3 Inspecting `kermit` now shows that the object it references has the attribute `position` with value `3` and the attribute `colour` with the value `OUColour.BROWN`. In programming terms we say that its *instance variable* `position` has the value `3` and that its *instance variable* `colour` has the value `OUColour.BROWN`.

4 Inspecting the object referenced by `kermit` now shows that its instance variable `position` has the value `1` and that its instance variable `colour` has the value `OUColour.GREEN`. (To be exact, `colour` references the colour `OUColour.GREEN`, because `colour` is a reference variable.)

The reason for this sudden change in `colour` and `position` is that the code

```
kermit = new Frog();
```

has made `kermit` reference a *new* `Frog` object. The frog that `kermit` referenced initially, in parts 2 and 3, is no longer accessible as no variable now references it.

5   When you opened the `Amphibians` window from the `Graphical Display` menu it displayed a graphical representation of the `Frog` object referenced by `kermit`. Sending state changing messages in the OUWorkspace to the `Frog` object referenced by `kermit` resulted in the `Amphibians` window graphically displaying those state changes.

6   Assignment of a new `Frog` object to `gribbit` is accompanied by the display of a second frog in the `Amphibians` window.

Garbage collection

Something interesting happened in step 4 of Activity 2. The `Frog` object referenced by `kermit` in step 3 wound up with no variables referencing it at the end of step 4. Such objects are no use to anyone, because there is no way of communicating with them. If they were allowed to remain in memory indefinitely more and more of them would accumulate until the system actually ran out of memory! Running out of memory in this way is sometimes called a *memory leak*.

In some languages, it is the programmer's responsibility to keep track of all their objects and to ensure that any memory they occupy is reclaimed when the objects are no longer needed. This is a tricky and risky business, because if the programmer gets it wrong, they may accidentally remove an object that is still needed. In Java there is a much safer (though possibly less efficient) system, which is that from time to time the Java Virtual Machine will hunt to see if there are any objects without references and, if so, it will remove them altogether so that the memory they occupied can be reused. This process is called **garbage collection**.

So, after step 4 of Activity 2, the object that `kermit` referenced in steps 2 and 3 is available for garbage collection because no variable is holding its reference.

The `Amphibians` window (graphical display)

The `Amphibians` window that you encountered in Activity 2 models the (possibly empty) collection of variables shown in the `Variables` pane of the OUWorkspace. Hence, as soon as you created a new `Frog` object and assigned it to the variable `gribbit`, it was displayed in the `Amphibians` window. However, the `Amphibians` window 'knows' how to display only `Frog`, `HoverFrog` and `Toad` objects graphically. It ignores any variables that hold values of primitive types or any variables that reference non-amphibian objects. You will learn more about how all this happens in *Unit 4*.

Note that you can open an `Amphibians` window from the OUWorkspace's `Graphical Display` menu to view graphical representations of `Frog`, `HoverFrog` and `Toad` objects if any project that includes those classes is open in BlueJ.

2.6   Variable identifiers

You have now seen how to declare and initialise variables, and we said that you could choose a name for each variable. These names, technically called identifiers, should be chosen so that they tell a reader what their purpose is. However, there is not a totally free choice because Java imposes rules on valid names.

Valid identifiers must:

- begin with an upper- or lower-case letter (that is, A...Z, a...z), or the underscore or dollar characters (_, $);
- subsequent characters may be an upper- or lower-case letter or a digit (0, 1, 2...9) or the underscore or dollar characters.

In M250 we follow the common convention of not using the underscore or dollar characters, because they are less readable, and we ask that you also avoid them – for more about coding style see the *M250 Code Conventions* document.

Identifiers must not:

- contain spaces;
- be **keywords** (keywords have special meanings in Java – a full list of them is shown in Table 2; however, you are not required to memorise them);
- be the words `true`, `false` or `null` because they are reserved words that are literals used to indicate values.

Table 2   Java keywords

abstract	continue	for	new	switch
assert	default	goto	package	synchronized
boolean	do	if	private	this
break	double	implements	protected	throw
byte	else	import	public	throws
case	enum	instanceof	return	transient
catch	extends	int	short	try
char	final	interface	static	void
class	finally	long	strictfp	volatile
const	float	native	super	while

In M250 we would also encourage you to respect the following style guidelines when choosing identifiers for your variables. Keeping to these guidelines should make your programs much easier to read and maintain.

- Although there is no upper limit on the number of characters that can be used in an identifier, in general you should avoid very short identifiers, such as `a`, `b`, `x`, or `ch` because such names are not very informative.

- Identifiers composed entirely of letters are usually the most meaningful to human readers, although it might sometimes be appropriate to use digits in identifiers for a number of similar values; for example, `frog1`, `frog2`, `frog3`. Always choose meaningful names, that is, identifiers which give some indication as to the role played by the variable.

- Identifiers should start with lower-case letters. This helps to distinguish them from classes, whose names start with an upper-case letter. Where an identifier is composed of two or more English words or abbreviations, then we suggest the use of a single upper-case letter to mark the start of each word after the first. We used this style of identifier (known as a camel-backed identifier) for `myNumber` and `yourNumber` in Section 2. Here are a few more examples: `totalCost`, `dateToday` and `myFamilyName`.

Note that M250 assessment materials may include marks for adhering to the given style.

SAQ 2

Which of the following are valid variable identifiers in Java? Give a reason in each of the cases where you consider that the text is not an identifier.

(a) `kermit`
(b) `hover frog`
(c) `hoverFrog1`
(d) `my+Frog`
(e) `myAcc`
(f) `3.2`
(g) `"iAmAVariable"`
(h) `MyNumber`
(i) `$myMoney`

Answer

(a) `kermit` is a valid variable identifier.
(b) `hover frog` is not valid; it contains a space character.
(c) `hoverFrog1` is a valid variable identifier.
(d) `my+Frog` is not a valid identifier since it contains the illegal character +.
(e) `myAcc` is a valid variable identifier.
(f) `3.2` is not valid; it does not start with a letter; in fact it is a number literal.
(g) `"iAmAVariable"` is not valid; it does not start with a letter; in fact it is a string literal.
(h) `MyNumber` is valid. However, it breaks an almost universal programming convention that variable names should start with a lower-case letter.
(i) `$myMoney` is a valid identifier, although it does not conform to M250 style rules.

Although the Java compiler will accept the identifier names shown in both (h) and (i) you should avoid these kinds of name.

In this section you have seen that Java has reference types, which are defined by classes (including ones we write ourselves) as well as built-in primitive data types. From classes we can create objects.

You have learnt how to:

- declare primitive variables that store values of primitive types;
- declare reference variables that are used to store references to objects;
- assign values of the appropriate type to these variables by using assignment statements.

You have also learnt that the attributes of objects can be implemented by instance variables, which may be of primitive or reference types.

It is very important to bear in mind the distinction between primitive variables and references: references can be used to send messages to objects, whilst primitive values are used to perform general calculations.

You have seen examples of how an assignment statement allows you to assign a value (such as a simple literal or a newly created object) to a variable. You will see in Section 3 that the right-hand side of an assignment statement can be more complex than the examples we have seen so far.

3

Expressions

An **expression** is a piece of code that can be evaluated to produce a single value. (**Evaluating** an expression simply means determining its value.) We have already used expressions on the right-hand side of an assignment statement, but they can be used in other places as well. In fact, although we have previously talked about assigning a value to a variable with an assignment statement, an assignment statement can be represented more generally as follows:

```
aVariable = anExpression;
```

The right-hand side must evaluate to a primitive value (such as an `int`, or a `float`) or a reference value (such as a reference to a `Frog`).

The simplest examples of expressions in Java are literals such as `17` or `'c'`. The literal `17` evaluates to the `int` value `17`; the character literal `'c'` evaluates to the character `c` (a value of type `char`). An example of an expression that evaluates to an object reference is `new Frog()`.

A variable that has been assigned a value is also an example of a simple expression. Thus, if `myNumber` has been assigned the value `34`, when the expression `myNumber` is evaluated, it has the value `34`. Similarly if a `Frog` object has been assigned to the reference variable `kermit`, then, when `kermit` is evaluated, its value is the stored `Frog` object reference.

3.1   Expressions involving primitive data types

You can build more complex expressions involving values of primitive data types by combining literals and variables using **operators**. In this section we will discuss some of the different kinds of operator present in Java.

Arithmetic operators

The operators most people are familiar with are the arithmetic operators used with numbers. For example,

```
17 + 12
```

is an expression built from the two literals `17` and `12` using the operator `+` (addition). The value it returns when evaluated is `29`. In this expression we call `17` and `12` the **operands** and `+` the operator. In fact `+` is termed a **binary operator** because it has two operands.

In the above expression both operands are integers (in fact they are of type `int`); however, you can also use addition with values of type `float` and `double` and, indeed, with a mixture of different types of number. The type of the value returned by the evaluation of such expressions will depend on the type of the operands.

For example,

`1.7 + 3.4`	evaluates to a value of type `double`,
`5 + 1.7`	also evaluates to a value of type `double` as the `5` gets converted by the Java interpreter from an `int` to a `double` before the addition is carried out,
`5 + 17`	evaluates to a value of type `int` as both the operands are of type `int`.

The other arithmetic operators are similar. These are – (subtraction), * (multiplication) and / (division). Examples of expressions using them are:

`17 - 5`	evaluates to the `int` value `12`,
`7.1 - 5`	evaluates to the `double` value `2.1`,
`3 * 2`	evaluates to the `int` value `6`,
`1.5 * 2`	evaluates to the `double` value `3.0`,
`6 / 2`	evaluates to the `int` value `3`,
`7 / 2`	evaluates to the `int` value `3`,
`7.0 / 2`	evaluates to the `double` value `3.5`.

The only surprising aspect of the above examples is the result when `7 / 2` is evaluated. The expression evaluates to `3` rather than `3.5` because when an `int` is divided by an `int` the answer produced is an `int` and any decimal places are dropped off the end – this is termed *integer division*. In the last example, because one of the arguments is a `double`, the result is a `double` and not an `int`. Java assumes in this case that the more accurate answer is required.

The minus operator

The minus operator is just a minus sign (as used for subtraction), but when it is put in front of a single number (instead of being put between two numbers), it produces the negative of that number when the expression is evaluated. This is an example of a **unary operator**, which means that it has only one operand. For example, `-(-7)` evaluates to the `int` value `7`.

The minus operator can also be used with more complex numerical expressions; for example, if `x` is of type `int` and holds the value `-10` then `-x` will evaluate to `10`.

The remainder operator

One other arithmetical operator that is sometimes useful is the remainder operator, `%`, which gives the value of the remainder when one number is divided by another (this operator is also loosely called the *modulus* operator, but technically modulus is not the same as remainder).

For example,

7 % 2	evaluates to the int value 1 (the remainder when 7 is divided by 2),
-17 % 3	evaluates to the int value -2,
5.3 % 10	evaluates to the double value 5.3 (do not confuse this with 5.3 / 10 which gives 0.53).

The sign of the result is the same as the sign of the dividend (the left-hand number).

Comparison operators

Because we often want to compare values and find out relationships between them, there is another group of operators called **comparison operators** that have numerical operands, but which return a value of type boolean when the expression is evaluated (see Table 3).

Table 3   Java comparison operators

Operator	Meaning
==	equal to
!=	not equal to
<	less than
<=	less than or equal to
>	greater than
>=	greater than or equal to

Some examples of how these operators are used are given in Table 4.

Table 4   Example expressions with comparison operators

Expression	Value
3 == 3	true
7.1 == 2.5	false
7 == 7.0	true
3 != 3	false
7.1 != 2.5	true
2 < 3	true
2 <= 3	true
3 <= 3	true
4 < 3	false
4 > 3	true

Note that the operators consisting of two symbols, such as >=, must not have a space between the symbols. However, although not strictly necessary, it is good practice to have space on each side of a binary operator for readability.

As with the arithmetic operators, an int value is converted to a double value when using the comparison operators if the one of the operands is a double.

The *equality operators* (== and !=) can be used with other types of operands as well. When used with reference types, == will evaluate to true if both sides evaluate to the *same* object reference. In other words, == will return true if both sides reference the same object.

The *relational operators* (<, <=, > and >=) can also be used with operands of type char. Thus an expression using < evaluates to true if the character on the left is less than the character on the right. For our purposes it is sufficient to know that character values are arranged in the following order

    '0' '1' '2' ... '9' ... (other characters)
    ... 'A' 'B' ... 'Z' ... (other characters)
    ... 'a' 'b' ... 'z' ... .

For example, 'A' < 'z' evaluates to true.

Logical operators

There are three important operators that can be used with Booleans only. These are && (logical *and*), || (logical *or*), and ! (*not*).

The behaviour of these **logical operators** is shown in Table 5 (note that ! is another example of a unary operator).

Table 5 Expressions using logical operators

Expression	Value
true && true	true
true && false	false
false && true	false
false && false	false
false || false	false
true || true	true
true || false	true
false || true	true
!true	false
!false	true

In the examples in Tables 4 and 5 above, the operands in the expressions are literals. However, the operands do not need to be literals; an operand can be a variable or indeed any expression that evaluates to a value of an appropriate type.

Before you can use a variable in an expression you will, of course, need to ensure that it has been declared *and* given a value.

For example, declaring the variable `myNumber` and assigning it a value thus:

```
int myNumber = 15;
```

would allow the following expressions to be constructed:

```
myNumber + 12
myNumber < 17
```

In fact, an assignment is also an expression, because = is also an operator. For example,

```
myNumber = 12;
```

evaluates to 12. An assignment evaluates to its left-hand side's value after the assignment has taken place.

Exercise 2

Assume that `myNumber` and `yourNumber` have been declared and initialised by executing the following statements.

```
int myNumber = 17;
int yourNumber = 5;
```

What are the values of each of the following expressions?

(a) `myNumber - 15`

(b) `myNumber * yourNumber`

(c) `myNumber / yourNumber`

(d) `yourNumber > myNumber`

(e) `yourNumber != myNumber`

Parentheses and precedence

When you use one expression as an operand in another expression, it is sensible to enclose the expression being used as an operand in parentheses (round brackets) unless it is a simple literal or variable. This will avoid any misunderstanding about which part of the expression should be evaluated first. For example, to evaluate the expression

```
(17 - 5) - 2
```

we first evaluate `17 - 5` to obtain `12`; this is then the value of the first operand for the right-hand subtraction, which becomes `12 - 2`, giving the value `10`.

On the other hand, in the expression

```
17 - (5 - 2)
```

it is the `5 - 2` that gets evaluated first giving the value `3` for the second operand of the left-hand subtraction, which becomes `17 - 3` giving the value `14`.

If you write such an expression without parentheses, such as `17 - 5 - 2`, then it might not be clear to a human reader which of the evaluations is meant. In fact, there are rules, called **precedence rules**, that determine the order in which things are worked out when there are no parentheses to help determine the order. According to these rules `17 - 5 - 2` would be worked out as if it were `(17 - 5) - 2`. You can read more about these rules in Appendix 2.

When an expression is built up using other expressions as its operands we say that the operand expressions are *sub-expressions* of a **compound expression**. For example, in the compound expression

```
(3 + 2) * 6
```

the left-hand operand to the `*` operator `(3 + 2)` is an example of a sub-expression. Such sub-expressions can themselves be made up of further sub-expressions, a little like Russian dolls; for example, in the compound expression

```
4 * (5 + (6 / 2))
```

we say that `(6 / 2)` is nested within the sub-expression `(5 + (6 / 2))`.

Such nested expressions should be read from the inside out. So, in this example, `6` is first divided by `2`. Then `5` is added to that result, which is finally multiplied by `4`.

More generally, as each nested expression is evaluated, the resulting value is used at the next level, so that by the time the outer level is reached the entire compound expression will evaluate to a single value.

There is no limit to the level of nesting; however, it is sensible to limit the amount of nesting since if too much nesting is used it can become very difficult for a human to interpret the expression. As code becomes less readable it is easier to make mistakes.

Exercise 3

In your head, or using pencil and paper, evaluate each of the following expressions.

(a) `3 * (7 + 2)`

(b) `(3 * 7) + 2`

(c) `(7 - (5 - 2)) > (8 / 2)`

(d) `(3 <= 7) && (7 < 9)`

(e) `(6 + 4) / (6 - 4)`

Activity 3

Launch BlueJ, if it is not already open, and then from the `Tools` menu select `OUWorkspace`.

Enter, select and execute the following variable declarations, one at a time.

```
int anInt;
double aDouble;
boolean aBool;
int myNumber = 17;
int yourNumber = 5;
```

In each of the following statements an expression is evaluated and then assigned to a variable of an appropriate type. When an assignment statement is executed, the value assigned is returned as the answer. Make sure that `Show Results` is checked; you will then be able to read the value of the expression that was evaluated from its textual representation in the `Display Pane`.

Enter and execute each of the following statements in turn; make sure that the parentheses are in pairs. (These statements can be seen in the `README.TXT` file associated with Unit3_Project_1.)

```
1  anInt = myNumber - 15;

2  anInt = myNumber * yourNumber;

3  anInt = myNumber / yourNumber;

4  aDouble = myNumber / yourNumber;

5  aBool = yourNumber > myNumber;

6  aBool = yourNumber != myNumber;

7  anInt = myNumber % yourNumber;

8  aDouble = 7 / 2;

9  aDouble = 7.0 / 2;

10 anInt = 3 * (7 + 2);

11 anInt = (3 * 7) + 2;

12 aBool = (7 - (5 - 2)) > (-8 / 2);

13 aBool = (3 <= 7) && (7 < 9);

14 anInt = (6 + 4) / (6 - 4);
```

```
15 anInt = 3 * (2 + 11);
16 anInt = (13 + 2) % 7;
17 anInt = 25 - (6 - 2);
```

In the next two statements we have deliberately introduced errors. In each case a bracket (parenthesis) is missing. Type in the statements just as you see them and then execute them, one at a time.

Can you understand the error messages?

```
18 anInt = 22 / 11) + 4;
19 aBool = (22 / 11 + 4;
```

Discussion

1 anInt is assigned the value 2.

2 anInt is assigned the value 85.

3 anInt is assigned the value 3.

4 myNumber / yourNumber evaluates to 3, which is converted to 3.0 before being assigned to aDouble.

5 aBool is assigned the value false.

6 aBool is assigned the value true.

7 anInt is assigned the value 2.

8 7 / 2 evaluates to 3 (integer division), which is converted to 3.0 before being assigned to aDouble.

9 aDouble is assigned the value 3.5.

10 anInt is assigned the value 27.

11 anInt is assigned the value 23.

12 aBool is assigned the value true.

13 aBool is assigned the value true.

14 anInt is assigned the value 5.

15 anInt is assigned the value 39.

16 anInt is assigned the value 1.

17 anInt is assigned the value 21.

18 When the left parenthesis of a pair is omitted, the Display Pane reports an error:

```
Error: line 1 - ';' expected
```

This rather confusing error message is caused by the compiler expecting to have found a semicolon, based on what it had seen so far (before it reached the right parenthesis).

Note that when you see this message it does not always mean that there is a missing semicolon! In this case it was due to the mismatched parentheses.

19 When the right parenthesis of a pair is omitted, the following error report is written in the `Display Pane`:

```
Error: line 1 - ')' expected
```

In this case the compiler recognised that it had seen a left parenthesis, and so it expected to see a right one.

3.2   Expressions involving objects and their references

You have seen how operators are used with values of primitive types to build up complex expressions from simple ones. However, with objects and their references the only kinds of expression we have mentioned explicitly are ones of the form

```
kermit
```

and

```
new Frog()
```

The first expression is simply a reference variable's name; it evaluates to the reference that it stores, which may be `null` or a reference to an object. The second expression uses the keyword `new` together with the `Frog` constructor; this expression evaluates to a reference to a newly created and initialised `Frog` object.

We have been quite careful up to now to point out that a reference variable stores a reference to an object, and *not* the object itself. However, as mentioned earlier, programmers will often informally blur the distinction between a reference and the object it references for the sake of brevity.

Thus although `new Frog()` evaluates to a reference to an object and not to the object itself, informally we can say that `new Frog()` evaluates to a `Frog` object. Most of the time this informality is safe, but particularly when dealing with assignments and comparisons involving object references, you will need to bear the distinction in mind.

Unlike values of primitive data types, objects are not normally used with operators. The most common operators generally available for use with objects are the equality operators `==` and `!=`. For example, if `kermit` and `gribbit` are reference type variables then

```
kermit == gribbit
```

will evaluate to `true` if the operands reference the same object; otherwise the expression will evaluate to `false`. In other words, the `==` operator just compares the reference values that `kermit` and `gribbit` hold for equality. Another way of thinking about this is that it compares the object *identities* (whether `kermit` and `gribbit` reference the same object or not).

The operator `!=` is the opposite of `==`. You can read it as 'not equals'. That is, `!=` will be `true` if its two operands are references to *different* objects and `false` if the two operands are references to the same object.

Message expressions

There is another type of expression – one that does not involve operators – that is used with objects. As you will recall from *Unit 2*, when certain messages are sent to an object a message answer is returned. For example, if `kermit` references a `Frog` object then the message-send

```
kermit.getColour()
```

returns an answer which is a reference to the colour attribute of `kermit`. Similarly if `myAccount` references an instance of `Account` then the message-send

```
myAccount.debit(100)
```

returns an answer which is either `true` or `false` depending on the state of the receiver.

Message-sends that return a value (that is, they return a message answer of some sort) are called **message expressions**. You can think of them as evaluating to the returned answer.

On the other hand, message-sends such as

```
kermit.right()
```

and

```
myAccount.credit(100)
```

do not return answers; they simply change the state of the receiver.

SAQ 3

Some message-sends return answers, some change the state of the receiver and some do both. Based on the above discussion, give an example of a message-send for an `Account` object that would both return an answer and change the state of the receiver.

Answer

`myAccount.debit(100)` does both, assuming that `myAccount` is an instance of `Account` with a large enough balance. The message-send will cause the state of `myAccount` to change by reducing its attribute `balance` by `100` and the answer returned will be `true`.

SAQ 4

What types of value, if any, do you think each of these snippets of Java code would evaluate to? You can assume that `kermit` references a `Frog` object, `myAccount` references an `Account` object, `myNumber` holds an int, and that the `balance` of an `Account` object is represented using an instance variable of type `double`.

(a) `kermit.left()`
(b) `myAccount.getBalance()`
(c) `myAccount.credit(50)`
(d) `kermit.getPosition()`
(e) `myNumber > myAccount.getBalance()`
(f) `myAccount.debit(kermit.getPosition())`
(g) `myAccount.debit(70) == true`
(h) `kermit.getPosition() + 2`
(i) `myAccount.getBalance() * (kermit.getPosition() + 2)`

Answer

(a) None, the message `left()` does not return a message answer.
(b) A value of type `double` as the message `getBalance()` returns the `balance` of an `Account` object.
(c) None, the message `credit()` does not return a message answer.
(d) A value of type `int` as the message `getPosition()` returns the `position` of a `Frog` object.
(e) A value of type `boolean`. The left-hand operand evaluates to an `int` which is then converted to a `double` to compare to the right-hand operand which is a message-send that evaluates to a `double`.
(f) A value of type `boolean`. The message `debit()` returns either `true` or `false`. In this example the argument to the `debit()` message is also an expression which evaluates to an integer.
(g) A value of type `boolean`. The message `debit()` returns either `true` or `false` which is compared for equality against the right-hand operand which is a `boolean` literal value.
(h) A value of type `int`. The left-hand operand to the + operator is a message-send which evaluates to an integer. The right-hand operand is an integer literal. The expression returns the addition of the two operands.
(i) A value of type `double`. The left-hand operand to the * operator is a message-send which evaluates to a `double`. The right-hand operand to the * operator is an `int` type sub-expression because both of the operands for + are of type `int`, but this value is converted to a `double` because the left-hand operand is a `double`.

A very important point to note is that you cannot tell simply by looking at a message-send whether or not it is a message expression. In other words, unless you know what the message-send 'means' or 'does' you cannot work out whether or not it returns an answer. Often the name might give a clue, but sometimes message names can be misleading. Before you can use a message correctly by writing a message-send you need to know what it does when sent to that type of receiver and whether or not it returns an answer.

It is important to realise that a message-send can be used as a statement on its own whether or not it returns a message answer.

For example, both the following are Java statements:

```
kermit.left();
kermit.getPosition();
```

Both are instructions to send a message to an instance of `Frog`. However, it would be unusual to find the second one in a genuine program. The whole purpose of the message-send `kermit.getPosition()` is to return the value of the receiver's position, but in the above statement the message answer that is returned is simply ignored. So the statement achieves nothing. You would only send the message `getPosition()` to a `Frog` object if you were going to:

- assign the message answer to a suitable variable for use later in the program; for example, you might write:

  ```
  int aNumber = kermit.getPosition();
  ```

  or similarly as part of a more complex expression such as:

```
int frogSum = kermit.getPosition() + gribbit.getPosition();
```

- use the message answer as the argument to another message such as:

  ```
  gribbit.setPosition(kermit.getPosition());
  ```

3.3 Strings

Although many classes such as `Frog` and `Account` are developed by programmers for particular applications, there are some classes that are used for creating objects that are useful in most, if not all, applications. There are many sorts of these *general-purpose classes* and they are provided in various libraries as part of the Java language. One important example is the `String` class.

Instances of the `String` class model sequences of characters. In other words, an instance of `String` is a collection of characters in a particular order. In Java a string can be represented by enclosing its characters in double quotes. For example, `"cat"` is a string literal representing a `String` object whose characters are `'c'`, `'a'` and `'t'` in that order. Other examples of strings are `"Hello Mum!"`, `"Whitehall 1212"` and `"013683795"`.

`String` objects are used for many purposes; for example, as file names, names of products for sale, addresses of businesses and descriptions of holiday resorts. You have already met `String` objects in the `Account` class – the attribute `holder` of an `Account` object is of type `String`. In fact, executing the statement

```
myAccount.setHolder("Grendel Barty");
```

makes the `holder` attribute of `myAccount` reference a 13 character `String` object whose characters are `'G'` `'r'` `'e'` `'n'` `'d'` `'e'` `'l'` `' '` `'B'` `'a'` `'r'` `'t'` `'y'`.

SAQ 5

In the `String` literal `"Grendel Barty"`, write down the following:
(a) the first character
(b) the fourth character
(c) the eighth character

Answer

(a) `'G'`
(b) `'n'`
(c) `' '` (a space)

Note that a `String` literal is a sequence of characters enclosed in double quotes, and a `char` literal is an individual character enclosed in single quotes. A more technical way of expressing this is to say that `String` literals are *delimited* by double quotes and individual `char` literals are *delimited* by single quotes. The term delimit is more accurate than *enclosed* because the quotes are used to tell the Java compiler where a string starts and ends so that the interpreter can determine that the series of characters is not a variable name or a keyword. In a similar way the semicolon (`;`) is a **delimiter**, as it tells the Java compiler where a single program statement ends.

If you wish to include the double quotes character in a string literal, a backslash (\) must precede each double quote, as in `"say \"hello\" to me"`, for example. The reason for the backslash is that if a double quote is to be included in a string, then there must be some way of signalling to the Java compiler that the end of the string has not been encountered yet and that it should consider the double quote as just a character rather than a delimiter.

The sequence of characters `\"` is an example of an **escape sequence**. Escape sequences are a common technique used in programming languages to tell the compiler that some text needs to be treated in a special way. Escape sequences begin with an **escape character**, which in Java is the backslash.

3.4   Messages to string objects

`String` objects understand many messages including, for example, `toUpperCase()` and `toLowerCase()`. The message answer from each of these messages (when sent to a `String` object) is a newly created and distinct `String` object showing the effect suggested by the name of message. For example, sending the string `"Milton Keynes"` the message `toUpperCase()` results in the message returning a new `String` object `"MILTON KEYNES"`. (To be technically accurate, these messages return references to strings, but we are now starting to blur the distinction.)

Another message in the protocol of `String` objects **concatenates** (joins) two `String` objects. To join two `String` objects, the message `concat()` is sent to a `String` object receiver, using another `String` object as the message argument. This results in a message answer that is a `String` object made up from the combination, in order, of the characters of the receiver and the argument. For example, `"Java".concat(" programming")` results in a `String` object `"Java programming"`.

The concatenation operator +

Since concatenation is used frequently when programming with `String` objects, a shorthand alternative is provided by Java. Instead of using the message `concat()`, the operator + (plus) placed between two strings will return a new string that is a concatenation of those two strings. For example, `"Java" + " programming"` will return the string `"Java programming"`.

In fact, if just *one* of the operands to + is a `String` object then the other operand is automatically converted to a `String` object and the + is interpreted as meaning 'concatenation'. For primitive types, such as numbers, Booleans and characters, the resulting string is made up of the characters of the concatenated value. For example:

- `"cat" + 's'` evaluates to `"cats"` (`'s'` is converted to `"s"`)
- `"The answer is " + 17` evaluates to `"The answer is 17"` (17 is converted to `"17"`)
- `10 + "66"` evaluates to `"1066"` (the number 10 is converted to the string `"10"`)
- `"17 > 8 is " + (17 > 8)` evaluates to the string `"17 > 8 is true"` (17 > 8 is in parentheses and therefore is evaluated first to give `true`; then `true` is converted to `"true"` before being concatenated with `"17 > 8 is "`)

Note that `10 + 66` evaluates to the integer value `76` (there are no string operands so no conversion takes place; here the + results in ordinary integer addition).

Displaying information in the OUWorkspace

Although you can always see the value of the last expression executed in the OUWorkspace `Display Pane` (if it has a value), it can be useful to just 'print out' values as well. A simple way of doing this is using a 'print statement'. The OUWorkspace will insert a print statement for you if you choose `System.out.println(…)` from the `Edit` menu.

You can think of `System.out` as being a reference to the OUWorkspace's `Display Pane` so that you are sending a message to the `Display Pane` to display something.

For example, the statement

```
System.out.println("1" + "2 = " + (1 + 2));
```

produces the output

```
12 = 3
```

in the `Display Pane`.

Don't worry about the syntax of this statement for now: all you need to know at this point is that any expression can be used as the argument, and when you execute the print statement the expression will be evaluated and displayed as text in the `Display Pane`.

The `ln` in the name `println` indicates that a newline character is appended after the provided argument, so that any subsequent output in the `Display Pane` will appear on the next line (and not directly after the previous output).

There is another kind of print statement named `print()`, which does not append a newline character after its argument. For example:

```
System.out.print("Some text");
System.out.print("Some text");
```

results in the following text being displayed:

```
Some textSome text
```

Equality of strings

It is important to remember that strings are *not* primitive data values. This means that it is possible for two distinct `String` objects to end up with exactly the same characters (i.e. having the same state) although the strings are different objects. Thus, when an expression such as

```
string1 == string2
```

where `string1` and `string2` reference `String` objects, evaluates to `false` it does not necessarily mean that the objects referenced by `string1` and `string2` contain different characters (or that they contain the same characters in a different order). It simply means that the two variables happen to reference *two distinct objects*. It is quite possible that these distinct objects may contain exactly the same characters, in exactly the same order. (Remember, when using `==` with reference variables, the operator only compares whether two variables reference the same object; it does not compare the state of objects.)

In order to find out if two string objects contain exactly the same characters in the same order, rather than whether two variables reference the same `String` object, there is an `equals()` message that you can use with strings. It is used as follows:

```
string1.equals(string2)
```

This message expression returns the value `true` if the receiver (`string1`) and the argument (`string2`) both reference `String` objects that have the same characters in the same order, that is, if the String objects have the same state.

As you will see later in the module, the equals() method can also be used with objects of other classes with its meaning varying from one class of object to another.

> Without going into the details here, we need to point out that the handling of String storage in Java is unusual because of a feature called *interning*. However, if you remember to use equals() to compare string contents, you should not run into any problems. There is seldom a need to use the == operator with strings. *Unit 9* will discuss this topic further.

SAQ 6

Suppose that the following statement has been executed:

```
String fred = "bill";
```

What would be returned by the following message expressions?

(a) "fred".toUpperCase()
(b) fred.toUpperCase()

Answer

(a) "FRED", i.e. a string whose characters are 'F' 'R' 'E' 'D' in that order.
(b) "BILL"

Note the difference between the literal "fred" that is a string with characters 'f' 'r' 'e' 'd' and the variable fred that references a String "bill" with characters 'b' 'i' 'l' 'l'.

SAQ 7

Explain why 'h' and "h" are literal representations of different types.

Answer

The expression 'h' is a literal that represents the single char value h, and "h" is a literal representing a String object with just the single character 'h' in it. So 'h' represents a primitive data value, not an object, whereas "h" will evaluate to a reference to a String object containing the single character 'h'.

SAQ 8

What types and values do the following expressions evaluate to?

(a) `"The answer to Life, the Universe and Everything is "`
` + 42`

(b) `76 + " Trombones led the big parade"`

(c) `56 + 23`

(d) `"56" + 23`

Answer

(a) The string `"The answer to Life, the Universe and Everything is 42"`.

(b) The string `"76 Trombones led the big parade"`.

(c) The integer `79`.

(d) The string `"5623"`.

Activity 4

Launch BlueJ and select **Open Project...** from the **Project** menu. Navigate to the folder containing your M250 projects and open the project named Unit3_Project_1.

After selecting **OUWorkspace** from the **Tools** menu, enter, select and execute the following statements. (If you already have this project open you may need to reset the workspace so that you have a fresh start. The **Reset OUWorkspace** command is in the **Action** menu.) Remember you can view graphical representations of `Frog` objects in the **Amphibians** window (accessible via the **Graphical Display** menu).

```
Frog kermit = new Frog();
kermit.right();
kermit.setColour(OUColour.RED);
```

Make sure **Show Results** is checked. Enter, select and execute each of the following statements, one at a time, noting the value that is returned in each case.

```
1  System.out.println(kermit.getPosition());

2  System.out.println(kermit.getColour());

3  System.out.println("Milk".concat("Wood"));

4  System.out.println("Milk ".concat("Wood"));

5  System.out.println("Milk".concat(" Wood"));

6  System.out.println("Under Milk ".concat("Wood"));

7  System.out.println("Milk " + "Wood");

8  System.out.println("It is " + "raining.");

9  System.out.println("He wouldn't say \"boo\" to a goose");

10 System.out.println("The End of the Line".toUpperCase());
```

Next, execute the following variable declarations and **variable initialisations** and then explain what you see in the Display Pane when you execute the statements numbered 11–15.

```
String cat1 = "cat";
String cat2 = "CAT".toLowerCase();
String cat3 = cat1;
String dog = "dog";
```

11 `System.out.println(cat1 == cat2);`

12 `System.out.println(cat1 == cat3);`

13 `System.out.println(cat1.equals(cat2));`

14 `System.out.println(cat1 == dog);`

15 `System.out.println(cat1.equals(dog));`

Discussion

You should have observed the following output:

1 `2`

2 `OUColour.RED`

3 `MilkWood`

4 `Milk Wood`

5 `Milk Wood`

6 `Under Milk Wood`

7 `Milk Wood`

8 `It is raining.`

9 `He wouldn't say "boo" to a goose`

10 `THE END OF THE LINE`

11 `false` because `cat1` and `cat2` reference different `String` objects.

12 `true` because `cat1` and `cat3` reference the same `String` object, because the reference held by `cat1` was assigned to `cat3` earlier.

13 `true`, because both strings contain the same characters in the same order, even though they are distinct objects (as we saw in step 11).

14 `false`, because `cat1` and `dog` reference two different string objects (and not because these objects have different characters, although they do).

15 `false`, because `cat1` and `dog` reference string objects containing different character sequences.

4   Type compatibility and assignment

So far in this unit we have introduced the concepts of data types, variables and assignment. You have seen how variables must be declared as being of some particular type, and how values are assigned to them using assignment statements (which themselves might involve either simple or complex expressions).

We now need to look at the restrictions that declaring a variable as a given data type places on the values that can be assigned to that variable and what happens if we attempt to break these restrictions.

4.1   Compatibility of primitive types

You might think that if a variable has been declared to be of a certain type, then only values of that type can be assigned to it. However, as you have seen, for operators like + it is not necessary for both operands to be of the same type; for example, you can use + to add two numbers of different types (an `int` and a `double`), and you can also use + to concatenate a `String` object with a value of any type. Similarly with assignment, you will find that it is sometimes possible to assign a value to a variable that is of a different type to the variable's declared type. In the next few activities you will investigate what is possible.

We will restrict ourselves to the types `int` and `double`, but there are similar rules that apply to the other primitive types we discussed in Subsection 2.1.

Activity 5

Launch BlueJ and from the `Tools` menu select `OUWorkspace`. If necessary, reset the workspace first. Remember that the type of a floating-point number literal is `double`, and the type of an integer literal is `int`.

1   Enter and execute the following statement. Note what happens.

```
int anInt = 17.5;
```

2   Enter and execute the following, then inspect `aDouble`.

```
double aDouble;
aDouble = 17;
```

3   Enter and execute the following. Can you explain what happens?

```
int anotherInt = aDouble;
```

4   Enter and execute the following, then inspect `aDouble`.

```
aDouble = 17.5;
```

Discussion

1 A compilation error message containing the following text is written in the
   `Display Pane`:

   ```
   Error: line 1 - possible loss of precision
   required: int
   found: double
   ```

   The message is telling you that this is not valid Java code. `17.5` cannot be
   assigned to the variable `anInt` because `17.5` is a `double` and `anInt` has
   been declared as an `int`. Loss of precision would result if a `double`
   number is squeezed into the space reserved for an `int`. Some information
   would have to be discarded, and thus the compiler will not let you do this
   accidentally.

   Since it was not possible to run the code (it could not be compiled), the
   variable `anInt` did not appear in the `Variables` pane.

2 The `int` value `17` is converted to a `double` by Java and assigned to
   `aDouble`, which now has the value `17.0`.

   After the code compiled successfully (you know this because there was no
   compilation error message) it was run, and the variable `aDouble` appeared
   in the `Variables` pane. The value of `aDouble` is also displayed in the
   `Display Pane`.

3 A compilation error message including the following text is written in the
   `Display Pane`:

   ```
   Error: line 1 - possible loss of precision
   required: int
   found: double
   ```

   The message is telling you that this is not valid code. A variable of type
   `double` cannot be assigned to a variable of type `int` such as `anInt`. As
   the code could not be compiled, it could not be executed, and
   `anotherInt` was not created.

4 `17.5` is of type `double` and can be assigned to the variable `aDouble`.
   This is confirmed by the inspector.

Automatic type conversion

Activity 5 shows that it is sometimes possible to assign a value of one
numeric type to a variable of a different numeric type. For example, you can
assign an `int` value to a `double` variable, but you cannot assign a `double`
value to an `int` variable (even if the value seems equivalent).

More generally, if we arrange the most commonly used numerical types in the
order

```
double, float, long, int
```

then it is permissible to assign a variable a value of its own type as well as a
value of any type to the right. (For example, you can assign a value of type
`float`, `long` or `int` to a `float`, but not a value of type `double` to a

`float`.) When such type conversions take place it is called **automatic type conversion** as the conversion is automatically carried out by the JVM.

For example, if we write

```
int anInt = 17;
double aDouble = anInt;
```

then, in the second line,

- `anInt` evaluates to `17`,
- then the value `17` is converted to the `double` value `17.0`,
- and the value `17.0` is stored in `aDouble`.

After this, the value held by `aDouble` is still of type `double`, and the value held by `anInt` is still the same `int` value that it was before. The variables only ever store a value of their declared type.

Although the rules are more complex than we have explained here, it is worth remembering that it is never possible to automatically assign a value of a larger type to a variable of a smaller type (even if the actual value seems to allow it). Thus, although `17.0` (a `double`) would seem to have the same value as `17` (an `int`) you cannot store `17.0` in a variable of type `int`, because a `double` occupies 64 bits while an `int` occupies 32 bits. There just isn't room in the variable to store the larger value.

Conversion from one primitive type to another is, however, often possible, using a mechanism called a *cast*. This topic is discussed in Appendix 3.

The `char` type as an integer

With the advent of the internet a desire to support all the different characters that are used in all of the world's written languages led to a rethink of early computer character representations (which were generally limited to a mere 128 characters) and, as a result, a new character representation, Unicode, has been gaining ground since 1987. Unicode characters were originally stored in 16 bits (allowing for 65,536 different values) and, because the Java language designers wished to support international use, this is what Java chose for the primitive type `char`.

Unicode values can be represented as unsigned integers (an integer type with only non-negative values), and so a Java `char` value can in fact be safely used anywhere an `int`, `long`, `float` or `double` value is required.

For example, the code

```
char myChar = 'a';
int myInt;
myInt = myChar;
```

will assign the value `97` to `myInt`, because the integer value for `'a'` in Unicode is `97`.

This integer-like characteristic means that you can do things such as add 1 to a character to find the next character in a character set. It also helps to explain how you can perform comparisons such as `'a'` < `'b'`, which are useful for sorting characters (and strings) into alphabetical order: the order is simply a numerical one 'underneath'. However, for most purposes you will not need to worry about the actual implementation of `char` values. Just be aware that Java characters are a little odd in this respect, and that automatic type conversion can sometimes take place.

Activity 6

Launch BlueJ and open the OUWorkspace. Then enter and execute the following declarations:

```
int anInt = 0;
double aDouble = 0;
```

Notice that we used automatic type conversion to assign the value 0 to the different variables. After this, `anInt` will contain the `int` value 0 and `aDouble` will contain the `double` value 0.0 due to automatic type conversion.

Enter and execute the following statements in the OUWorkspace, doing one statement at a time. If no error is reported, inspect the relevant variable; in all cases try to explain what has happened.

1   `aDouble = 17 / 5;`
2   `anInt = 17;`
    `aDouble = anInt / 5;`
3   `double anotherDouble = 17;`
    `aDouble = anotherDouble / 5;`
4   `aDouble = 23E456;`
5   `aDouble = 17 / 0;`

Discussion

In this discussion when we write, for example, 'anInt is 17' we mean that inspecting `anInt` shows it has the value 17.

1   `aDouble` is 3.0. Although `aDouble` is a `double` the expression 17 / 5 involves integer division so it evaluates to 3. This integer value is automatically converted to the `double` 3.0 before being assigned to `aDouble`. To get the decimal places you could have used 17.0 / 5 (at least one of the operands for the division must be a `double` for the result to be a `double`).
2   `aDouble` is 3.0. Because `anInt` is an `int`, the explanation is just the same as for part 1.
3   `aDouble` is 3.4. This time the calculation is done using doubles.
4   Here an error message of the following form is given.
```
Compilation failed (25/11/2011 12:36:35)
Error: line 1 - floating point number too large
```
    The literal 23E456 is too large to store in a double variable, so the code could not be executed and so the value of `aDouble` in the **variables** pane did not change. (See Appendix 1 if you're not familiar with exponential notation.)

5   This code compiled successfully but when it was run it produced an
    exception message

```
java.lang.ArithmeticException: / by zero
in (OUWorkspace:1)
```

Exceptions are discussed in *Unit 8*. This error arose because you cannot
perform integer division by 0.

4.2   Compatibility of class types

The previous subsection involved only values of primitive data types being
assigned to primitive type variables. In this subsection you will use the `Frog`
and `HoverFrog` classes to investigate assignment using reference type
variables and objects.

Just as with any other assignment, assignment involving reference type
variables involves a value being copied from the right-hand side of the
assignment to the left-hand side. However, in this case the value being copied
is a reference. As a result, it is quite possible that many reference variables
can all contain a reference referring to the *same* object, even though each
variable has its own *copy* of that reference.

There are also rules for compatibility of reference types. You cannot arbitrarily
assign a reference to an object of some type to a reference variable of another
type: sometimes the operation is legal, sometimes not.

In Activity 7 you will explore how this works with some real objects and
reference variables.

Activity 7

From the `Project` menu of BlueJ select `Open Project...`, then navigate to
and open the project Unit3_Project_1.

1   From the `Tools` menu select `OUWorkspace`. Then enter and execute the
    following declarations:

```
Frog kermit = null;
Frog gribbit = null;
HoverFrog happy = null;
HoverFrog bouncy = null;
```

You might find it helpful at this stage to open the OUWorkspace's
graphical display, as this will allow you to see graphical representations of
the `Frog` and `HoverFrog` objects that will be created during this activity.

2   Enter each of the following statements in turn, select it and execute it.
    After each execution inspect the objects referenced by each of the
    variables `kermit`, `gribbit`, `happy` and `bouncy` and note any changes.

If executing the statement results in an error message being written in the `Display Pane`, make a note of the problem.

(a) `kermit = new Frog();`

(b) `happy = new HoverFrog();`

(c) `kermit.right();`

(d) `kermit.right();`

(e) `happy.setColour(OUColour.RED);`

(f) `gribbit = kermit;`

(g) `gribbit.setColour(OUColour.BLUE);`

(h) `kermit.right();`

(i) `bouncy = kermit;`

(j) `kermit = happy;`

(k) `happy.up();`

(l) `kermit.up();`

Discussion

1   The first step creates `Frog` and `HoverFrog` reference variables initialised to the value `null`.

2   When you execute the statements in part 2, the following effects are observed:

(a) `kermit` references a `Frog` with `position` set to `1` and `colour` set to `OUColour.GREEN`. (Note that the inspector shows the colour, rather than the name of the colour.)

(b) `happy` references a `HoverFrog` with `position` set to `1`, `colour` set to `OUColour.GREEN` and `height` set to `0`.

(c) The `Frog` object referenced by `kermit` now has `position` set to `2`.

(d) The `Frog` object referenced by `kermit` now has `position` set to `3`.

(e) The `HoverFrog` object referenced by `happy` now has `colour` set to `OUColour.RED`.

(f) `gribbit` now references the *same* `Frog` object as `kermit`. That object has `position` set to `3` and `colour` set to `OUColour.GREEN`. What happened here was that the reference stored in `kermit` was *copied* into `gribbit`.

(g) The `Frog` object referenced by both `kermit` and `gribbit` now has `colour` set to `OUColour.BLUE`.

(h) The `Frog` object referenced by both `kermit` and `gribbit` now has `position` set to `4`.

(i) This code does not compile and so `bouncy` has not been assigned any value.
The reference `kermit` is of type `Frog` and you cannot assign a `Frog` type reference to a variable of type `HoverFrog`. More informally we say, you cannot assign a `Frog` object to a `HoverFrog` variable. You should have seen an error message that

included the words: `incompatible types - found Frog but expected HoverFrog`.
We will explain in more detail shortly why this is so.

(j) It turns out that you can assign a reference to a `HoverFrog` object to a variable of type `Frog`. So `kermit = happy` results in the reference in `happy` being *copied* into `kermit`. This results in both `kermit` and `happy` referencing the same hoverfrog. The `HoverFrog` object has `position` set to `1`, `colour` set to `OUColour.RED`, and `height` set to `0`.

(k) The `HoverFrog` object referenced by both `happy` and `kermit` now has `height` set to `1`.

(l) Although the variable `kermit` now references an instance of `HoverFrog`, the variable was declared as being of type `Frog`. As `up()` is not in the protocol of `Frog`, the compiler rejects the statement with an error message including the words:
`cannot find symbol - method up()`

The previous activity illustrates that if a reference variable is of type `T` (where `T` is a class such as `Frog`), then an instance of a subclass of `T` (such as `HoverFrog`) can be assigned to the variable. To remember this, remind yourself that we could say that a hoverfrog 'is a' frog, so it is okay to assign a `HoverFrog` object to a `Frog` variable. The subclass relationship guarantees this *is-a* relationship. Whenever you need to ask yourself if you can assign a reference to some reference variable, ask yourself if the *is-a* relationship applies.

However, it is *not* valid to assign a `Frog` object to a `HoverFrog` variable. More generally we can say that an instance of a class `T` (such as `Frog`) cannot be automatically assigned to a variable whose type is a subclass of `T` (such as `HoverFrog`).

Notice that the assignment that is valid is the one with the more specific type on the right-hand side of the assignment.

A real-world example may help to illustrate this more clearly: a trout is a kind of fish, so assuming `Trout` is a subclass of `Fish`, you could assign a reference to an object of type `Trout` to a variable of type `Fish`. However, a fish doesn't have to be a trout, so the compiler will not accept an assignment of a `Fish` object to a `Trout` type reference variable (even though some kinds of fish are trout).

Bear in mind also that a reference variable usually refers to some object. An object is *completely unaffected* by assignment. For example, if you create an instance of `HoverFrog` and assign its reference to a variable of type `Frog`, as follows:

```
Frog kermit = new HoverFrog();
```

then the `HoverFrog` object doesn't stop being a `HoverFrog` and the variable `kermit` is still of type `Frog`.

The fact that this assignment is legal results in a very interesting circumstance – the Java compiler will not know when it sees a `Frog` type reference variable whether, when the bytecode is executing in the JVM, `kermit` will be referencing a `Frog` or a `HoverFrog` object. By default, the compiler assumes that the `Frog` variable must reference a `Frog` object. Therefore, when you compile code such as `kermit.up()`, as in the last step of Activity 7, the compiler assumes it is not possible, because `Frog` objects don't understand the message `up()`. That is why we had the compilation error 'cannot find ... method up()'. Frogs can't go up, only hoverfrogs can, and the compiler doesn't know that `kermit` might actually be referencing a `HoverFrog` object.

Exercise 4

Suppose that we have a class of type `X` and a reference variable of type `Y`. Under what circumstances can you assign a reference to an object of class `X` to the variable `Y`?

4.3   Visualising references to objects

It can often be useful to use variable reference diagrams to visualise what is going on when dealing with reference type variables and assignment. We now repeat the statements that were used in Activity 7 and after each show the state of the relevant objects using variable reference diagrams. Note that in these diagrams we have added a reminder of the type of each amphibian reference variable below its circle.

After the variables have been declared and initialised (part 1 of Activity 7), they all initially hold the value `null` (Figure 14).

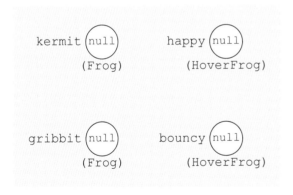

Figure 14 All variables hold `null`

Then, running through the statements used in part 2, we have the following.

(a) `kermit = new Frog();`

`kermit` now references a `Frog` object. This is shown in Figure 15 by the arrow between the block of memory labelled by the variable `kermit` and the `Frog` object.

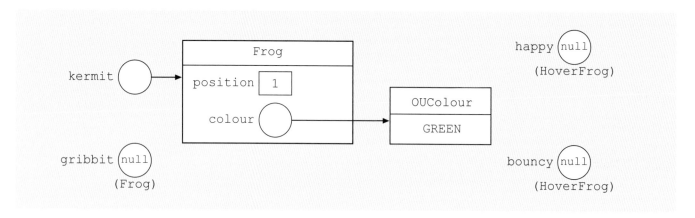

Figure 15 `kermit` references a `Frog` object

Note that in Figure 15, the instance variable `colour` of the `Frog` object is shown referencing an instance of `OUColour`, and the instance variable `position` directly holds the value 1. To prevent our variable reference diagrams in this discussion of Activity 7 becoming too cluttered, we will simplify the representation of `OUColour` objects to a rectangle with the name of a colour in it (see Figure 16). For the same reason, we have not shown the type of `colour` in Figure 16.

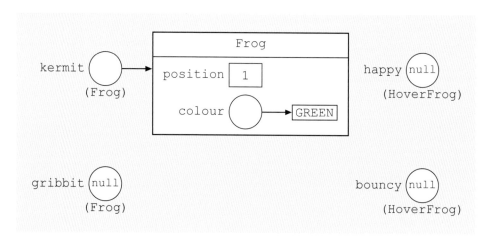

Figure 16 `kermit` references a `Frog` object (simplified)

(b) `happy = new HoverFrog();`

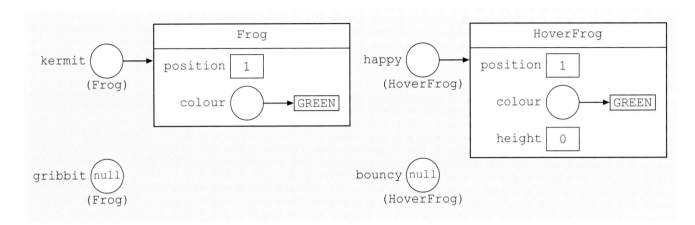

Figure 17 Now `happy` references a `HoverFrog` object

(c) `kermit.right();`

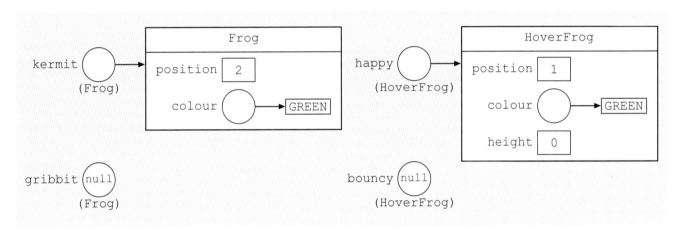

Figure 18 The `position` of the `Frog` object referenced by `kermit` has now been set to 2

(d) `kermit.right();`

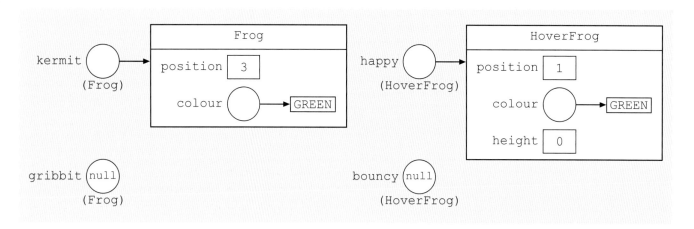

Figure 19 The `position` of the `Frog` object referenced by `kermit` has now been set to 3

(e) `happy.setColour(OUColour.RED);`

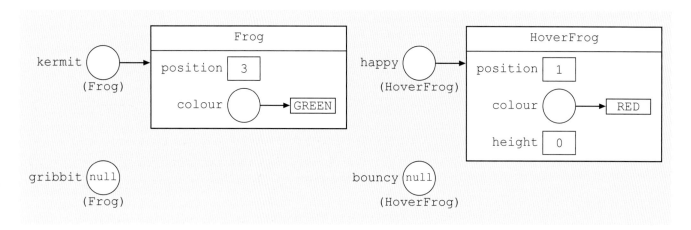

Figure 20 The `colour` of the `HoverFrog` object referenced by `happy` has now been set to `OUColour.RED`

(f) `gribbit = kermit;`

The reference stored in `kermit` has been copied into `gribbit`.

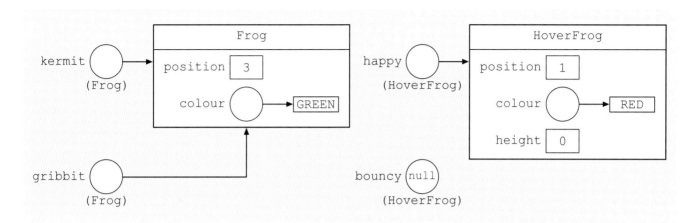

Figure 21 Now `gribbit` and `kermit` reference the same `Frog` object; `bouncy` still holds the value `null`

(g) `gribbit.setColour(OUColour.BLUE);`

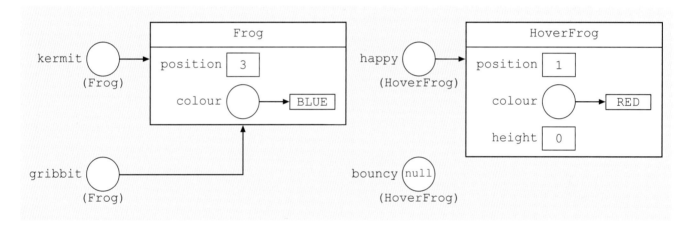

Figure 22 The `colour` of the `Frog` object referenced by both `gribbit` and `kermit` has now been set to `OUColour.BLUE`

(h) `kermit.right();`

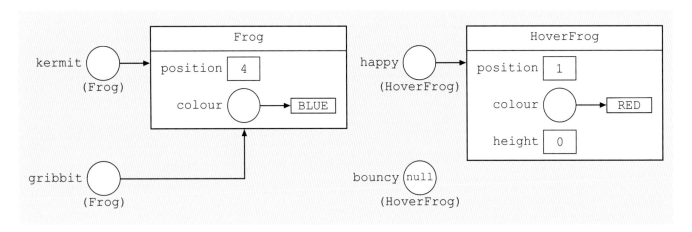

Figure 23   The `position` of the `Frog` object referenced by both `gribbit` and `kermit` has now been set to 4

(i) `bouncy = kermit;`

This produces a compilation error message as `kermit` is of type `Frog` while the left-hand side is of type `HoverFrog`.

(j) `kermit = happy;`

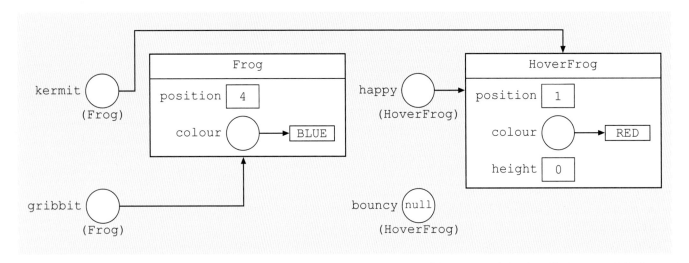

Figure 24   `kermit` and `happy` now reference the same `HoverFrog` object; `gribbit` references a `Frog` object and `bouncy` still holds the value `null`

Notice that, in Figure 24, the arrow from `kermit` to the `Frog` object has gone, as this reference has been overwritten by the reference to the `HoverFrog` object. Note that the type of the variable `kermit` is unchanged by the assignment.

(k) `happy.up();`

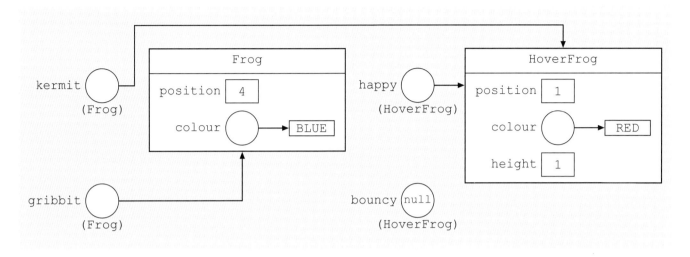

Figure 25 The `height` of the `HoverFrog` object referenced by both `kermit` and `happy` has now been set to 1

(l) `kermit.up();`

This produces an error because, although `kermit` now references a `HoverFrog` object, `kermit` has been declared as being of type `Frog`. The compiler knows that the message is not in the protocol of `Frog` objects and so it cannot be sent using a `Frog` type reference.

In the above sequence of statements note that although there were four variables involved only two objects were created.

It is important to distinguish assigning a reference to a variable from sending a message to the object that a variable references. We will now consider this further.

Assignment compared to messages with references

When you assign a non-null reference to a reference variable, you associate that variable with a particular object. In this way you determine which object will receive any messages sent using that variable. Assigning a value to a reference variable is therefore quite different from sending a message using that variable. The following example illustrates this idea further.

Suppose the following statements have been executed (starting from a reset OUWorkspace).

```
Frog kermit = new Frog();
Frog gribbit;
kermit.right();
kermit.setColour(OUColour.RED);
gribbit = kermit;
```

The situation is shown in Figure 26.

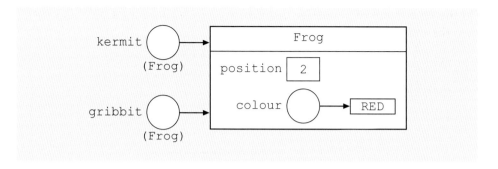

Figure 26 `kermit` and `gribbit` are referencing the same `Frog` object

If we now send a message using either `kermit` or `gribbit` as the receiver, the *same* object will be the actual receiver of the message. Thus

```
gribbit.right();
```

produces the situation shown in Figure 27.

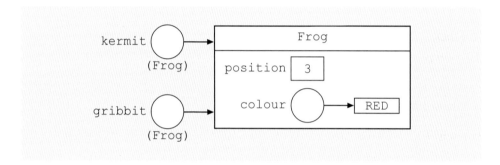

Figure 27 `kermit` and `gribbit` are still referencing the same `Frog` object

The message–send

```
kermit.setColour(OUColour.BLUE);
```

results in Figure 28.

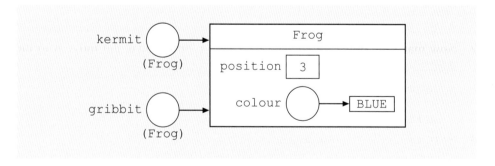

Figure 28 `kermit` and `gribbit` are now blue

On the other hand, if we assign a different reference to one of the variables, then the other one is unaffected. Thus

```
kermit = new Frog();
```

results in Figure 29.

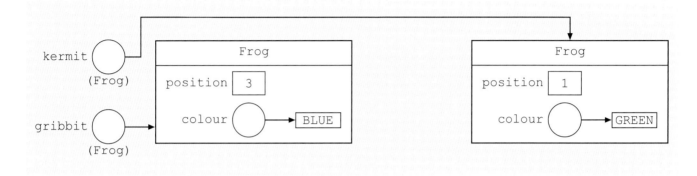

Figure 29 `kermit` and `gribbit` are now referencing different `Frog` objects

Another technique for visualising references to objects is to make use of the `Amphibians` graphical display window, which you will do in the next activity.

Activity 8

Launch BlueJ if necessary. From the `Project` menu navigate to and open the project called Unit3_Project_1. From BlueJ's `Tools` menu open the OUWorkspace. From the `Graphical Display` menu of the OUWorkspace choose `Open` to bring up the `Amphibians` window.

1 In the OUWorkspace declare two variables for `Frog` objects by typing and executing the following:

```
Frog kermit;
Frog perseus;
```

Next create and assign a new `Frog` object to the variable `kermit` by executing the following code:

```
kermit = new Frog();
```

2 Now make the object referenced by `kermit` turn brown and move it to the third stone to the right by executing:

```
kermit.setColour(OUColour.BROWN);
kermit.right();
kermit.right();
```

3 Next assign the `Frog` object referenced by `kermit` to the variable `perseus` by executing the following statement:

```
perseus = kermit;
```

Now execute the following statements one by one and observe what happens in the Amphibians window.

```
perseus.setPosition(1);
perseus.right();
kermit.right();
perseus.right();
kermit.right();
```

What is the resulting behaviour in the Amphibians window? What is the resulting state (use the inspector to inspect kermit and perseus)? How do you account for what you observe?

4   Now execute the code

```
perseus = new Frog();
```

What do you observe in the Amphibians window?

5   Now execute

```
kermit.right();
```

What do you observe in the Amphibians window?

6   Now execute

```
perseus.setColour(OUColour.BLUE);
```

What do you observe in the Amphibians window?

7   Finally, execute the following assignment statement:

```
perseus = kermit;
```

What do you observe in the Amphibians window?

Discussion

1   The code kermit = new Frog(); creates a new instance of the class Frog, which you could observe in the Amphibians window.

2   Inspecting kermit shows the expected position and colour.

3   The statement perseus = kermit; copied the reference to the Frog object held by kermit to the variable perseus. Now both variables, perseus and kermit, reference the same Frog object. You can have as many variables as you like referencing a given object.

Because perseus and kermit reference the same object there is still only one Frog object visible in the Amphibians window.

To demonstrate further that the assignment statement really did make the variable named perseus reference the same Frog object that is referenced by kermit you should have observed that sending messages using either the variable perseus or the variable kermit made the same single Frog object change state (as observed in the Amphibians window).

4   perseus = new Frog();
After the execution of this assignment statement, the variable perseus references a new instance of Frog, which is displayed in the Amphibians window – there are now two frogs in the Amphibians window.

5 `kermit.right();`
The variable `kermit` evidently still references the original `Frog` object. This is demonstrated by the fact that when you send the `right()` message, the original `Frog` object moves right.

6 `perseus.colour(OUColour.BLUE);`
This demonstrates that the variable `perseus` really does reference the new `Frog` object, as the second `Frog` object in the `Amphibians` window turns blue.

7 `perseus = kermit;`
As soon as this assignment statement is evaluated, the second `Frog` object disappears from the `Amphibians` window. The variable `perseus` once again references the same object as `kermit`, and the `Frog` object that was referenced by `perseus` prior to the assignment statement is no longer available as it is no longer referenced by a variable. At some later stage the Java Virtual Machine will remove it from memory by garbage collection.

5

Textual representations of objects and primitive values

Throughout this unit you have seen how the value obtained from evaluating an expression is displayed in the `Display Pane` of the OUWorkspace. When these values have literal value equivalents, like numbers (e.g. `1`), Booleans (e.g. `true`) and strings (e.g. `"Fred"`), this is fairly straightforward, as Java knows how to display (as text) values that have literal equivalents. But what about complex data like `Frog` objects? If a message returns a reference to a `Frog` object as its answer, how could that be displayed in the `Display Pane`? How would the JVM know what to display? This section explains how to give an object a textual representation of your choice, which can be used to describe that object in the `Display Pane`.

5.1   The message `toString()`

In Java every object is able to understand a message called `toString()`. On receiving such a message an object will return as the message answer a textual representation of itself.

The nature of the textual representation varies with the class of the object and by default indicates:

- the class of the object (in the first part of the representation);
- its address in memory (in the second part of the representation – this will vary from one object to another).

This is the case for `Account` objects: the message expression `myAccount.toString()` might return the string `"Account@bb0f79"`, where `Account` is the class name and the string `bb0f79` represents the memory address at which the object is stored.

This default representation is used if the programmer has not provided for a more meaningful descriptive text in designing the class. Instead, it is possible to provide information on the state of the object, for example. This is the case with the `Frog` class so that the message expression `kermit.toString()` returns a textual representation dependent on the state of the `Frog` object referenced by `kermit`, such as:

```
"An instance of class Frog: position 1, colour
OUColour.GREEN"
```

As a result of this choice of representation, unlike `Account` objects, `Frog` objects cannot be distinguished by their textual representations since all frogs with the same state will have the same textual representation. It is up to the programmer to decide what text to provide.

In the next activity, message answers are revisited and you will examine the way in which the message `toString()` is used to obtain the textual representation of an object.

Activity 9

Every object has a textual representation associated with it. You will now investigate how textual representations are generated in the Display Pane by using the message toString().

Open Unit3_Project_2 and note the four rectangles, labelled Frog, HoverFrog, Toad and Account, in the main BlueJ window. You will be able to create instances of these classes in the OUWorkspace.

Open the OUWorkspace and make sure that Show Results is checked.

1   Declare a variable of type Frog called kermit and assign a new Frog object to it as follows:

```
Frog kermit = new Frog();
```

Next type and execute the following statement to declare a String variable named str:

```
String str;
```

Next type and execute:

```
str = kermit.toString();
```

What has been written in the Display Pane?

From the list of variables double-click on str to inspect it. What does the inspector show?

2   Now execute a statement that consists of just the variable name and the toString() message:

```
kermit.toString();
```

Note the textual representation of the result shown in the Display Pane.

Why do you think that the results shown in the Display Pane are similar for steps 1 and 2?

3   To confirm your ideas, repeat steps 1 and 2 with an Account object.

Discussion

1   When you execute str = kermit.toString(); the text "An instance of class Frog: position 1, colour OUColour. GREEN" is displayed in the Display Pane. This string is the value to which the message expression kermit.toString() evaluates.

Inspecting the variable str shows that the result of evaluating kermit.toString() has been assigned to the variable str.

2   The result of evaluating just kermit.toString(); is the string returned by the toString message, which is the same value that was assigned to str in step 1. Both expressions have the same value therefore. The difference is that in step 1 the value was also stored in str.

3   You should have found that `Account` objects behave the same way; for example, if you create an `Account` object referenced by `myAccount`, and execute

```
myAccount.toString();
```

or if you execute

```
str = myAccount.toString();
```

in both cases you see the textual representation of the account object displayed in the `Display Pane`

Just as the icons that represent the `Frog`, `Toad` and `HoverFrog` objects in the `Amphibians` window and the various microworlds encountered in *Units 1* and *2* are not the objects themselves but are graphical representations, the results of evaluating expressions that are shown in the `Display Pane` of the OUWorkspace are textual representations of objects or primitive values and are not the objects themselves.

Summary

Variables and types

- Data is stored in named memory locations. These named memory locations are called variables because they can contain different values, at different times, during the execution of a program. Variable names must follow the rules for Java identifiers.

- A type is a set of values and the set of operations that are permitted on those values. Java has two very different kinds of type – primitive data types and reference types (classes).

- Primitive variables hold values of primitive data types. Reference type variables hold references to instances of classes (objects) – we say they reference objects.

- Variables are declared to be of a particular type and can only be assigned values of a compatible type.

- Each variable can hold a value independently of every other variable.

- Assignment is a process whereby the value of an expression on the right-hand side of the assignment is copied to the left-hand side variable. This does not change the types of the variables or objects involved.

- A reference variable can only reference a single object at any one time, but many variables can reference the same object. Variable reference diagrams can be useful for visualising a series of assignments.

- An object does not know what variables it is referenced by. Objects whose references are not held by any reference variables are garbage collected (destroyed) by the Java Virtual Machine.

- A reference variable can reference an object of the reference variable's type, or a subclass of that type.

- Any changes to the state of an object referenced by more than one reference variable can be seen using any of those reference variables.

- Primitive data types can be considered to be general-purpose data types from which objects are built.

- In Java, any sequence of characters enclosed in double quotes is an instance of the class `String`. The individual characters in a string are values of the primitive type `char`.

Expressions

- Expressions are a way of performing work in a Java program. Among other things, expressions are used to compute values and to help control the execution flow of a program. The job of an expression is twofold: to perform the computation indicated by the elements of the expression and to return some value that is the result of the computation.

- Expressions are built using operands and operators.
- Sub-expressions can be combined using parentheses to create compound expressions that evaluate to a single value.
- A message that returns a message answer is called a message expression.

Objects

- Objects are created by using the keyword `new` and a constructor.
- Every object has an associated textual (string) description. The default description gives the class and memory address of the object. A programmer may choose to provide a fuller description for instances of some classes.
- All objects understand the message `toString()`, which returns the textual representation of the receiver.
- A compilation error will result if you compile a message-send where the message is not in the protocol of the object reference type.

BlueJ and the OUWorkspace

- BlueJ encompasses a programming language, a library of classes and a development environment. All commercial software development systems contain these three parts.
- The OUWorkspace is a tool (integrated into BlueJ) that enables the writing and testing of code in a quick and convenient way.
- The `Display Pane` is used to display output from executing your code, including the value of the last expression evaluated (when `Show Results` is checked). If your code does not compile, the `Display Pane` displays a compiler error message. You may also see an error message (exception) resulting from executing your code.

Learning outcomes

After studying this unit you should be able to:

- explain the meaning of, and make appropriate use of, *type*;
- explain what a variable is and how it is declared and assigned a value;
- explain the difference between primitive data types and reference types, and how assignment is used to set such values;
- explain the difference between a primitive type variable and a reference type variable;
- draw or accurately describe variable reference diagrams and answer questions about the practical effects of assignments;
- use the OUWorkspace to execute statements that evaluate expressions and assign the results to variables;
- explain the purpose of a constructor;
- create instances of a class by using the keyword `new` and a constructor;
- explain the purpose of garbage collection and when it takes place;
- use the OUWorkspace's inspector to inspect the state of an object;
- use print statements to display the values of expressions;
- use the message `toString()` to obtain the textual description of an object;
- use simple and compound expressions;
- control (using parentheses) the precedence of evaluation in Java;
- explain the difference between the `==` operator and the `equals()` message when applied to strings.

Appendix 1 Literals

This appendix contains additional information about types in Java – this material is included mainly for interest.

Integer types

A `long` can be represented using a literal ending in the letter `1` or `L`. For example, `17L` represents a long precision integer value 17. (`L` is preferred as it is more readable.)

There are no special literals for representing the smaller types of integer; to store an integer as a `byte` or a `short` you need to assign the integer to a variable of the appropriate type.

Floating-point types

A `float` can be represented using a literal ending in the letter `f` or `F`, e.g. `17.0f` represents a float literal. Such a number will be converted to a `double` if assigned to a double type variable.

A `double` can be used to store a maximum value greater than 17 followed by 307 zeros, i.e. 17×10^{307}, compared with the much smaller 3 followed by 38 zeros, i.e. 3×10^{38}, for `float`.

There is another way of representing floating-point numbers that is useful for very large or very small numbers. This is known as exponential notation. For example, `3.17E15` represents the number 3 170 000 000 000 000 (stored as a `double`), which could also be written 3.17×10^{15}. The `E15` means that the decimal point should be moved 15 places to the right.

Similarly, `3.17E-15` represents the number 0.000 000 000 000 003 17 or 3.17×10^{-15}, as the `E-15` means the point has to be moved 15 places to the left.

Character types

There are two ways of representing literal values of the data type `char`. One is to enclose the character in single quotes; for example, `'c'` or `'%'`. The other method is to use the actual Unicode code for the character. This is done by writing the 'escape sequence' `\u` followed by the character's hexadecimal code, all within single quotes. So for example, `'\u0063'` represents the character `'c'` and `'\u0061'` represents the character `'a'`. This second approach is particularly useful for representing characters that don't appear on your keyboard, such as characters from other languages.

Hexadecimal Numbers

Hexadecimal is the base-16 number system, in which there are 16 unique symbols: the digits 0 to 9 and the letters A to F. For example, the number 15 is represented as F in the hexadecimal numbering system. One use of the hexadecimal system is that it can represent every byte (8 bits) as two consecutive hexadecimal digits.

Appendix 2 Precedence rules

Table 6 summarises the order of precedence for the operators you have met so far. However, it is always better to use parentheses in a complex expression to make the order of evaluation clear. This helps the readability of the code that you write as well as making it less likely that you will make mistakes with the precedence rules.

In the table the operators in any row all have higher precedence than those in the rows below. Apart from the assignment operator, if binary operators of equal precedence appear (without parentheses) in succession in an expression they are evaluated from left to right.

Table 6   The precedence of the main operators in Java

Purpose of operator	Operator
multiplicative	* /
additive	+ -
relational	< > <= >=
equality	== !=
logical AND	&&
logical OR	||
assignment	=

Appendix 3 Casting with primitive types

Whilst you cannot always automatically assign a value of some primitive type to a variable of another primitive type, it is possible to *force* a value of some numeric data type to be converted to another numeric data type (typically to a type occupying fewer bits, so risking loss of precision) by using what is known as **casting**. A cast comprises a type name enclosed in parentheses. Thus you can use the cast `(int)` to 'convert' a non-integer value into a value of type `int`. For example:

```
double aDouble;
int anInt;
aDouble = 17.6;
anInt = (int) aDouble;
```

In the last line above, what happens is this:

- `aDouble` is evaluated, and returns the value `17.6` as a `double`;
- the cast `(int)` converts the value `17.6` into an `int` by simply throwing away everything after the decimal point;
- the `int` value `17` gets assigned to the variable `anInt`.

After this `anInt` is still of type `int`, and contains an `int` value. Likewise `aDouble` is still of type `double`, and still contains a `double` value `17.6`. The types of the variables never change.

Finally, it is worth mentioning that you can use a cast in cases where automatic type conversion would take place anyway and in cases where a cast is not required at all, although it would be poor style to do so. In these cases the cast doesn't have any effect.

Unit 4

Methods and messages

Contents

Introduction

In earlier units you interacted with objects by sending them messages. In this unit you are going to be looking 'behind the scenes' at the code that allows an object to perform some action in response to a message. This code is termed a method – it is a method that is executed when the corresponding message is sent to an instance of that class. Thus creating new object behaviours is about writing new methods or changing existing ones.

We will also investigate how object attributes are implemented using instance variables, and see how methods can be used to interact with those variables. It will become clear that methods allow us to reuse code, reducing the amount of work we need to do when developing classes.

This unit will introduce you to two important concepts in object-oriented programming: encapsulation and data hiding. You will see that access modifiers such as `public` and `private` are important in implementing these features.

Sections 2 to 5 may look short on paper, but the computer activities will take time to complete as you will be developing your ability to use the BlueJ editor and the techniques necessary for writing code.

Sections 6 and 7 are mainly discursive, but the concepts they introduce are fundamental to your understanding of the principles of object-oriented programming and so need careful study.

Section 8 is a consolidation section. It consists of a few activities and aims to draw together, in one extended example, techniques and ideas that you have learnt in this unit. It is important to complete this section as it will give you practice in the types of activity that may arise in practical TMA questions.

2

Classes and methods

In this section we will start by exploring the code for the `Frog` class, concentrating on the methods. We will then extend the protocol for `Frog` objects by adding a new method, `catchFly()`, and add a new method, `doubleLeft()`, to the `Toad` class. Two discussions complete the section: a short look at documenting a class, and a description of the edit, compile, execute cycle.

2.1   A look inside the `Frog` class

First, we will look at how the `Frog` class is constructed, and use the editor in BlueJ to scroll through the source code for the `Frog` class and look at the various parts. In this unit we will only be concerned with writing some new methods and changing the code for others – the explanations for the various parts of the code in a class are only sufficient to enable you to carry out these simple editing tasks.

Activity 1

This activity introduces you to the way classes are written through an exploration. As such, no specific 'exercise' is set: the activity contains a discussion of what you should see in your exploration.

Launch BlueJ and open the project named Unit4_Project_1 from the Unit4 folder (remember you can obtain help about using using BlueJ, from the *M250 Software Guide*). You should see a window containing rectangles representing the classes `Toad`, `Frog` and `HoverFrog`. You will notice that the classes `Frog` and `HoverFrog` are connected by an open-headed arrow. This indicates that `HoverFrog` is a subclass of `Frog`.

Double-click on the rectangle that represents the `Frog` class to view its code in the BlueJ editor. The window that opens should look something like Figure 1. If it does not, make sure the text in the dropdown list at the top right-hand corner of the window is labelled **Source Code**.

Figure 1 and the accompanying text identify and explain some of the major elements of the code for the class `Frog`. For now, just make sure you can identify the different parts of the code in the editor, then close the editor and return to this text.

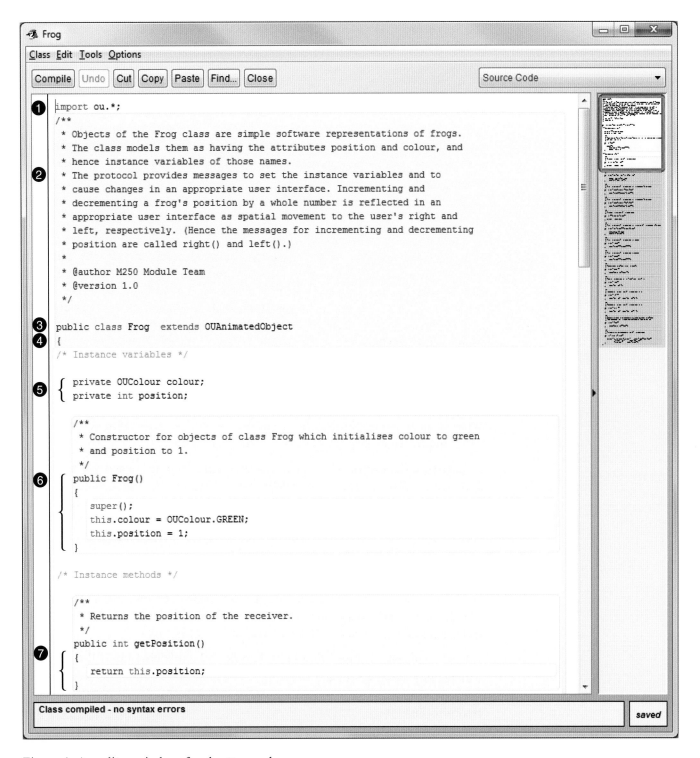

Figure 1 An editor window for the Frog class

The seven important elements of the code for the class `Frog` numbered from top to bottom in Figure 1 are as follows.

1   The first line of the code:

```
import ou.*;
```

makes use of the Java keyword `import` to tell the Java compiler that one or more library classes (previously developed code) may be needed within this class. We will discuss the use of Java libraries in Subsection 6.1.

2   The next section of code is a lengthy comment about the `Frog` class. The comment begins with the characters `/**` and ends with the characters `*/` and contains information about the purpose of the class, the author and the version number.

3   The third item is the **class header**

```
public class Frog extends OUAnimatedObject
```

This tells the compiler that the class is called `Frog` and has a superclass called `OUAnimatedObject`.

4   The fourth number points out the next line of code: an opening brace (`{`) for the `Frog` class definition, which is matched right at the end of the class (not visible in the figure) by a closing brace (`}`). Braces are important as they enclose blocks of code that belong together logically.

5   After a short comment (`/* Instance variables */`) comes the fifth numbered item, which consists of the lines of code:

```
private OUColour colour;
private int position;
```

These are declarations for the instance variables of `Frog` and every object of the class will have its own copy of these variables. Instance variables are explained further in Section 3.

6   The sixth area of code immediately below the instance variables, and after a further comment, begins with the text `public Frog()` and ends with a closing curly brace.

This area of code is the class constructor – it tells the Java Virtual Machine (JVM) how to create a `Frog` object. Note again that braces are used to enclose the constructor code.

7   The seventh and final area of code begins with the text `public int getPosition()` and ends with a closing curly brace.

This item is the method `getPosition()`. Methods define the behaviours of objects.

2.2   Messages and methods

In the activities in the previous units you sent messages to `Frog` and `Toad` objects that caused them to behave in a certain manner: if a `Frog` object is sent the message `jump()` it will seem to jump in the `Amphibians` graphics window.

Adding a message to the protocol of an object involves writing a piece of program code called a **method**. Every message must have a corresponding method. So, for the class `Frog`, whose methods include `right()`, `left()` and `green()`, there are corresponding messages `right()`, `left()` and `green()`. Notice that the message and the corresponding method have the same name.

The structure of a method

Let us use the message `right()` as an example. You have already used this part of the protocol for `Frog` with message-sends such as `kermit.right()`.

The method `right()` — the program code that is executed whenever a `Frog` object is sent the message `right()` — is shown below.

```
public void right()
{
    this.setPosition(this.getPosition() + 1);
}
```

A method consists of a **method header** and the **method body**.

The method header is:

```
public void right()
```

and the method body is:

```
{
    this.setPosition(this.getPosition() + 1);
}
```

Note that the braces are part of the method body.

The method header gives important information to the compiler about the method, including its name. We will describe the meanings of the different parts of the header shortly.

The method body contains the code that describes what to do when the method is executed.

A method should usually also be preceded by a **comment**. For the method `right()` the comment is:

```
/**
 * Increments the position of the receiver by 1.
 */
```

The compiler will ignore the comment, which is intended for human readers; it will compile only the header and body of the method.

Method comments

Our method comments begin with an opening forward slash followed by two asterisks (/**) and end with a closing asterisk and forward slash (*/). This form of comment (really a special form of multi-line comment – see below) is called a **Javadoc comment**, and it allows web page documentation for the method to be created automatically (as you will see in Subsection 2.3).

There are two other forms of comment a programmer can write, which will not appear in the web page documentation.

- Within the method body, **end-of-line comments** are sometimes used to explain what is intended by a section of code. They start with a double forward slash (//) and continue until the end of the line on which they begin. They may begin after some code on the same line, or they may be on a line by themselves.

- You can also write a **multi-line comment** in between the symbols /* and */. The syntactical difference between an ordinary multi-line comment and a Javadoc comment is that the latter has two asterisks at its start.

The method header

The method header has three parts:

1   The first part is the **access modifier**; it tells the Java compiler what other groups of objects can send the corresponding message. For now, all the methods we use will be declared `public`, which means that objects of any class may send the corresponding message to objects of the class defining the method (including you, from the OUWorkspace!).

2   The second word in the method header tells the Java compiler the type of the value returned, if any, when the method is used. The methods we consider in this section return no value, which is indicated by the keyword `void`. (`void` is termed a pseudo-type: it is used in some circumstances where type information is required, however, there are no values of this type).

3   The final word is the name of the method, in this case `right`, followed by parentheses. In some methods there will be extra information between the parentheses, but for now all you need to remember is that you must put the parentheses after the name of the method.

The method body

A method body is a block of code enclosed between braces, containing one or more Java statements, each ending with a semicolon. These statements comprise the code that is executed whenever the corresponding message is sent to an object of the class. We say that when a message is sent to an object, the corresponding method of the same name is executed (or 'invoked'). Notice that there is no semicolon after the method body.

The keyword `this` is used when there is a need to refer to the object that is executing the method and is an expression; it evaluates to an object reference. You may find it helpful to think of `this` as meaning 'me' or 'myself'.

At the time the method is executed (when the program is running), `this` evaluates to a reference to the particular object that received the message that caused the execution of the method. The reference `this` is also sometimes called a *pseudo-variable*, as it has a different value for each object.

SAQ 1

The following is the method `home()` (and its comment) in the class `Frog`.

```
/**
 * Resets the receiver to its "home" position of 1.
 */
public void home()
{
    this.setPosition(1);
}
```

Write down:

(a) the comment
(b) the method header
(c) the method body.

Answer

(a) The comment is:

```
/**
 * Resets the receiver to its "home" position of 1.
 */
```

(b) The method header is:

```
public void home()
```

(c) The method body is:

```
{
    this.setPosition(1);
}
```

Activity 2

Open Unit4_Project_1 in BlueJ and then open the `Frog` class. Notice that there is a method `whoAreYou()` in the `Frog` class as follows:

```
/**
 * Returns a reference to the receiver object
 */
public Frog whoAreYou()
{
    return this;
}
```

Note that all the method does is to return `this`.

1   In the OUWorkspace execute the following code (which can be seen in the
    README.TXT file associated with this project):

```
Frog kermit = new Frog();
Frog kermella = new Frog();
Frog frogulika = new Frog();
kermit.setColour(OUColour.RED);
kermella.setColour(OUColour.YELLOW);
frogulika.setColour(OUColour.BLUE);
```

Next, execute the following statements **one at a time**, each time observing
the results in the Display Pane:

```
kermit.whoAreYou();
kermella.whoAreYou();
frogulika.whoAreYou();
```

2   Explain what you see when you execute the following code in the
    OUWorkspace:

```
System.out.println(kermit == kermit.whoAreYou()); //A
System.out.println(kermella == kermella.whoAreYou()); //B
System.out.println(kermit == kermella.whoAreYou()); //C
```

Discussion

1   The frog referenced by kermit had its colour set to OUColour.RED.
    Sending whoAreYou() to kermit resulted in

```
An instance of class Frog: position 1, colour
OUColour.RED
```

being printed to the Display Pane (note the colour).

The frog referenced by kermella had its colour set to
OUColour.YELLOW. Sending whoAreYou() to kermella resulted in

```
An instance of class Frog: position 1, colour
OUColour.YELLOW
```

being printed to the Display Pane.

The frog referenced by frogulika had its colour set to OUColour.BLUE.
Sending whoAreYou() to frogulika resulted in

```
An instance of class Frog: position 1, colour
OUColour.BLUE
```

being printed to the Display Pane.

2   Considering the commented lines in turn:

(i)   Line //A
      The expression kermit == kermit.whoAreYou() evaluates to
      true, since all the method whoAreYou() does is to return the
      receiver reference, and kermit is the receiver in this case. The
      println statement receives the Boolean value as an argument and
      prints it as text in the Display Pane.

(ii) Line `//B`
Likewise, `kermella == kermella.whoAreYou()` also evaluates to `true`, because `kermella` is the receiver and `whoAreYou()` returns the receiver reference.

(iii) Line `//C`
However, `kermit == kermella.whoAreYou()` evaluates to `false`, because the receiver of `whoAreYou()` in this case is `kermella`, and `kermit` and `kermella` do not reference the same frog objects.

This activity should have convinced you that when the keyword `this` appears in a method it references the object that was sent the corresponding message.

`this.x`, **the object's own** `x`

In fact, you can access variables and methods of a class without using the word `this`. For example, you could write simply `x` instead of `this.x` to access an object's variable `x`, or `x()` instead of `this.x()` to access an object's method `x()`.

In M250 we use the word `this` to clarify that the variable or method we are referring to belongs to a particular object. In *Unit 5* you will see another kind of variable called a local variable that is accessed without using `this`, and it should then become clearer why it is helpful to use `this` to remove ambiguity from your code.

Each message in the protocol of `Frog` has a corresponding method that is similar in its overall structure to that of the method `right()`. A method provides the behaviour that occurs in response to a message – it describes what takes place when a message is received.

SAQ 2

What is the difference between a message and a method?

Answer

A method is a piece of code that is executed when an object receives a message. A message is the event that results from a message-send; it is a request for an object to do something (execute a method).

Exercise 1

The comment and method header for the method `left()` of the class `Frog` is given below.

```
/**
 * Decrements the position of the receiver by 1.
 */
public void left()
```

Write down the method body for the method `left()`.

Activity 3

This activity introduces you to the way methods are written through a second exploration using the BlueJ editor. Again, the activity just describes what you see in your exploration.

Open the project named Unit4_Project_1 from the Unit4 folder and then open the `Frog` class to view its code in the editor.

The instance methods are all set out after the constructor. Scroll down to the method `left()`. You will see the following code.

```
/**
 * Decrements the position of the receiver by 1.
 */
public void left()
{
    this.setPosition(this.getPosition() - 1);
}
```

Browse through all the methods that are available for `Frog` objects. Note how all the methods have the same format: the method header followed by the method body. Read the comments for the methods. Do not worry if you cannot understand the code at the moment – all will be revealed in the next few units.

Now open the `Toad` class to view its code in the editor and to see how the method `left()` for `Toad` differs from the method `left()` for `Frog`. Try to arrange the windows so that you can see both methods. (You can open an editor window for each class and have them on the screen at the same time.)

Coding a new method

Let us now consider a message that is not yet part of the protocol for the `Frog` class. Suppose that we want `Frog` objects to understand a new message called `catchFly()`. The effect of `catchFly()` – the new behaviour it will provide – is that a `Frog` object that receives a `catchFly()` message will perform its jump behaviour, perform its croak behaviour, and then perform its 'move to the right' behaviour. In order to extend the protocol of Frog objects in this fashion, a method for catchFly() must be written.

Exercise 2

On paper, write a suitable comment and method header for the method catchFly().

Exercise 3

On paper, write a body for the catchFly() method that will provide the required behaviour. Remember the braces and the semicolons.

The following activities will give you more practice in using methods and messages.

Activity 4

You are now going to write the catchFly() method for the Frog class in the BlueJ editor. Here is the complete code for catchFly(), as developed above:

```
/**
 * Causes the receiver to perform its jump, croak
 * and right behaviours.
 */
public void catchFly()
{
    this.jump();
    this.croak();
    this.right();
}
```

In order to create a new method, you need to edit the source code for the class. Open the Frog class in Unit4_Project_1 in the BlueJ editor. Scroll down to the end of the code. What you see now should look like Figure 2.

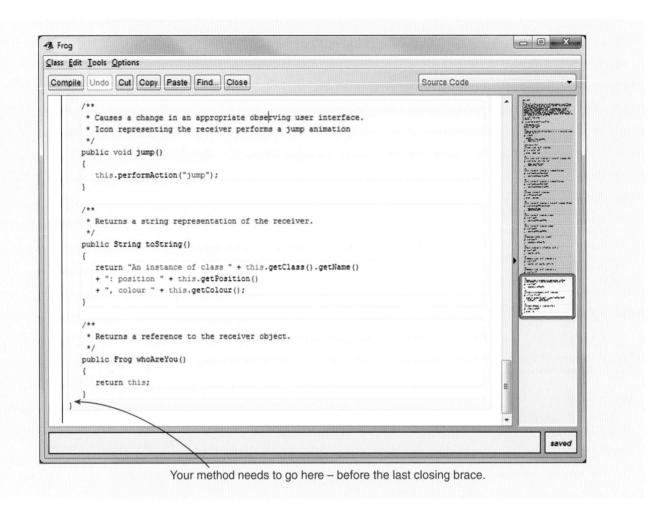

Figure 2 The source code for the `Frog` class before the method `catchFly()` has been inserted

Position your cursor after the brace that ends the last method in the class. There will be a brace below your cursor. This is correct – the class needs a final closing brace. Insert the method code for `catchFly()`. Your editor window should now look like Figure 3.

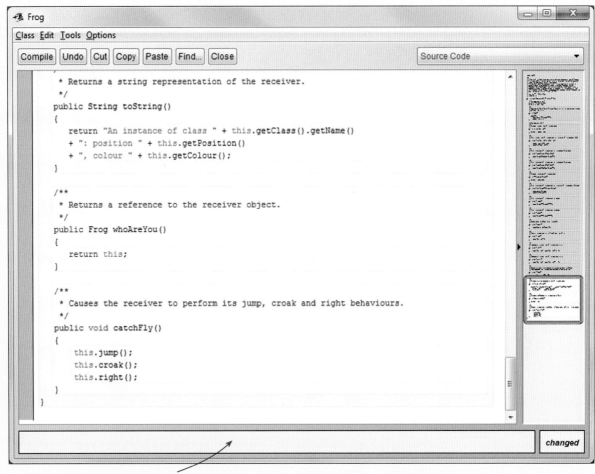

The message area, where messages from the Java compiler may appear.

Figure 3 The source code for the `Frog` class after the method `catchFly()` has been inserted

Now click on the **Compile** button at the top left of the editor window, and look at the message area at the foot of the window. You should see either the word 'compiling ...' or the phrase 'File saved' in the message area. After a short time that will be replaced by 'Class compiled – no syntax errors'.

If you have made a mistake when typing in the `catchFly()` method, an error message will appear in the message area and the code somewhere near the error will be highlighted. Check your code very carefully, making sure you have placed the semicolons and braces correctly and used correct capitalisation, then press the **Compile** button again.

> Note that after receiving an error message, in some cases clicking on the '?' icon on the right-hand side of the message area will give more information about the error.

Continue correcting and recompiling your code until there are no more compilation errors.

In fact you could have placed our new method before or after *any* of the existing methods in the class. The order in which the methods appear in a class does not matter. Usually methods are grouped together in what seems a logical order to the person writing the code. As catchFly() does not seem to belong to a logical grouping with any existing methods, we asked you to place it at the end of the class.

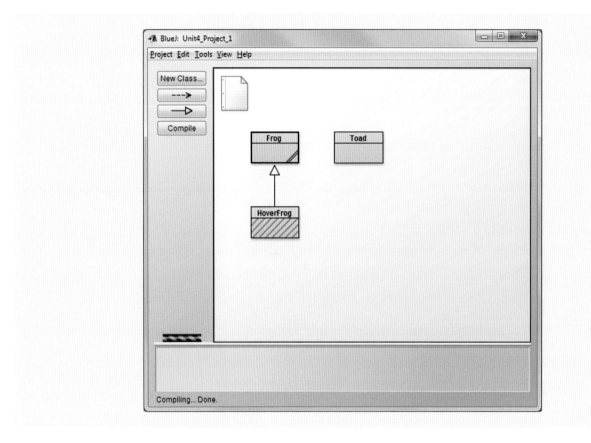

Figure 4 The project window after the Frog class has been recompiled

Now close the editor. You will find that the rectangle representing the HoverFrog class is shaded with diagonal lines, as in Figure 4. This shading is to alert you that, as it is the subclass of a class that has been changed, the HoverFrog class needs to be recompiled. Press the **Compile** button in the BlueJ window. The HoverFrog class should now look like the other classes.

Congratulations – you have created your first method in the BlueJ Java environment.

Activity 5

You now need to test your new method in order to ensure that it produces the desired behaviour when the message catchFly() is sent to an instance of Frog. To do that, you will need to create some Frog objects in the OUWorkspace.

With Unit4_Project_1 open, select OUWorkspace from the BlueJ Tools menu. The OUWorkspace will open. In order to see, graphically, the effect of sending messages to Frog, Toad and HoverFrog objects, you will need to open an Amphibians window. Do this by selecting Open from the OUWorkspace's Graphical Display menu.

Make a note of this process since in future we will just ask you to execute statements in the OUWorkspace and to view their effect in the graphical display.

In the Code Pane of the OUWorkspace window, type the following code and execute it. (Remember to execute code, select it and then either press Ctrl+E or select Execute Selected from the Action menu.)

```
Frog kermit = new Frog();
```

You should see the variable name kermit appear in the Variables pane, and a representation of the frog that kermit references should appear in the Amphibians window.

Create some more Frog objects (give them different names) in the same way. Send each object a catchFly() message, for example:

```
kermit.catchFly();
```

and observe the behaviour.

Now create some HoverFrog objects and send them catchFly() messages. Observe the result.

Finally, create a Toad object referenced by croaker. Execute the following statement in the OUWorkspace and observe what happens.

```
croaker.catchFly();
```

Try to explain why there is a difference between what happens when you send a catchFly() message to a Frog or HoverFrog object and what happens when you try to send the same message to a Toad object.

Discussion

You may have noticed several things.

All the instances of the Frog class that you create can understand a catchFly() message.

Instances of HoverFrog also understand the message catchFly(). This is because HoverFrog is a subclass of Frog and so any method with public access that is defined for Frog is also available for HoverFrog.

The statement croaker.catchFly(); does not compile (or run). Instead you get an error message in the Display Pane that contains the text:

```
cannot find symbol - method catchFly()
```

Remember that the actual error message displayed includes the number of the line within the selected code on which the error occurred.

The error message occurs because `Toad` is not a subclass of `Frog` and therefore behaviours defined for `Frog` objects will not necessarily be defined for `Toad` objects. (In this case, `Toad` doesn't provide this behaviour itself.)

Note that when your selected code does not compile in the OUWorkspace, none of the selected code is executed, even if the compilation error is only in one line of the code.

Note that before you can test any changes made to a class within the BlueJ editor you will need to compile the class. If you compile a class while the OUWorkspace is open you may find that the OUWorkspace is reset. All the variables will be removed from the `Variables` list and the `Display Pane` will be cleared; however, any statements in the `Code Pane` will remain. Any associated `Graphics Display` window will also be closed. The reset is necessary because current instances of the class in the OUWorkspace may not be consistent with the revised class, and how those instances interact with instances of other classes in the OUWorkspace may also have changed. The OUWorkspace only resets automatically for classes that it 'knows' about (such as the amphibian classes), so there are occasions where a manual reset will be needed before recompiled classes can be properly tested. To reset manually, use the `Reset OUWorkspace` function in the `Action` menu.

Activity 6

This activity continues to use the project Unit4_Project_1.

You are now going to write a new method, called `doubleLeft()`, for the `Toad` class. This method will perform the `Toad` class's left behaviour twice. However, before defining this new method, satisfy yourself that `Toad` objects do not currently understand a `doubleLeft()` message.

1   In the OUWorkspace, execute the following statements:

```
Toad toad1 = new Toad();
toad1.doubleLeft();
```

2   We will now guide you through the code for the new method.

The comment and method header for your new method `doubleLeft()` are given below.

```
/**
 * Performs the left behaviour twice.
 */
public void doubleLeft()
```

Open the `Toad` class in the editor. Start writing the new method after the other methods in the `Toad` class, just as you added the method `catchFly()` to the `Frog` class.

You now need to write the method body to achieve the effect indicated in the comment. This can be done by sending the message `left()` twice to the object referenced by `this` (the object whose method is being executed).

Complete your method by writing the two statements and the enclosing braces. Compile the `Toad` class (correcting any errors you may have made).

3   Test your new method by sending `doubleLeft()` messages to some `Toad` instances you create in the OUWorkspace. You might like to use the following code to start with.

```
Toad toad1 = new Toad();
toad1.doubleLeft();
```

Discussion

1   You should see an error message containing the words:

```
cannot find symbol - method doubleLeft()
```

2   Here is the complete `doubleLeft()` method.

```
/**
 * Performs the left behaviour twice.
 */
public void doubleLeft()
{
    this.left();
    this.left();
}
```

3   Check that the `doubleLeft()` messages have worked by inspecting the `position` for `toad1` or by watching the progress of the toad icon in the **Amphibians** window. To inspect, double-click on `toad1` in the OUWorkspace **Variables** pane (or press **ENTER** when it is selected).

Now you have completed these activities, you have:

• used the BlueJ editor and examined existing methods for a selected class;

• defined new methods for a class, compiled and tested them;

• seen that if a method is defined for a particular class and declared as `public`, then the corresponding message can be sent to objects of that class and its subclasses.

If you have had difficulties with Activities 3–5, Unit4_Project_2 incorporates all the changes made to the classes `Frog` and `Toad` in this set of activities (note that the `whoAreYou()` method has been omitted).

SAQ 3

What do you need to do to add a new message to the protocol of an object?

Answer

Adding a message to the protocol requires editing the related class definition to add a new method and recompiling the class.

SAQ 4

How can an object send a message to itself?

Answer

In a method you can use the keyword `this` whenever you want to refer to the object currently executing the method. So `this` is a 'self' reference.

2.3   Documenting methods with Javadoc

When writing a large program it is important that there is some form of document recording how the program works; however, if the program changes the documentation must change as well. For large programs that are constantly being changed and improved, it would be a tedious and error-prone task to separately maintain documentation and keep it consistent with the source code. There are many tools available to help ease this task, and a standard tool for Java is **Javadoc**, a program documentation tool that comes with Java and that can be run directly from BlueJ.

Each time we have asked you to write a method, we have given a description of what the method is intended to do in the form of a Javadoc comment. Javadoc comments can also be used to document classes and constructors.

When you run the Javadoc tool it picks up information from these specially formatted comments and they are used to create an HTML file, which documents the class in a widely accepted, industry standard way. This documentation is aimed at human readers (including possibly the writer of the code, as they might well forget what the methods do). Since Javadoc documentation is aimed mainly at people who want to make use of the code, by default it only includes items that can be accessed from outside the class itself.

Activity 7

Open Unit4_Project_2. As previously indicated, this project incorporates all the changes made to the classes `Frog` and `Toad` in Activities 3–5 (although the `whoAreYou()` method has been removed).

1   From the `Tools` menu select `Project Documentation` (or press `Ctrl+J` on your keyboard).

A dialogue box may appear; if it does, click on `Regenerate`. This causes the Javadoc tool to run.

After a short while a browser window will appear containing the Javadoc documentation for the project. The left-hand frame of the browser window will display an alphabetical list of all the classes in the project. The right-hand pane will display the documentation for the selected class in the left-hand frame, in this case the documentation for the class `Frog`.

Try clicking on another class name and on a method name.

Can you explain what you see? For now, ignore the links at the top of the right-hand frame, above the class documentation.

2   Close the browser window, open the `Frog` class in the editor, and move (cut and paste) the comment for `catchFly()` to after the method header. Recompile the `Frog` class. Did `Frog` recompile successfully?

Once the class has recompiled, select **Project Documentation** from the BlueJ **Tools** menu. Click on **Regenerate** in the dialogue box that appears. Look at the Javadoc entry for `catchFly()`. What do you notice?

Return the comment for `catchFly()` to the correct position and recompile the `Frog` class. Close the editor and the browser, and exit from BlueJ.

Discussion

1   Here is a short explanation of the main parts of the documentation that you might find useful as you scroll downwards.

The first section under the title 'Class Frog' shows where `Frog` comes in the class hierarchy. It is a subclass of `OUAnimatedObject` and has one subclass, called `HoverFrog`.

The second section shows the class comment.

Next, the constructor summary displays the first sentence of the constructor's comment. This is followed by a summary of methods, in alphabetical order. These summaries consist of:

o   the return type

o   the name of the method

o   any arguments the method requires when it is executed

o   the first sentence in the method's comment.

Inherited methods are displayed in the next section, beginning with `Frog`'s superclass `OUAnimatedObject`. The second section lists methods inherited from the class `Observable`, and the last from class `Object`.

Clicking on the name of a method or constructor will display the full information available about that item in your web browser (including its full header). In fact, these 'method details' are in the same document after the constructor and method summaries, as you can see if you continue to scroll down the page.

Note particularly the method `catchFly()`. You should see the comment you typed in for the method.

2   You should have been able to recompile the `Frog` class without difficulty – the Java compiler takes no notice of the comment or where it is placed. However, you should find that the Javadoc tool has now failed to pick up

the comment, and so it is missing from the entry for the method `catchFly()`.

As Activity 7 shows, documentation will be picked up by Javadoc only if it is in a particular form *and* position. So far you have learnt that:

- you must enclose a Javadoc method comment between /** and */, and
- you must place a method comment directly before the method header.

Method comments serve several purposes.

- They help focus your mind on the purpose of the method, that is, on the behaviour the corresponding message will cause.
- Months later, when as a student you are revising, or as a programmer you are reviewing this method among dozens of other methods you have written previously, comments can be enormously helpful in giving you a quick reminder of what the code is about.
- They support reuse of code as they help anyone else looking at your code to understand how to use the method and what the method should do.

Notice that a method comment should not focus on *how* the code works; it should focus on the code's purpose or effect.

Although you should always include a method comment, you need not use comments within a method body. As a general rule, comments other than the initial one are more about how a method is implemented. You should use these when you think that something is tricky to understand, so that the person reading the code will know what was intended.

2.4   Editing, compiling and executing methods

This section explains the relationship between what you write in a class, code compilation and code execution, and reviews some material from *Unit 1*.

Java is a high-level programming language: it is designed so that human beings can read it. A Java program is written, or modified, using an editor. This could be a simple text editor such as Notepad, but in this module you use the editor provided by the BlueJ environment. The code you write is called the source code. For example, earlier in this unit you used the editor to modify the source code for the Frog class by adding a method catchFly(). Source code file names have the extension .java.

For the code to be executed on a computer, the Java compiler must first compile it into an intermediate form called bytecode. In BlueJ, the compilation is done when the **Compile** button is pressed. Bytecode file names have the extension .class. In the case of the Frog class, the compiler will create the file Frog.class from the source code file Frog.java. The bytecode for a class must be recreated when its source code is modified and may also need recompiling when other related classes are changed.

The bytecode file is portable, because each computer that can run Java programs has a JVM – which is itself a program – that understands bytecode and converts it into the machine code required for that particular computer. So any computer with a suitable JVM will be able to execute the bytecode for our compiled class `Frog`.

When an object receives a message (while a program is running, that is at *run-time*), the JVM selects the appropriate method to be executed (determined by the class of the object). We call this **invoking** the method or **method invocation**. The first time a method is used at run-time, the JVM converts the corresponding bytecode into the machine code appropriate for that particular computer.

Once the bytecode for a method has been translated into machine code, the JVM retains the machine code for the next time the method is required, so it does not have to do the translation over and over again. If a method is never used at run-time, it is never compiled to machine code.

A bit of bytecode

Java programmers almost never have to be concerned with bytecode – the compiler and the JVM deal with that side of things. However, purely for interest, here is a snippet of bytecode. Can you guess what it is?

```
0: aload_0

1: aload_0

2: invokevirtual #28; //Method getPosition:()I

5: iconst_1

6: isub

7: invokevirtual #27; //Method setPosition:(I)V

10: return
```

3

Instance variables

You have seen that when a message is sent to a `Frog` object a method with the same name is executed. Some methods, such as `left()`, result in the state of the object changing, while some methods may answer with (that is, *return*) some information relating to the state of the object. The current state of an object is represented by the values of its instance variables.

You have already seen a pictorial representation of instance variables in the variable reference diagrams we introduced in *Unit 3*. Here, for example, is a diagram that represents a potential state of a `Frog` object referenced by `gribbit`.

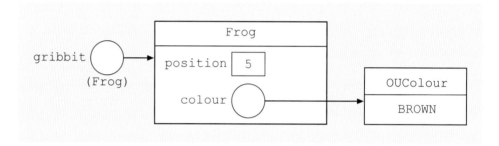

Figure 5 Diagrammatic representation of a `Frog` object referenced by `gribbit`

The diagram shows that the `Frog` object has two instance variables, `position` and `colour`, and that the value of `position` is 5. The instance variable `colour` references a separate object, of type `OUColour`. Its state is BROWN. (We omit details of the state of `OUColour` for simplicity.)

This section looks at how we implement state using instance variables and at how we can use methods to interact with instance variables. We conclude by showing how to add a new instance variable to a class.

Activity 8

Open the class `Frog` in the project Unit4_Project_2. Find all the Java statements that use the instance variable `colour`. (You might like to use the `Find …` option under the `Tools` menu in the editor.)

What do you think each statement does?

Discussion

The Java statements that use the instance variable `colour` directly are as follows.

1   `private OUColour colour;`

   The above statement appears immediately after the class header and before the constructor. This statement and the following statement:

   `private int position;`

   are the variable declarations that define the instance variables for all `Frog` objects. That is, they tell the Java compiler the name of each instance variable and the type of value it can hold. In this case, the instance variable `colour` is defined to hold a reference to an instance of the class `OUColour`.

   The access modifier `private` tells the Java compiler that the instance variable can be accessed directly only within the class itself. (Once objects of the class have been created, their `private` instance variables will be accessible only to objects of the same class.)

2   `this.colour = OUColour.GREEN;`

   This statement is in the constructor for the class `Frog`. It accesses the instance variable `colour` and assigns to it a reference to the object `OUColour.GREEN`.

3   `return this.colour;`

   This statement is in the method `getColour()`. It accesses the `colour` instance variable of the receiver and returns its value. We discuss methods that return values in Section 4.

4   `this.colour = aColour;`

   This statement is in the method `setColour()`. It copies the reference held in `aColour` into `colour`. We discuss methods like `setColour()` in more detail in Subsection 3.2 and Section 5.

   An expression such as `this.colour` (or `colour`) is called a **direct access** of the `colour` instance variable of the object referenced by `this`. By direct access, we mean that we have not used a method to access the variable. When we speak of accessing a variable, we normally mean directly accessing it.

3.1   Constructors and initialisation

Activity 8 illustrated how instance variables are declared and how they can be used. When an instance of a class is created – using, as you saw in *Unit 3*, Subsection 2.5, the keyword `new` – all of its instance variables have to be given an initial state. This is done by a constructor.

SAQ 5

Write down a Java statement to create an instance of the class `Frog` referenced by a newly declared variable called `aFrog`.

Answer

```
Frog aFrog = new Frog();
```

As an example of how to write a constructor, we look at the constructor for the `Frog` class in Exercise 4.

Exercise 4

The `Frog` constructor is shown below. The statement `super();` will be explained in *Unit 6*; for the moment we will ignore it. What is the purpose of the other two statements?

```
/**
 * Constructor for objects of class Frog which
 * initialises colour to green and position to 1.
 */
public Frog()
{
    super();
    this.colour = OUColour.GREEN;
    this.position = 1;
}
```

3.2   Setter and getter methods

Now we will look at how you can interact with instance variables using setter and getter methods, which are the methods corresponding to the setter and getter messages you first saw in *Unit 2*.

For these methods the access modifier in the method header is often `public` so that objects of any class can send the corresponding messages. The implication of this design decision is that objects of any class will be able to discover information about and to indirectly interact with the state of the objects of a given class. Here we look at the `Frog` class as an example.

Activity 9

You have seen in Activity 8 that the method `setColour()` sets the instance variable `colour`. It does this by means of the following assignment statement:

```
this.colour = aColour;
```

Are there any other methods defined for the `Frog` class that also change the value of instance variables directly by assignment? Use the BlueJ editor to examine all the methods defined for `Frog` in the project Unit4_Project_2.

Discussion

You should have identified `setPosition()` as the only other method that sets an instance variable directly, using assignment. (Note that although the constructor also directly assigns values to the instance variables, constructors are not methods.)

Setter methods

Methods that directly access and set values of instance variables, such as `setPosition()` and `setColour()`, are called **setter methods** or setters (also sometimes known as **mutator methods**).

You will have noticed that `setColour()` assigned a value to the instance variable called `colour`, and `setPosition()` assigned a value to the instance variable called `position`. This method naming is typical: a setter's name is usually formed from the word `set` followed by the name of the instance variable (with its initial letter capitalised) to which it assigns a value. This method naming is purely a convention, but it is one that is strongly adhered to by Java programmers (indeed, setter and getter methods in a certain type of class called a JavaBean, which lies outside the scope of M250, *must* follow the conventions outlined here).

As they need to set an instance variable to some value, setter methods also typically receive a single argument. The ability to receive a value in this way is indicated in the setter method's header; for example, by the text `int aPosition` in the case of `setPosition()`. (Arguments are discussed in more detail in Section 5.)

Note that whilst other methods in a class can also be written so that they directly set instance variables, we do not recommend this, and in M250 we will normally allow *only* setter methods and constructors to directly set instance variables.

Getter methods

We also often require methods, called **getter methods** or getters (also sometimes called **accessor methods**), to facilitate the discovery of the values of instance variables – these methods will also directly access instance variables.

In the case of the `Frog` class, we have a getter called `getColour()`, whose purpose is to return the `colour` of the `Frog` object that receives the message.

Getter methods also follow a simple naming convention: they normally begin with the word `get`, and that is followed by the name of the instance variable whose value they return. If the variable in question is a Boolean, the getter conventionally begins with the word `is` instead. For example, `isHappy()` could be used as a getter for a Boolean instance variable called `happy`. This is merely to provide more readable code: `kermit.isHappy()` is more readable and informative than `kermit.getHappy()`.

There are also other cases where more helpful names for getter methods are chosen; for example, collection classes (which you will meet for the first time in *Unit 9*) provide a method called size(), to tell the size of a collection of objects, and size() is also a getter method.

Both setter and getter methods may do more than simply setting an instance variable or accessing its value. For example, in setPosition(), the last statement in the method (this.update("position");) causes the update() method defined in the superclass (OUAnimatedObject) to be executed. This method informs any object that has registered an interest, such as the OUWorkspace's graphical display, that the frog has moved position. Similarly the setColour() method in Frog has the statement this.update("colour");.

A common additional task carried out by setter methods is to check the validity of the argument used when the corresponding message is received. For example, the setHeight() method of HoverFrog checks that its argument is between 1 and 6 (inclusive).

We will look at getter methods in more detail in Section 4, where we consider methods that return values.

Activity 10

Here is the code for the method brown(), which demonstrates how the setter setColour() can be used to change the colour of a Frog.

```
/**
 * Sets the colour of the receiver to brown.
 */
public void brown()
{
    this.setColour(OUColour.BROWN);
}
```

Suppose that you need to add the message yellow() to the protocol of Frog objects. This message will cause the state of a Frog object to change so that its instance variable colour references OUColour.YELLOW (rather than, say, the initial OUColour.GREEN). This new message requires a new method, yellow(), to be written. Your task is to write the code for this method, using the method brown() above to guide you.

Open the Frog class in the project Unit4_Project_2 in BlueJ. Add your code for the yellow() method to the class and recompile. Now test your new method in the OUWorkspace by creating a Frog object and sending it the message yellow() – view the effect in the graphical display.

Discussion

Here is the code that you should have written for `yellow()`.

```
/**
 * Sets the colour of the receiver to yellow.
 */
public void yellow()
{
    this.setColour(OUColour.YELLOW);
}
```

In the OUWorkspace you could use the following statements to test your new method:

```
Frog kermit = new Frog();
kermit.yellow();
```

Notice that it was not necessary for us to use an `update()` message in the `yellow()` method to inform the graphical display that the frog's colour had changed because `setColour()` already does this for us. By reusing `setColour()` we saved ourselves some work.

Check that if you create some more `Frog` objects they can each have a different colour from `kermit` or each other. You can use the `setColour()` method if you wish, since it is `public`. Give each frog a different name. Amongst the colours you can use are orange, pink, purple, white and red, i.e. `OUColour.ORANGE`, `OUColour.PINK`, etc.

3.3   Implementation of instance variables and methods

You have seen that, after initialisation by a constructor, each instance variable contains a value of its declared type. Reference variables will contain a reference value (typically a reference to an object) and primitive variables will contain a value of some primitive data type. For example, using the provided `Frog` constructor, the instance variable `colour` was initialised to contain a reference to an instance of the class `OUColour`, in this case `OUColour.GREEN`; while the instance variable `position` contains a value of the primitive type `int`, in this case `1`.

The values of instance variables represent the state of an object of a class and each object must be able to have its own unique state. The JVM therefore stores a separate set of instance variables for each object of the class that is created. However, in practice we are not concerned with how such data is stored and you can imagine that an object contains its own instance variables.

The way in which methods are treated is quite different. Informally, you can imagine that when an object receives a message it looks in its class (and, if necessary, its superclass and so on) to find the corresponding method to execute. The important point to note is that, in practice, just one copy of the class serves to define the methods for all objects of that class.

3.4 Adding an instance variable to a class

To consolidate what you have learnt about instance variables, in the following three activities you will define an additional instance variable, `flyCount`, for `Frog` objects, which will be used to record the number of times the message `catchFly()` has been received since the object was created. You will need to initialise `flyCount` and you should provide `public` getter and setter methods. Also, you will need to add code to the method `catchFly()` to increment the value of `flyCount` every time `catchFly()` is executed.

Activity 11

Continue working with project Unit4_Project_2 and open the `Frog` class in the editor.

1 Find the instance variable declarations. Add the variable declaration for `flyCount`, making it `private`. What would be a good type for it? Include a comment describing the variable's purpose.

2 You now need to initialise `flyCount`. Find the constructor for the `Frog` class and locate the following statements.

```
super();
this.colour = OUColour.GREEN;
this.position = 1;
```

Add a statement to set the initial value of `flyCount` to `0` after the other assignment statements. Also alter the constructor's comment to reflect what you have done.

3 Recompile the `Frog` class, create a new `Frog` object in the OUWorkspace and assign it to a variable named `kermit`. Inspect the object referenced by `kermit` and check that the new instance variable is listed.

Discussion

1 Because you can catch only a whole number of flies (we assume), we decided to make `flyCount` an `int`. Your comment and variable declaration should be something like the following.

```
//Number of flies caught since the Frog was created.
private int flyCount;
```

2   The constructor and its comment should now look like the following.

```
/**
 * Constructor for objects of class Frog that
 * initialises colour to green, position to 1
 * and flyCount to 0.
 */
public Frog()
{
    super();
    this.colour = OUColour.GREEN;
    this.position = 1;
    this.flyCount = 0;
}
```

3   To create a Frog object you will have executed a statement such as the following.

```
Frog kermit = new Frog();
```

Inspecting the object referenced by kermit should show you that flyCount has been added to the object's list of attributes, and that flyCount has been initialised to 0.

Activity 12

Continue using Unit4_Project_2 and write getter and setter methods for flyCount. The comments and method headers for the new methods are shown below.

```
/**
 * Returns the flyCount of the receiver.
 */
public int getFlyCount()

/**
 * Sets the flyCount of the receiver to the value
 * of the argument aFlycount.
 */
public void setFlyCount(int aFlyCount)
```

Add the full code for the methods setFlyCount() and getFlyCount() to the Frog class. Use other getter and setter methods in the class to guide you.

Note that you do not need an update() message in the code of your setter method, as the value of flycount is not represented in the graphical display (the Amphibians window).

Test your methods in the OUWorkspace by sending appropriate messages to instances of the Frog class.

Discussion

You should have written something like the following.

```
/**
 * Returns the flyCount of the receiver.
 */
public int getFlyCount()
{
    return this.flyCount;
}


/**
 * Sets the flyCount of the receiver to the value
 * of the argument aFlyCount.
 */
public void setFlyCount(int aFlyCount)
{
    this.flyCount = aFlyCount;
}
```

You could test the new methods with the following code in the OUWorkspace.

```
int count;
Frog kermit = new Frog();
kermit.setFlyCount(3);
count = kermit.getFlyCount();
```

In the OUWorkspace's list of variables you could double-click on either count or kermit to determine the value of flyCount.

The Frog class now has a declaration for a new instance variable, flyCount, which is initialised by the class constructor, and for which you have written getter and setter methods. In the next activity you will modify the method catchfly() to increment flyCount.

Activity 13

Again using Unit4_Project_2, open the Frog class in the BlueJ editor and find the method catchFly(). Add a statement to the method that will increment the value of flyCount each time the method is executed. Recompile the class and then test your method in the OUWorkspace.

Discussion

The additional statement needed in catchFly() is:

```
this.setFlyCount(this.getFlyCount() + 1);
```

This will increment the instance variable flyCount each time the method catchFly() is executed.

You could test the modified method with the following statements in the OUWorkspace.

```
Frog kermit = new Frog();
kermit.catchFly();
```

Then you could inspect `kermit` to check the value of the instance variable `flyCount` after each execution of the statement `kermit.catchFly();`.

If you have had difficulties with Activities 6–13, Unit4_Project_3 incorporates all the changes made to the classes in this set of activities.

In this section you have studied instance variables, learnt how to add them to a class, and seen how to write simple getter and setter methods. In doing so, you have written a method that requires an argument and a method that returns a value. We now go on to consider such methods in more detail.

Methods that return values

We have already seen that getter methods are one example of methods that return instance variable values. In this section we examine how to write methods that return a value in more detail.

The programmer will need to declare the type of value that the method will return, called its **return type**, and also to provide a statement within the method that returns a value of an appropriate type.

4.1   Message answers and method return values

The effect of sending a message right() to an instance of Frog is to cause the object to execute the method right(), which will change the state of the object so that its position instance variable is incremented by 1. This change in state is reflected in the Amphibians window (if you have it open): the Frog icon moves one stone to the right. The right() message does not return a message answer, but you will recall that there are other messages in the protocol for the Frog class that *do* have message answers. An example of such a message is getColour(), which, if sent to a Frog object, answers with the colour of the receiver, such as OUColour.GREEN.

So how do you write methods that return values (that is return either a value of some primitive type or a reference to an object)? How do you control what they return? To answer this, look at how getColour() is written.

```
/**
 * Returns the colour of the receiver.
 */
public OUColour getColour()
{
    return this.colour;
}
```

Every method must have a defined return type and in this case it is OUColour. This information comes before the name of the method. If the method returns no value then its return type must be given as void.

In the statement

```
return this.colour;
```

the Java keyword return instructs the Java system that the value of the expression that follows is to be returned by the method. This value must be compatible with the declared return type of the method, in this case OUColour. In this case, the value of the colour instance variable of the receiver is returned.

As you learnt in Section 3, instance variables can hold references to objects or they can hold the value of a primitive data type. Here, the instance variable colour will hold a reference to some instance of OUColour; for example, OUColour.GREEN.

In practice, this means that an expression such as `kermit.getColour()` (where `kermit` references a `Frog` object) will reference the same `OUColour` object as kermit's `colour` instance variable.

You are now going to carry out a series of activities in which you will use and investigate `return` statements in methods.

Activity 14

You have just seen that methods that return a value always contain a statement beginning with the Java keyword `return`. Using Unit4_Project_3, use the BlueJ editor to examine the classes `Frog`, `HoverFrog` and `Toad` and make a note of the methods that return a value.

Discussion

You should have identified the following methods in each class.

Class name	Methods that return a value
Frog	getColour(), getFlyCount(), getPosition(), toString()
HoverFrog	getHeight(), toString()
Toad	getColour(), getPosition(), toString()

Activity 15

The method `getHeight()` for `HoverFrog` (shown below) is typical of getters:

```
public int getHeight()
{
    return this.height;
}
```

The method simply returns the value of the primitive instance variable `height` of the object that received the message `getHeight()`.

In this activity you are going to define a new `Frog` method in which the value returned is a computed value that depends on the value of an instance variable.

In the project Unit4_Project_3, use the BlueJ editor to define a new method `positionReport()` for the class `Frog` with the following comment and header.

```
/**
 * Return the String "The position is " concatenated
 * with the value of the position of the receiver.
 */
public String positionReport()
```

Complete the method assuming that you wish to obtain the value of the instance variable `position` reported as part of a `String` rather than as an integer. To help you with this, recall from *Unit 3* that if one of the operands of the + operator is a `String` object then the other operand is automatically converted to a `String`.

Once you have completed this method and recompiled the `Frog` class, satisfy yourself that `Frog` objects respond appropriately to the new message in the OUWorkspace.

Discussion

Your method `positionReport()` should look like the following.

```
public String positionReport()
{
    return "The position is " + this.getPosition();
}
```

The following statements illustrate one way of testing your new method.

```
Frog kermit = new Frog();
System.out.println(kermit.positionReport());
```

For the method `positionReport()` the return type is `String`, which is a predefined class in the Java language. Remember that primitive types such as `int`, `double` and `boolean` start with a lower-case letter and that classes start with an upper-case letter by convention, so remember to use upper- or lower-case initial letters for your return types as appropriate.

Activity 16

Continue using Unit4_Project_3 and define and test a similar method named `heightReport()` for instances of the class `HoverFrog`, which returns the height of a hoverfrog using a string.

Discussion

Your method `heightReport()` should look similar to the following.

```
/**
 * Returns the String "The height is " concatenated
 * with the value of the height of the receiver.
 */
public String heightReport()
{
    return "The height is " + this.getHeight();
}
```

After recompiling, the following statements could be used to test your new method in the OUWorkspace.

```
String frogHeight;
HoverFrog wizzy = new HoverFrog();
wizzy.up();
frogHeight = wizzy.heightReport();
```

Then you could inspect the value of the variable `frogHeight`. (This is a bit more of a roundabout approach than our test in Activity 15, but illustrates that you can assign a value returned by a message-send to a variable.)

You have now written and tested several methods that return a value by means of a `return` statement.

In a method that returns a value, the last statement to be executed *must* be a `return` statement. This is a rule that is built into the syntax of the Java language, and the Java compiler will not accept as valid any method that breaks this rule. To illustrate this, you are now going to define a new `Frog` method that will cause a `Frog` object to move right and then report the new position. Having written this method correctly you will then see what happens if you write the statements in the wrong order.

Activity 17

Using the project Unit4_Project_3, define a new method called `moveRightAndReport()` for the class `Frog`. The comment and code for the method is given below.

```
/**
 * Causes the receiver to move right then
 * returns a position report.
 */
public String moveRightAndReport()
{
    this.right();
    return this.positionReport();
}
```

Note that we reused the `positionReport()` method we defined in Activity 15. You should look out for opportunities to reuse code in this way.

Once you have added this method, recompile the class.

Now rewrite the method with the order of the two statements in the body of the method reversed, i.e.:

```
return this.positionReport()
this.right();
```

Then attempt to recompile the class.

Discussion

When you compile the first version there should be no problems and you should find the corresponding message can be sent from the OUWorkspace.

When you rewrite the method with the order of the two statements reversed and click on the `Compile` button in BlueJ, the compiler should respond by displaying `unreachable statement` in the message area and highlighting the statement `this.right();` in the code. The compiler is indicating that it is a mistake to have another statement after the `return` statement and thus the code cannot be compiled.

We have seen that it is not possible to have further statements executed after a `return` statement. What will happen if we attempt to return a value of an incompatible type?

Activity 18

In this activity you will investigate what happens if a return value is not of a type compatible with that declared in the method header.

Still using Unit4_Project_3, open the `Frog` class and change the `return` expression for the method `moveRightAndReport()` from

```
return this.positionReport();
```

to

```
return this.getPosition();
```

What happens when you try to compile? Before you leave the editor, correct the method and recompile.

Discussion

The Java compiler highlights the return expression and gives the following error message.

```
incompatible types
```

When you correct the method it should compile without an error message.

The error message also reveals that it may be possible to use a different, but compatible type of value in a return statement. As you saw in *Unit 3*, for example, it is possible to assign an `int` value to a variable of type `double`. So the compiler is actually checking that the type in the return statement is compatible with the declared return type.

It is important to realise that, although the compiler highlighted the `return` statement here, it could have been the type declaration in the method header that was incorrect. When you get this error message you need to check both places and decide which type you need the return value to be.

If you have had difficulties with Activities 14–18, Unit4_Project_4 incorporates all the changes made to the classes in this set of activities.

SAQ 6

What is the declared return type for the method `getColour()` in the class `Frog`?

Answer

The declared return type is `OUColour`.

SAQ 7

Write down the method header for a method that has the name `myMethod()`, has no arguments, and returns an `int` value. Objects of any class should be able to send the corresponding message.

Answer

```
public int myMethod()
```

Exercise 5

Using pen and paper, write a new method for the `Frog` class called `redness()` that returns the value of the red component of a frog's colour. You will need to use a message we have not mentioned before, `getRed()`, which can be sent to an `OUColour` object. This method returns an `int` value representing how red the colour is, on a scale from 0 to 255.

Don't spend too long on this; it's a bit tricky.

4.2 Methods that do not return a value

The keyword `void` is used in a method header in the position of the return type to tell the Java compiler not to expect a return value from the method. In such cases the method cannot return a value.

SAQ 8

Think back over the methods you have looked at in the class `Frog`. Which methods do not have a return value? Look at the method headers for these methods. What do they all have in common?

Discussion

The methods `setPosition()`, `sameColourAs()`, `setColour()`, `brown()`, `green()`, `croak()`, `home()`, `left()`, `right()`, `jump()`, `catchFly()`, `yellow()` and `setFlyCount()` do not have a return value. They all have the keyword `void` as the second part of their header.

SAQ 9

Write down the method header for a method that has the name
`myMethod()` that is accessible to any object, has no arguments, and has no
return value.

Answer

```
public void myMethod()
```

Methods with arguments

In Activity 8 you discovered that setter methods can be used to change the values of instance variables. A typical setter method does this by being provided with a new value for the instance variable using an argument.

In this section we investigate how to write methods that require arguments. A method that requires an argument will declare an identifier of some type to receive the argument provided by a corresponding message. Some messages have more than one argument, and therefore their corresponding methods have more than one such declaration. You will see the syntax for this shortly. First we will give you a reminder of how arguments are used.

The activities in this section use the project Unit4_Project_4.

5.1   Formal arguments and actual arguments

You will now have seen many examples of messages that require a value to be supplied to them in the form of an argument. An argument, or more properly, an **actual argument**, supplies some information that a method needs in order to complete its job, and a **formal argument** (see below) receives that information and makes it available to the code in the method's body. (Note that the term 'argument' is used as an abbreviation for *actual argument*.)

A method can be written to receive any type of argument. For example, when using the message `sameColourAs()` you must specify which `Frog`, `HoverFrog` or `Toad` object the receiver should copy its colour from. So you might have written (and executed) the statement

```
kermit.sameColourAs(gribbit);
```

in order to get the object referenced by `kermit` to change its state so that it is the same colour as the object referenced by `gribbit`.

The value of `gribbit` (a reference to a `Frog` object) is the *actual argument* of the message.

Likewise, if you want `kermit` to change its colour to that of, say, `bonny`, then you send a similar message but with `bonny` as the argument:

```
kermit.sameColourAs(bonny);
```

Again, it is the value of `bonny`, the reference that the variable holds, that the method receives as an actual argument, but you may find it simpler just to think of the method as receiving the object referenced by `bonny`, or just read it as receiving `bonny`. We will use this less formal language often, to keep things simple.

SAQ 10

Write down the receivers and the arguments of the following message-sends.

(a) `frog1.sameColourAs(frog3);`

(b) `frog4.setPosition(3);`

Answer

(a) `frog1` is the receiver and `frog3` is the argument.

(b) `frog4` is the receiver and `3` is the argument.

Formal argument declaration

So how does a method receive the information it needs? Let us look at the method `setPosition()` as an example.

```
/**
 * Sets the position of the receiver to the value of
 * the argument aPosition.
 */
public void setPosition(int aPosition)
{
    this.position = aPosition;
    this.update("position");
}
```

The method header here is

```
public void setPosition(int aPosition)
```

The name of the method is `setPosition()` and the declaration `int aPosition` inside the parentheses indicates that this method expects an argument.

The argument `aPosition` given in the method header is the *formal argument* (also known as a formal parameter). It is always necessary to declare both a name for each formal argument and its type. In this case, the formal argument has the identifier `aPosition` and it is declared as being of the primitive type `int`. The type of a formal argument can also be a class, such as `String`.

When writing setter methods in M250, we typically use the convention for naming formal arguments of using the name of the variable they set preceded by 'a' or 'an'. Hence `aPosition` is the name of the formal argument for the `setPosition()` method, to be used to assign a value to `position`. In other kinds of method we may name a formal argument for the type of thing it represents (a name, an icon, a frog's leg and so on) preceded by the text 'a' or 'an', giving names such as `aName`, `anIcon`, or `aFrogLeg`. However, as long as the choice of formal argument name is legal and does not conflict with any other names, it will compile. As with any other variable name, you should choose a name that is meaningful, readable and helpful.

Note that the declaration of a formal argument is similar to the declaration of a variable, and, in fact, the JVM will create this variable every time the method is executed. The formal argument can be used within the method body and you can assume that when it is used it will have been initialised using an actual argument, as explained below.

When the message `setPosition()` is sent to a `Frog` object the actual argument must be compatible with the type of the formal argument in the method header. For example, in the message

```
kermit.setPosition(3);
```

the integer 3 is the actual argument for the message and is of type `int`, the same as the formal argument type.

On receiving the message `setPosition(3)`, the `Frog` object referenced (in this case the object referenced by `kermit`) causes the method `setPosition()` to be executed with its formal argument `aPosition` set to the value of the message's actual argument, in this case 3.

This is always the case with methods that use arguments in Java: when a message is sent, the values of any actual arguments are *copied* into any formal argument variables so that they can be used within the method body. This approach to handling of arguments is technically called 'passing by value'. In Java all arguments are passed by value.

After this the `update()` message is sent to the receiver using the argument `"position"`. There is no need to consider how the `update()` method works, just remember that it lets the graphical display know that the frog needs to be redrawn. In this case, the `String` argument `"position"` informs the display that the frog's position has changed.

Activity 19

You have just learnt that methods that take arguments have matching formal arguments declared in their method header. Using the BlueJ editor and Unit4_Project_4, make a list of the methods that take arguments in the `Frog` class.

Discussion

You should have identified the following methods: `setPosition()`, `sameColourAs()`, `setColour()` and `setFlyCount()`.

Exercise 6

What do you think would happen if you tried to execute the following statements in the OUWorkspace?

```
Frog kermit = new Frog();
kermit.setPosition(OUColour.RED);
```

Exercise 7

Assuming that `kermit` references an instance of the `Frog` class, explain in detail what happens when the message `left()` is sent to the object referenced by `kermit`.

Exercise 8

Suppose you wish to add a new method `increasePosition()` to the `Frog` class. The method will increase the value of the instance variable `position` by an amount provided by an `int` argument, which we will call `step`.

Using pen and paper, write a suitable comment and method that will support this behaviour. Remember to use the getter and setter messages for the instance variable. You can use the method `left()` as a guide.

Activity 20

Reopen Unit4_Project_4, and open the `Frog` class in the editor. Add your new method `increasePosition()` from Exercise 8 and compile.

Satisfy yourself that `Frog` and `HoverFrog` objects perform the appropriate behaviour by executing message-sends in the OUWorkspace, such as `frog1.increasePosition(3)`. Remember that you can check visually on the behaviour of `Frog` and `HoverFrog` objects if you open the graphical display.

There is no discussion for this activity.

Exercise 9

Using pen and paper, write a new method called `toadGoHome()` for the `Frog` class, which will send a message to a `Toad` object to tell it to go to its home position (frogs can be a bit bossy around toads sometimes). The method will need an appropriate formal argument to allow it to communicate with a `Toad` object. The method should return the toad's `position` after it goes home, which is an `int` value. Remember that toads understand the messages `home()` and `getPosition()`.

5.2   Method signatures and overloading

The name of a method including the parentheses and the type of any
arguments is called the **method signature**. For example, the **signature** of
`setPosition()` is `setPosition(int)`. The signature shows clearly the
type of the expected argument.

Note that the `Frog` class defines *two* methods with the name
`sameColourAs()`. They have the headers:

```
public void sameColourAs(Frog aFrog)
public void sameColourAs(Toad aToad)
```

One has the formal argument `aFrog` of class `Frog` and the other has the
formal argument `aToad` of class `Toad`. In cases such as this, when methods
that have the same name but different signatures are present, we say that the
method name is **overloaded**. (Informally, programmers generally say a method
is overloaded e.g. we can informally say that `sameColourAs()` is an
overloaded method, even though, really, it is the *name* `sameColourAs()` that
is overloaded).

If there were a single `sameColourAs()` method whose formal argument was
declared as being of class `Frog`, then we would only be able to send a
`sameColourAs()` message to a `Frog` object with an actual argument that was
an instance of `Frog` (or a subclass of `Frog`, since instances of subclasses of
`Frog` are compatible). We would not be able to send a message
`sameColourAs()` to a `Frog` object with an actual argument that was an
instance of `Toad`. However, in this case the programmer wanted to be able to
set frog colours using toads as well, so a second method was required.

As long as the methods have different signatures, the compiler can decide
which one should be used based on the types of any actual arguments; that is,
any `sameColourAs()` message-send is unambiguous.

Conversely, two methods within the same class *cannot* have the same
signature. For example, two hypothetical methods with the following method
headers:

```
public void doSomething(int marks)
private int doSomething(int commission)
```

have the same signature, namely `doSomething(int)`. (The access modifier
and return type is not part of the signature, nor are the names of any formal
arguments.) The Java compiler would report an error if you attempted to
compile a class that defined two such methods.

Some utility methods in Java are very heavily overloaded. For example, the
method `println()`, which allows you to display some text, has ten different
signatures in Java 7. This means you can use `println()` with many actual
argument types without having to convert any of them to another type.
Constructors can also be overloaded.

Activity 21

With Unit4_Project_4 open, select Save As from the BlueJ Project menu and save the project with a different name, such as Unit4_Project_4_Act_21. After you have done this, open the OUWorkspace and from its Graphical Display menu open the Amphibians window.

1   Execute the following statements one at a time in the OUWorkspace.

```
Frog kermit = new Frog();
Frog gribbit = new Frog();
Toad toady = new Toad();
kermit.setColour(OUColour.RED);
gribbit.sameColourAs(kermit);
gribbit.sameColourAs(toady);
```

Now execute the following two statements in the OUWorkspace.

```
HoverFrog wizzy = new HoverFrog();
gribbit.sameColourAs(wizzy);
```

2   Use the BlueJ editor to comment out the method sameColourAs() that has a formal argument type of Toad from the class Frog. (Select the method's code then select Comment from the Edit menu.) Recompile the classes Frog and HoverFrog and execute the statements given in step 1 again. What happens this time?

Close the project when you have finished this activity.

Discussion

1   The first set of statements should all work correctly, and you should end up with gribbit coloured brown.

The second set of statements (using a HoverFrog object as the actual argument) should also work and gribbit should return to being coloured green.

2   You should have found that the message

```
gribbit.sameColourAs(toady);
```

no longer works and you get an error message containing the text:

```
method sameColourAs in class Frog cannot be applied to
given types;
    required: Frog
    found: Toad
    reason: actual argument Toad cannot be converted to
    Frog by method invocation conversion
```

Since gribbit is of type Frog, the compiler looks for a suitable sameColourAs() method in the Frog class and reports that the remaining sameColourAs() method in the Frog class (whose formal argument is of type Frog) cannot take an argument of type Toad, the type of toady.

SAQ 11

What are the signatures of the `getColour()` and `setColour()` methods in the `Frog` class?

Answer

Since the getter takes no arguments, its signature is `getColour()`. The setter has the signature `setColour(OUColour)`.

5.3   Methods with two arguments

Activities 22 and 23 introduce a method with two arguments. In a method with more than one formal argument, the arguments are separated by commas. There is no great difference in terms of the operation of methods with more than one argument. If there are two formal arguments then the corresponding message must use two actual arguments, and each is copied into the corresponding formal argument for use inside the method.

Activity 22

Suppose that there is (another) requirement for `Frog` objects – to set both the position of a frog to a given value and its colour to a given instance of `OUColour`, using a single message. To implement this behaviour you will need a new method, say `setPositionAndColour()`, that will take two arguments. One argument will give the position the frog must go to and the other argument will give the colour that the frog must assume.

Using the project Unit4_Project_4, write the code for this new method for the `Frog` class using the BlueJ editor, then recompile.

Then, using the OUWorkspace, satisfy yourself that `Frog` and `HoverFrog` objects respond appropriately to the new message you have added to the protocol of the `Frog` class.

Discussion

Here is our version of `setPositionAndColour()`.

```
/**
 * Sets the position of the receiver
 * to the argument aPosition and the
 * colour of the receiver to the argument aColour.
 */
public void setPositionAndColour(int aPosition, OUColour aColour)
{
  this.setPosition(aPosition);
  this.setColour(aColour);
}
```

You could have tested your code in the OUWorkspace with statements such as the following (assuming suitable objects referenced by `frog1` and `frog3`).

```
frog1.setPositionAndColour(5, OUColour.BLUE);
frog3.setPositionAndColour(1, OUColour.MAGENTA);
```

Note that, from the point of view of M250, although the method name begins with the word 'set' it is not a setter, since it does not directly access the instance variables position and colour.

SAQ 12

What is the signature of the method given in the discussion of Activity 22?

Answer

```
setPositionAndColour(int, OUColour)
```

Note that the order of the arguments is important, as we will now see.

Activity 23

In this activity you will look at what can happen if the order of the arguments in a message is not the same as the order defined in the method header of the corresponding method.

With the project Unit4_Project_4 and the OUWorkspace open, execute the following statements one by one. What happens?

```
Frog kermit = new Frog();
kermit.setPositionAndColour(3, OUColour.BLUE);
kermit.setPositionAndColour(OUColour.BLUE, 3);
```

Discussion

The first two statements execute normally and (if you have the graphical display open) you will see the Frog object, kermit, change position and colour.

The third statement does not execute. Instead, an error message is displayed indicating that the compiler cannot find a method with the correct signature. The actual error message includes the text:

```
method setPositionAndColour in class Frog cannot be
applied to given types;
  required: int,ou.OUColour
  found: ou.OUColour,int
  reason: actual argument ou.OUColour cannot be
  converted to int by method invocation conversion
```

You can see from this that the order in which the arguments are defined in the method header is important. The actual arguments (the ones that were 'found') of a message must be of compatible types with those that are 'required'. The required arguments are those specified in the corresponding method header. In this case, the types of the two arguments were incompatible, and so only one order for the actual arguments was possible.

You could, of course, have a method that takes two arguments of the same type, for example, two `int` arguments, with a signature like this:

```
setMyIntValues(int, int)
```

In such a case if you get the order of the actual arguments wrong the compiler won't give an error message. Only the method's documentation and sensible naming of the formal arguments guide you as to the appropriate order of your actual arguments. For this reason it is generally best to avoid writing methods that have several arguments of the same type if possible.

Constructors with arguments

We will discuss constructors in detail in *Unit 6*; however, at this point it is worth mentioning that constructors are syntactically very like methods, except that they don't declare any return type and they always have the same name as the class whose objects they will construct.

Just as for a method, it is possible to write a constructor signature with formal arguments. Actual arguments can be provided to initialise the newly created object to some desired state. So, for example, we could have written a `Frog` constructor like the following:

```
/**
 * Constructor for objects of class Frog
 * which initialises colour to aColour
 * and position to aPosition.
 */
public Frog(OUColour aColour, int aPosition)
{
    super();
    this.colour = aColour;
    this.position = aPosition;
}
```

Activity 24

Using the project Unit4_Project_4 alter the `Frog` class so that the value for a frog's 'home' position can be stored using an instance variable of type `int` called `homePosition`.

We take 'home' to mean the starting position of a frog, and if you read the `Frog` class you will see that its constructor sets its `position` to 1. The `homePosition` should therefore also be initialised to 1. Although initially the `homePosition` is 1, it may later be assigned a different value from one frog object to another. So this instance variable will allow us to remember a home position and to restore individual frogs to their particular home positions easily after they have been moving around.

In each of the following steps make sure you provide adequate documentation in the form of comments.

1 Add the declaration for the instance variable `homePosition` in a logical place in the `Frog` class.

2 Add code to initialise `homePosition` to 1 in the `Frog` constructor.

3 Add a setter method `setHomePosition()` and a getter method `getHomePosition()` at the end of the class, and then compile so that your class is ready for testing.

4 Test your work so far by executing the following statements one by one in the OUWorkplace and inspecting the temporary variable `hPos`.

```
int hPos = 0;
Frog frog1 = new Frog();
hPos = frog1.getHomePosition(); //check hPos is now 1
frog1.setHomePosition(5);
hPos = frog1.getHomePosition(); //check hPos is now 5
```

5 Alter the method `home()` so that it sets the value of `position` to the value of `homePosition`. You will need to recompile after this alteration.

6 Test your work by executing the following statements one by one in the OUWorkspace and inspecting the variable `pos`.

```
int pos = 0;
Frog frog1 = new Frog();
frog1.setHomePosition(3);
frog1.home();
pos = frog1.getPosition(); //check pos is now 3
```

7 Regenerate the documentation for Unit4_Project_4 by selecting **Project Documentation** from the BlueJ **Tools** menu.

Discussion

1 The instance variable declarations should now look like the following.

```
private OUColour colour;
private int position;
private int flyCount;
private int homePosition;
```

2 The code for the constructor should now look like the following.

```
/**
 * Constructor for objects of class Frog which
 * initialises colour to green, position to 1,
 * flyCount to 0 and homePosition to 1.
 */
public Frog()
{
    super();
    this.colour = OUColour.GREEN;
    this.position = 1;
    this.flyCount = 0;
    this.homePosition = 1;
}
```

3 The new getter and setter methods should be similar to the following.

```
/**
 * Returns the home position of the receiver.
 */
public int getHomePosition()
{
    return this.homePosition;
}


/**
 * Sets the home position of the receiver to the value
 * of the argument aPosition.
 */
public void setHomePosition(int aPosition)
{
    this.homePosition = aPosition;
}
```

4 You should find that the new `Frog` object has an initial `homePosition` of `1`, and that you can use the getter and setter methods to get and set the value of `homePosition`.

5 The method `home()` should look like the following.

```
/**
 * Resets the receiver to its home position.
 */
public void home()
{
    this.setPosition(this.getHomePosition());
}
```

6 After executing the code you should find that `pos` holds the value `3`.

7 You should find that the documentation for the `Frog` class now includes information on the new methods.

6

Reuse of code

So far in this unit we have introduced techniques that enable Java programmers to write code in an object-oriented manner. In this section we discuss a major concept in object-oriented programming – reuse of code.

You have seen that the code for the `Frog` class includes several methods. Each method can be tested to ensure that it conforms to the specification given in the method comment. When you add a new method to a class you can reduce some of the complexity of the new method, and also make the new method easier to maintain, by reusing methods that have already been developed and tested for that class.

Consider the method `doubleLeft()` for the `Toad` class, which you met in Activity 6:

```
/**
 * Performs the left behaviour twice.
 */
public void doubleLeft()
{
    this.left();
    this.left();
}
```

As the method name suggests, and as the method comment documents, the intention is that the left *behaviour* is performed twice (as opposed to a move to the left a certain number of stones).

At present, the `Toad` class defines `left()` to mean changing `position` by -2, and so `doubleLeft()` changes the position by -4. Because of this, we could instead have written the following code for `doubleLeft()` to achieve the same effect:

```
/**
 * Moves the receiver left four places.
 */
public void doubleLeft()
{
    this.setPosition(this.getPosition() - 4);
}
```

You might think this is better, or as good. However, suppose the designers of the `Toad` class changed their minds, as they easily might, and decreed that the `left()` behaviour for toads means changing position by -3. 'Perform the left behaviour twice' would now mean changing position by -6.

Now the method using the statement

```
this.setPosition(this.getPosition() - 4);
```

would be wrong and would need to be altered. If the designers had a further change of mind, another modification would be needed and so on.

However, the earlier version of doubleLeft(), which uses this.left() twice, would continue to work perfectly without any changes. It will always produce the same effect as two 'left' behaviours. The designers of Toad could change their minds about what left() means as many times as they like, and this version of the method would always automatically produce the correct result, without requiring any modification.

This is very important, because there could be many different methods whose result depends on the definition of the 'left' behaviour. If the methods are written so that they manipulate the frog's position directly, then every time there is a change to the method left() you would need to identify all those methods and update their code. Quite apart from the effort involved, you might overlook some and it would be easy to make mistakes.

However, methods that *reuse* left() will not require any changes at all, and all these problems are entirely avoided! Reuse is a far superior strategy, and experienced object-oriented programmers employ it wherever they can. Although you are not yet an expert, you should look carefully for possible reuse and try to take advantage of it in the code you write.

6.1   Using libraries

The ability to reuse code goes beyond the simple example described above. One of the features of object-oriented languages that make them so powerful is that they usually include class libraries. Such libraries may contain hundreds, or even thousands, of classes that have proven useful to programmers in the past to write a wide range of applications. These classes have been robustly tested, and well documented, so that programmers can understand the purpose of each class and what each method in a class does, without having to know how the methods are implemented. Indeed, class libraries usually do not include source code, just the compiled code, so the programmer's only source of information is often the documentation.

Java comes with many such class libraries, which it calls *packages*. In addition, programmers can develop their own class libraries (packages) containing classes that are relevant to their own application area. Once tested and documented, these can be reused to form the basis of many applications.

You are already making use of a library of classes developed for M250. It is this reuse of code that enables you to have frogs moving in a graphical display at this early stage in the module. In the next activity, we look at the documentation for the simplest of these classes. As this is an exploratory activity, there is no discussion.

Activity 25

Open the `Frog` class in the BlueJ editor in Unit4_Project_4. At the top of the editor window the first statement is:

```
import ou.*;
```

This tells the compiler that classes contained in the package called `ou` may be needed in the `Frog` class. Now select OU Class Library from the BlueJ **Help** menu. The documentation for the library will soon appear in a browser window. You will notice that the package name is `ou` and that it contains four classes.

- `OUAnimatedObject` is the superclass of the classes `Frog` and `Toad`, and it contains the methods that enable `Frog`, `HoverFrog` and `Toad` objects to be visible and move around a graphical display.

- `OUColour` is the class that provides the colours we have used in our classes.

- `OUDialog` provides methods that you will use in *Unit 5* to communicate with a user via dialogue boxes.

- The fourth class, `OUFileChooser`, is not used until *Unit 12*.

Click on the link for `OUColour` in the left-hand frame. We have been using this class each time we write a statement such as

```
freddie.setColour(OUColour.GREEN);
```

Do not worry if you do not understand the detail. For now, note that the various colours we use are defined in this class as constants. You will learn more about constants in *Unit 7*. (The documentation uses the word 'Fields' to describe various kinds of data that a class can define, including constants.)

There is only one instance method in this class: `toString()`. Also notice that the method `getRed()` we mentioned in Exercise 5 was inherited from the class `Color`.

Click on the link for `OUAnimatedObject` in the left-hand frame of your browser window. This is a much more complex class, but it still contains many parts you might recognise, including a list of methods that include `update()` and `performAction()`.

Now, going back to the BlueJ editor, look at the code for the `Frog` class. You will see that we use `update()` in the methods `setPosition()` and `setColour()`, and we use `performAction()` in the methods `jump()` and `croak()`. There is no need to worry about how these methods are implemented. We have all the information we need in the documentation provided for the library – a description of what they do and the method header. Someone else has put in the time to code these methods and test them to ensure they work.

Later in the module we will make extensive use of the Java Class Libraries. You can see the documentation for these libraries in your browser by selecting **Java Class Libraries** from the **Help** menu in the BlueJ window. You do not need to access this documentation now, but you might like at some stage to look at what is provided. Depending on how your computer is set up you may need to be connected to the internet in order to access this documentation.

6.2   Advantages of using getter and setter methods

Earlier in this section you saw that you could rewrite the method `doubleLeft()` using `setPosition()` and `getPosition()` rather than reusing `left()`, although this might not be advisable. It is even possible to rewrite the method without reusing any methods at all, since we can work with the variable `position` directly, although you will see shortly that there are strong reasons why this is even less advisable. The resulting method would be as follows.

```
/**
 * Moves the receiver left four places.
 */
public void doubleLeft()
{
    this.position = this.position - 4;
    this.update("position");
}
```

This results in quite readable and efficient code, and it seems fine – as before we use `update()` to notify any interested objects (technically they are called *observers*) that something of interest to them has changed (which is how the graphical display is updated). However, what happens if you write a new method `tripleLeft()` and forget the statement containing the message `update()`? You will investigate this in the next activity.

Activity 26

Using the project Unit4_Project_4, open the BlueJ editor on the `Toad` class and add the following method.

```
/**
 * Moves the receiver left six places.
 */
public void tripleLeft()
{
    this.position = this.position - 6;
}
```

Recompile, open the OUWorkspace from the BlueJ `Tools` menu and then open an `Amphibians` window from the `Graphical Display` menu.

Execute the following statements one at a time in the OUWorkspace.

```
Toad dermot = new Toad();
dermot.tripleLeft();
```

Inspect the state of dermot by double-clicking on the name dermot in the Variables pane in the OUWorkspace. Is the state of dermot reflected in the Amphibians window?

Discussion

You should have found that the value of position for dermot had changed to 5, but that the icon of the toad representing dermot in the Amphibians window was still sitting on the 11th stone. We explain why in more detail below.

If you have had difficulties with Activities 18–26, Unit4_Project_4_Completed incorporates all the changes and additions made in this set of activities.

The graphical display

The graphical display illustrates one reason to use setters and getters. When developing the OUWorkspace for this module, we arranged for the Amphibians window to display a representation of any amphibian-like objects created in the OUWorkspace. However, the Amphibians window and the collection of objects in the OUWorkspace have to be kept in step. Therefore any method that directly changes an instance variable that is of importance to the Amphibians window must also send a message to notify that window (or indeed any other interested observing object) that this has happened. If this is not done, the Amphibians window will not know to refresh itself to reflect any changes to the state of that object. This is exactly what has happened with the method you tested in Activity 26.

You will have noticed that the setter methods setColour(), setPosition() and setHeight() all use the update() method to notify an observing object (in this case the Amphibians window) that a particular object's instance variable has changed its value. This has the important consequence that a method that makes use of these setter methods will have the Amphibians window notified automatically that the instance variable has changed.

In this case the setter methods are performing an extra duty beyond initialising instance variables; in general, setters and getters may often do such extra duties. Since such extra work is carried out as a result of using setters and getters, failing to reuse them appropriately can mean that some necessary action, such as updating a display or checking the validity of an argument before it is used, might be missed out.

Changes to instance variables

What would happen if, for some reason, a class such as Toad was changed so that position was stored as a float rather than an int? Clearly any code that uses `position` directly will need to be checked and perhaps rewritten. Methods that use `position` directly will have been written assuming that `position` is an `int`, and the change of type is very likely to 'break' them so that they stop working.

If the programmer of the `Toad` class makes the adjustments necessary *within* the setter and getter methods then they can ensure that the `setPosition()` and `getPosition()` headers remain identical, so that the getter still returns an `int`, and the setter still takes an `int` argument. In this way, any number conversions that are required for objects expecting an integer `position` value would be taken care of. Methods depending on the getters and setters would go on working precisely as before.

So, any programmers that had used direct access instead of getter and setter methods would have to track down every place where this had happened, check how the code was affected and rewrite their code if necessary. This obviously entails a lot of additional work, and is an error-prone process. Programmers who had reused the appropriate setters and getters could relax, secure in the knowledge they had employed a superior strategy.

Attributes versus instance variables

Continuing our discussion of why reuse is important, note that a getter method need not return the value of an instance variable, but may compute some value that depends on an instance variable. For example, it might have been decided that the `getPosition()` method should return a string, either `"left"` or `"right"`, depending on the numerical value of `position` relative to a frog's home position. So it is more correct to say that a getter returns an *attribute* of an object – that is, it returns a value describing some feature of an object and not necessarily the value of an instance variable.

Similarly, a setter method `setDateOfBirth(String)` might allow you to send the message `setDateOfBirth("1 Oct 2012")` or `setDateOfBirth("1.10.2012")` or `setDateOfBirth("1/10/2012")` and the object receiving the message might use a different format internally to store the date, such as the Java `Date` class. Thus an argument received by a setter is not necessarily directly used to set an instance variable either, although we can think of an attribute as having been set.

The distinction between attribute and instance variable values is a further reason to limit direct access of instance variables to getters and setters and to reuse setters and getters as appropriate.

Reuse in subclasses

The advantages of code reuse apply equally to subclasses. Furthermore, a programmer implementing a subclass should not, in general, need to know *how* attributes are implemented by a parent class. Subclasses (and their instances) cannot directly access `private` instance variables declared in a superclass in any case. Instead subclasses will have to make use of any provided `public` methods from their superclass to do their work.

This means that a subclass can be insulated from any changes that might be made to its superclasses in terms of how its attributes are implemented.

To recap, there are two major advantages to reuse of methods in general and to setters and getters in particular (if they are provided).

1   Methods aid code reuse by implementing behaviours that objects need to perform in a reusable way. In the case of a setter, you can write the code required to change an object's state just once, and then reuse that method to do the same job in future. Likewise a getter method may enclose some complex code to determine an attribute based on the state of an object, and rewriting this code everywhere the attribute is needed would be wasteful and error prone.

2   Methods in general (and getters and setters in particular) aid reuse at the class level. That is, they facilitate the process of changing a class or creating a subclass for use in a different situation. This is because changes to a class T can be confined to code *within* methods provided by the class T, whose signatures do not need to change. Other classes can just continue to use those methods.

In M250, as a rule of thumb, we suggest that wherever getter and setter methods are available you should use them in your code. This will mean the only place – other than in a constructor – where an instance variable is assigned a value directly is in its setter method, and the only place it is accessed directly is in its getter method. These two methods – the getter and setter – *have* to operate directly with the instance variable because there is no other way for them to work. They cannot use getters and setters, because they *are* the getters and setters!

The exception is that, for reasons that cannot be elaborated upon at this point, it is safer, where possible, to initialise instance variables directly in a constructor rather than by using setter messages.

In the following section we will consider when it is appropriate for a class to provide `public` setters and getters.

Encapsulation

So far in this unit you have seen how an object contains both state (the values of its instance variables) and behaviour (defined by its message protocol). This is an example of what is termed **encapsulation**; that is, a parcelling up of related data and behaviour into a single entity. Put another way, objects *encapsulate* state and behaviour. The concept of encapsulation is very powerful because it allows an efficient division of labour in large software projects. Each team member can work in isolation on the class(es) he/she is responsible for. All that team members need to know about other classes are the names and specifications of their `public` methods.

Related to encapsulation is the concept of **data hiding**, whereby details of an object's instance variables are hidden so that other objects must use messages to interact with that object's state.

In this section we explore these ideas further and see how the access modifiers `private` and `public` are involved in implementing data hiding.

7.1 Access modifiers – `public` or `private`?

Instance variables and methods are examples of what are called class **members**. Each instance variable and method is a class member. It is useful to introduce this term so that we can talk about access modifiers as they apply to both instance variables and methods. We can summarise the meaning of the access modifiers `private` and `public` as follows:

- if a member is declared as `private`, only code within the class itself can directly access it;
- if a member is declared as `public`, code within any class (and in M250 code within the OUWorkspace) can directly access it.

Private instance variables and public methods

It is usual to declare instance variables as `private` to provide data hiding. The internal details of an object's state are a matter for the programmer of the object's class and should not be unnecessarily exposed to programmers who want to use the class, or to objects of other classes that are sending messages to instances of the class.

Methods are declared as `public` when a programmer wishes to allow the methods to have general use for communicating with an object and to allow interaction with its internal state. Such interactions include discovering values of attributes (using getters), changing attributes (using setters and other methods such as `right()` in the `Frog` class) and getting an object to do other useful work (using other kinds of method).

If we follow these principles for the use of access modifiers, then our Java objects exhibit data hiding. Figure 6 illustrates the concepts of encapsulation and data hiding.

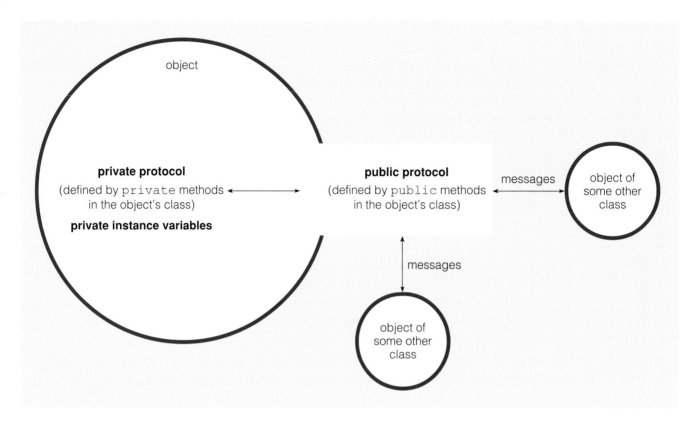

Figure 6 Encapsulation

Figure 6 shows that an object becomes a 'black box' – whatever is inside it is hidden, but public methods allow other objects to interact with the object's internal state.

The set of methods defined as `public` provide what we call the *public protocol* of an object (normally when we just say 'protocol' we are referring to the public protocol), whereas those that are defined as `private` provide the *private protocol* of an object. The public protocol of a class X refers to that set of messages that the user of an arbitrary class can send to an instance of class X (because the corresponding methods have been declared as `public` in class X). The private protocol refers to that set of messages whose corresponding methods have been declared as `private` and which normally an instance of a class would send only to itself inside one of its other methods (via `this`).

In programming terms this means access by objects of other classes to the data the object encapsulates (the instance variables) is possible *only* through a limited set of `public` methods.

The Millenium Bug

In the run up to the year 2000 there was much talk of the 'millennium' or 'Y2K' bug. This bug arose because some operating systems and some programming languages record time and dates as a number. (Compare this with Java, which has a `Date` class provided in the `java.util` package.) As time progresses the time number gets bigger – so a future date is always larger than a past date. The Y2K bug arose because many programmers writing commercial systems in the 1970s and 1980s had omitted the century digits from dates – such programmers did not think the century digits would be needed! For example, many COBOL programs represented the date 26 February 1990 as the number 900226, and the date 1 January 1991 as 910101, allowing the programs to compare the two numbers and correctly assume that the smaller number represented the earlier date. However, without the century digits, those comparisons would fall apart on 1 January 2000. The last day of the millennium was 991231, and after the stroke of midnight many computers would see 1 January 2000 as 000101 – a smaller number than the day before. Time would appear to have been reversed!

To avoid this disaster a lot of money was spent paying people to read programs line by line, checking how the programs implemented dates and, if need be, modifying the programs to include century digits. The cost of all this work is estimated to have exceeded 400 billion pounds worldwide! If all software had been written in an object-oriented language (or at least a language providing encapsulation and data hiding) the cost would have been considerably less, as it would have been necessary to check only objects that implemented dates.

Encapsulation is a powerful idea whose history is older than object-oriented programming. For example, languages such as Modula-2 and Pascal implemented similar ideas.

Finally, note that while objects and their classes are a highly developed form of reusable, encapsulated component, they themselves will generally form parts of larger reusable and encapsulated systems.

7.2 How `private` should we be?

You will see in *Unit 6* that there are other levels of access in addition to `public` and `private`, and that by using these access levels the programmer of a class has quite a fine degree of control over which other classes can directly access members of a class.

The M250 module team's suggestion that, when writing a class, instance variables should be `private` and that most methods should be `public` is just a rule of thumb (although we seldom break this rule, particularly with regard to instance variables). Without going into the detail of other levels of access, let us consider when we might not provide setters and getters, and when we might not make methods `public`. The answer is that it really depends on just how much access to instance variables you want to provide, and just what kinds of message you want to allow objects of other classes to send.

Setters and getters

Let us consider setter and getter methods as an example. Suppose that a `Frog` has a `boolean` instance variable called `happy` declared as follows:

```
private boolean happy;
```

A constructor might initialise this variable to `true` when we create a `Frog` object. At some point in a frog's life it might not be so happy, and it might (using a method) set this variable to `false`. For example, the `Frog` may have a `public poke()` method and when it receives that message it may, amongst other things, set `happy` to `false`. It may also have a `public stroke()` method, and when it receives the `stroke()` message it may set `happy` to `true`.

But, should we provide a `public setHappy(boolean)` method? Probably not. Objects of other classes should, most probably, not be able to dictate when a frog is happy, which they could do if we provided the ability to send this message. Other objects may use the `public` protocol of frogs, including using messages such as `poke()` and `stroke()`, and the `Frog` object itself can 'decide' (using its methods) when it is happy and when it is not.

Should the getter `isHappy()` be `public`? This is probably reasonable; however, it might be that we don't want to allow objects of other classes to know whether a frog is happy or not. A frog might just use its `happy` variable internally to make decisions, such as how high to jump when it receives the `jump()` message.

So, it is not necessary that every instance variable is gettable and settable using `public` methods. It is really up to us, as program designers, to decide which attributes we want to expose to other objects.

Likewise, if you have other methods that just do internal work for an object, you might not want other objects to be able to use them. Suppose frogs have a `tidyHouse()` method, you might not want objects of other classes to be able to send the corresponding message. A frog object might use this method when certain messages in its `public` protocol are sent (such as, perhaps, `offerToBuyHouse()`). Such methods that are for internal use, including ones used to break large tasks down into smaller pieces, are often called **helper methods**, and they should usually be declared as `private`.

So, to reiterate, if you are writing, say, the `Bananaquit` class, you should use `private` access for a method that should not be used by other kinds of object. Bear in mind that an object of the same class *can* use these methods to cause another `Bananaquit` to perform those behaviours. This is not as dangerous as it sounds because there is only one `Bananaquit` class to write, and you write it. So you decide which other methods might use these `private` methods.

Similarly, a `Frog` object *can* directly access another `Frog` object's `private` instance variables, within a method, if a method has been written that does that (using a reference to the other frog). But, again, this is not particularly problematic because frog objects don't get to decide what methods they have, or which of those methods access `private` instance variables: you decide this, when you write the `Frog` class.

SAQ 13

How is encapsulation implemented in Java?

Answer

In Java you can define classes that are templates for the creation of objects. These objects then encapsulate both state and behaviour.

SAQ 14

How do you implement data hiding in Java?

Answer

Data hiding is implemented by declaring instance variables as `private`.

Exercise 10

After completing Activity 12, the `Frog` class had a new instance variable, `flyCount`, which kept count of how many flies a `Frog` had caught. A method `catchfly()` was written that incremented `flyCount`. We wrote `public` getter and setter methods for `flyCount` so that you could examine, and change, the value of `flyCount` from the OUWorkspace for testing purposes. Was it a good choice to make `setFlyCount()` and `getFlyCount()` public?

8 Consolidation

This section contains activities designed to help you practise the techniques and explore some of the concepts you have learnt in this unit. The activities are all based on the project Unit4_Project_5 and involve drawing using simple shapes.

8.1 Shapes

To begin this section you will familiarise yourself with the `Circle`, `Triangle`, `Square` and `Diamond` classes, whose instances represent shapes that can be displayed in the OUWorkspace's graphical display. These classes can be seen in project Unit4_Project_5 along with the partially complete class called `Marionette`.

Activity 27

Open the project Unit4_Project_5 in BlueJ. Browse the code of the `Circle`, `Triangle`, `Square` and `Diamond` classes and note how, just like frogs, hoverfrogs and toads, the setter methods all have the final line of code of `this.update();` and that the classes are all subclasses of `OUAnimatedObject`.

Open the OUWorkspace and then select **Open** from the **Graphical Display** menu to open a window titled **Shapes**. This window will display graphical representations of `Circle`, `Triangle`, `Square` and `Diamond` objects provided that the workspace knows about them – that is, they *must* be referenced by variables in the OUWorkspace.

1   Execute the following statements in the OUWorkspace, one at a time, and check that they do what you might expect, both by inspecting the variables that reference the objects you create and by looking at their graphical representations in the **Shapes** window.

```
Circle aCircle = new Circle();
Diamond aDiamond = new Diamond();
Triangle aTriangle = new Triangle();
Square aSquare = new Square();
```

All shape objects are drawn relative to an *x* position and a *y* position in the **Shapes** window and have methods `setXPos()` and `setYPos()`. These methods each take one `int` argument, and allow you to alter the *x* or *y* location of the shape.

Now experiment by sending `setXPos()` and `setYPos()` messages to the objects you have created and observe the results in the **Shapes** window. Don't worry if the shapes disappear off the display, you can always recreate them.

2   In part 1, the shape objects were all created using a constructor that takes no arguments (that is, a *zero-argument constructor*). Each shape class also has an alternative constructor that takes a number of arguments that allow you to create shapes of different sizes and colours. Execute the following statements in the OUWorkspace, one at a time, and check that they do what you might expect, both by inspecting the variables that reference the objects you create and by observing their graphical representations in the Shapes window.

```
Circle aCircle = new Circle(50, OUColour.YELLOW);
Diamond aDiamond = new Diamond(75, 120, OUColour.RED);
Triangle aTriangle = new Triangle(20, 100, OUColour.PURPLE);
Square aSquare = new Square(60, OUColour.GREEN);
```

Once again experiment by sending setXPos() and setYPos() messages to the objects you have created and observing the results in the Shapes window. Also experiment by sending setColour() messages to the objects.

Discussion

1   On creating each shape (a circle, a diamond, a triangle and a square) you should have observed that they were all displayed in the top-left corner of the Shapes window, one on top of the other.

The Shapes window represents a drawing area in which each pixel has an *x*- and a *y*-coordinate. A pair of coordinates specifies a point in the Shapes window, and the point (0, 0) represents the top left-hand corner of the drawing area. Figure 7 shows the Shapes window 'drawing area' with one of each shape drawn in its default position, and the approximate dimensions of the drawing area.

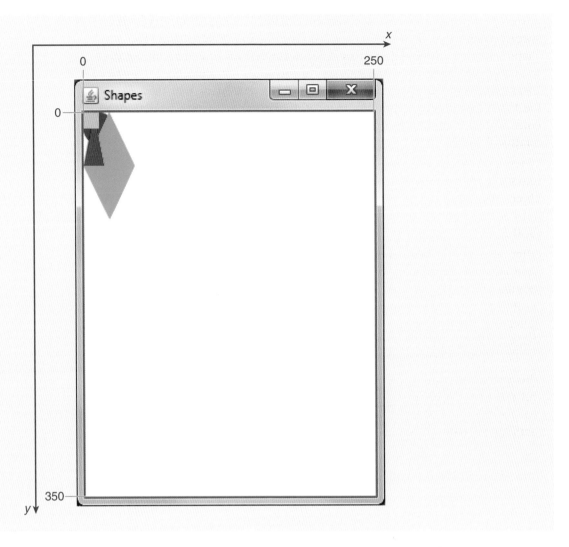

Figure 7 The **Shapes** window: the coordinates of the corners of the 'drawing area' are at (0,0), (250, 0), (0, 350) and (250, 350)

All graphical objects (of whatever shape) are enclosed by an invisible 'bounding box' that tightly encloses the graphical object (see Figure 8). A graphical object's bounding box is actually invisible, but in the figure we have outlined the bounding box of a circle.

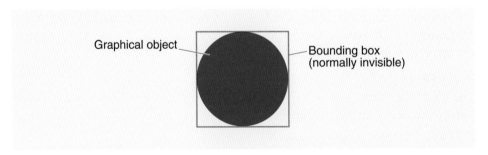

Figure 8 An illustration of the bounding box surrounding a circle

All shape objects have instance variables called xPos and yPos which specify where the shape should be displayed in the Shapes window. A shape's xPos is the number of units from the left-hand side of the Shapes drawing area to the left-hand side of its bounding box. Similarly a shape's yPos is the number of units from the top of the Shapes drawing area to the top of its bounding box. A shape is drawn relative to the top-left hand corner of its bounding box (as opposed to being drawn, for example, relative to its centre).

When any of the shape objects are created their xPos and yPos are both initialised to 0, so, when using the statements in step 1, all the shape objects were positioned in the top left of the Shapes window, with the top left-hand corner of the bounding boxes of each object located at the point (0, 0).

After sending setXPos() and setYPos() messages to the objects you have created you should have observed their graphical representations moving within the Shapes window. The Shapes window provides scrollbars to allow you to view shapes if they are displayed outside the default visible area. The Shapes window can also be resized to view shapes, but can only be closed using the Graphical Display menu in the OUWorkspace.

2   This second part of the activity has shown that shapes of different colours and sizes can be created by using the constructors that take arguments and that their colours and positions can subsequently be changed by sending them appropriate messages.

8.2 The Marionette class

Instances of the Marionette class represent puppet-like characters made up of Circle, Diamond and Triangle objects. The class at present is incomplete, but you will rectify that through a series of activities.

Activity 28

With the project Unit4_Project_5 open, from the BlueJ Tools menu select Project Documentation (if a dialogue box opens, click on the Regenerate button). When the browser opens to display the generated Javadoc documentation, select the link for the Marionette class in the left-hand frame. Now look at the documentation for the class in the main frame of the browser window. What method names can you see?

Discussion

The visible methods are: down(), getBody(), getHead(), getLeftLeg(), getRightLeg(), right() and up().

Activity 29

1   Open the class `Marionette` in the BlueJ editor. Read the class comment and look at the constructor. Note that the constructor creates a number of shape objects and assigns them to instance variables.

Notice that there are many more methods in the code than appeared in the documentation. Why don't all the methods appear in the documentation? What would happen if you tried to send a message that corresponded to one of the methods that isn't shown in the documentation to an instance of `Marionette` from the OUWorkspace?

2   Now open the OUWorkspace (if it is already open and contains statements select **Reset OUWorkspace** from the **Action** menu) and then select **Open** from the **Graphical Display** menu to open the **Shapes** window.

Execute the following statement and observe that nothing is displayed in the **Shapes** window.

```
Marionette woodenTop = new Marionette();
```

Inspect the `woodenTop` variable and, once you have an inspector open on the marionette, inspect its `body`, `head`, `rightLeg` and `leftLeg` attributes.

3   Now execute the following statements, one at a time, and again observe what is displayed in the **Shapes** window.

```
Circle circle1 = woodenTop.getHead();
Diamond diamond1 = woodenTop.getBody();
Triangle triangle1 = woodenTop.getLeftLeg();
Triangle triangle2 = woodenTop.getRightLeg();
woodenTop.right(20);
woodenTop.right(20);
```

Discussion

1   The methods that have been declared as `private` do not appear in the documentation. The methods have been made `private` because the corresponding messages are *not* to be part of the public behaviour of a marionette. If you tried to send these messages from the OUWorkspace to an instance of `Marionette()` you would get an error message.

2   When you created a `Marionette` object referenced by `woodenTop`, although nothing was displayed in the **Shapes** window `woodenTop` appeared in the **Variables** pane.

When you inspect `woodenTop` you should see that the `body` and `head` attributes of the marionette are of types `Diamond` and `Circle` respectively. The `rightLeg` and `leftLeg` attributes are both of type `Triangle`. You can further inspect these objects to see their attributes; for example, the `head` is a `Circle` whose `colour` is `OUColour.BLUE`, with xPos 95 and yPos 65.

3   When you declared variables in the OUWorkspace and then used getter messages to assign those variables the marionette's body parts, the shapes appeared in the **Shapes** window. This is because the **Shapes** window is designed to display any shape object that is referenced by a variable in the OUWorkspace (just as the **Amphibians** window is designed to display any amphibian object that is referenced by a variable in the OUWorkspace – see Subsection 6.2, 'The graphical display'). When you created a

Marionette object, even though its constructor created a number of shape objects, none of those shapes was referenced by a variable in the OUWorkspace.

By executing:

```
Circle circle1 = woodenTop.getHead();
Diamond diamond1 = woodenTop.getBody();
Triangle triangle1 = woodenTop.getLeftLeg();
Triangle triangle2 = woodenTop.getRightLeg();
```

the objects referenced by the various instance variables of woodenTop were assigned to OUWorkspace variables, and so immediately became known to the Shapes window and you were able to see the shapes arranged into a recognisable marionette-type figure.

This illustrates that a Marionette object encapsulates its body parts. It is only because we provided public getter methods for those parts that the workspace is able to see them.

Finally, sending right() messages to woodenTop caused this marionette figure to move to the right the specified number of pixels.

Instances of the Marionette class can understand the messages right(), up() and down(), but can't understand the message left() and have no arms. In the next two activities you will add the necessary instance variables and methods to complete the class.

Activity 30

Look at the code for the methods right(), up() and down(). Although it seems initially counter-intuitive, the up() method decrements yPos, and conversely down() increments yPos because, as illustrated in Figure 7, the y-coordinate increases going *down* the Shapes window, rather than going up.

1 Write a left() method for the Marionette class using the right() method as a template. Compile the class, then test your method by executing the following statements in the OUWorkspace. The method should be public so that you can send the corresponding message from the OUWorkspace. (Note that you will need to recreate any objects in the workspace.)

```
Marionette woodenTop = new Marionette();
Circle circle1 = woodenTop.getHead();
Diamond diamond1 = woodenTop.getBody();
Triangle triangle1 = woodenTop.getLeftLeg();
Triangle triangle2 = woodenTop.getRightLeg();
woodenTop.left(20);
```

2 What happens if you use negative valued arguments such as -20 when sending the messages left(), right(), up() and down()?

Discussion

1   Here is our code for the `left()` method .

```
/**
 * Decrements the xPos of the receiver
 * by the value of the argument.
 */
public void left(int decrement)
{
    this.setXPos(this.getXPos() - decrement);
}
```

2   The marionette moves the specified number of pixels in the opposite direction you would expect from the message name! This is because the method simply performs some arithmetic using the provided argument; it doesn't check to see whether the argument makes the marionette move a particular direction. Of course, you could have written methods to move horizontally or vertically (rather than say specifically right or left), and then the sign of the argument wouldn't have mattered.

In *Unit 5* you will see how we can write code that can do one thing or another depending on some conditions, so that a method such as `left()` could be constrained to behave in a certain way.

Activity 31

The body parts of a `Marionette` object are referenced by the following instance variables: `body`, `head`, `rightLeg` and `leftLeg`.

1   You are now going to add arms to a `Marionette` object. The arms of `Marionette` objects should be instances of the class `Diamond`. Look at the code for declaring the instance variable `leftLeg`. Write similar declarations for two new instance variables: `leftArm` and `rightArm`.

2   In the `Marionette` constructor add code (before the `alignAll()` message) to create two instances of the `Diamond` class, both of which should have a width of 40, a height of 15 and be coloured `OUColour.YELLOW`, and assign them to the instance variables `leftArm` and `rightArm`. You will need to use the three-argument `Diamond` constructor, whose signature is: `Diamond(int, int, OUColour)`. The first `int` argument is for the diamond's width, and the second is for its height.

3   Write `public` getter methods for the new instance variables.

4   In order to align the arms of a `Marionette` object to the rest of its body parts you will need to write two more methods: `alignLeftArm()` and `alignRightArm()`. Use the methods `alignLeftLeg()` and `alignRightLeg()` as templates. The xPos of the left arm should be set to the xPos of the marionette minus 35, and the yPos set to the yPos of the marionette plus 25. The xPos of the right arm should be set to the xPos of the marionette plus 25, and the yPos to the yPos of the marionette plus 25.

5   Finally, you will need to add two more statements to the `alignAll()` method that make use of `alignLeftArm()` and `alignRightArm()`.

After compiling your class (and resolving any errors), you should test that the code you have written in this activity works correctly by executing the following statements in the OUWorkspace.

```
Marionette woodenTop = new Marionette();
Circle aCircle = woodenTop.getHead();
Diamond diamond1 = woodenTop.getBody();
Triangle triangle1 = woodenTop.getLeftLeg();
Triangle triangle2 = woodenTop.getRightLeg();
Diamond diamond2 = woodenTop.getLeftArm();
Diamond diamond3 = woodenTop.getRightArm();
woodenTop.right(50);
woodenTop.left(50);
woodenTop.up(50);
woodenTop.down(50);
```

Discussion

1   You should have added the following code to the list of instance variables.

```
private Diamond leftArm;
private Diamond rightArm;
```

2   Here is our updated code for the constructor.

```
public Marionette()
{
    super();
    this.head = new Circle(40, OUColour.BLUE);
    this.body = new Diamond(30, 100, OUColour.RED);
    this.leftLeg = new Triangle(10, 100, OUColour.GREEN);
    this.rightLeg = new Triangle(10, 100, OUColour.GREEN);
    this.xPos = 100;
    this.yPos = 100;
    this.leftArm = new Diamond(40, 15, OUColour.YELLOW);
    this.rightArm = new Diamond(40, 15, OUColour.YELLOW);
    this.alignAll();
}
```

3   The code for the getter methods should be as follows.

```
/**
 * Returns the leftArm of the receiver.
 */
public Diamond getLeftArm()
{
    return this.leftArm;
}


/**
 * Returns the rightArm of the receiver.
 */
public Diamond getRightArm()
{
    return this.rightArm;
}
```

4   Here is our code for the methods `alignLeftArm()` and `alignRightArm()`.

```
/**
 * Aligns the leftArm of the receiver relative to the
 * xPos and yPos of the receiver.
 */
private void alignLeftArm()
{
    this.getLeftArm().setXPos(this.getXPos() - 35);
    this.getLeftArm().setYPos(this.getYPos() + 25);
}


/**
 * Aligns the rightArm of the receiver relative to the
 * xPos and yPos of thereceiver.
 */
private void alignRightArm()
{
    this.getRightArm().setXPos(this.getXPos() + 25);
    this.getRightArm().setYPos(this.getYPos() + 25);
}
```

5   Below is the updated code for the method `alignAll()`.

```
/**
 * Aligns all the body parts of the receiver.
 */
private void alignAll()
{
    this.alignBody();
    this.alignHead();
    this.alignLeftLeg();
    this.alignRightLeg();
    this.alignLeftArm();
    this.alignRightArm();
}
```

If you have had difficulties with Activities 28–31, Unit4_Project_5_Completed incorporates all the changes and additions made in this set of activities.

The marionette example illustrates a relationship between classes called **composition**. This occurs when objects of one class have instance variables that reference objects of other classes. Marionettes have instance variables that reference `Diamond`, `Circle` and `Triangle` objects. (Note, `Marionette`'s primitive instance variables `xPos` and `yPos` do not reference objects – they contain primitive values. If all instance variables of a class are of primitive types, then composition does not occur.)

In fact, we have seen examples of composition already, but we did not give a name to this relationship. For example, the `Frog` class has an instance variable called `colour`, which holds a reference to an object of the class `OUColour`. Another example is that the `Account` class has instance variables `holder` and `number` that reference `String` objects.

The composition relationship is also known as the *has-a* relationship, for example we can say that an account *has-a* holder and *has-a* number. This is quite different to the *is-a* relationship that inheritance gives us.

Composition is a powerful and frequently used object-oriented programming technique, because it reflects the way the real world is constructed. Sometimes we use Java library classes such as `String` in composition, and other times, as in `Marionette`, we have to write our own classes such as `Diamond` to achieve our purpose.

You should be able to think of many real-world examples of composition. For example, a car has wheels and has an engine, and this could be modelled in code using composition of `Car`, `Wheel` and `Engine` objects, by giving a `Car` class instance variables of type `Wheel` and `Engine`.

The activity in Unit4_Project_6 provides you with another example of composition, and of how objects related in this way can be initialised using their class constructors.

9   Summary

After studying this unit you should understand the following ideas.

- A `public` method defines a message for all instances of a class and for all instances of any subclasses.

- A `private` method is used to define a message that only instances of that class can send (to themselves or to other instances of the same class), but which other classes of objects cannot send.

- Although a method has to be defined only once to work for a whole class of objects, when a message causes a method to be executed, the method behaves as though it is inside exactly one object – namely the object that received the message that caused the execution of the method.

- Attributes are implemented in Java using instance variables. An instance variable holds either a primitive data value or a value that is a reference to an object. The declared type of the variable specifies what kind of value it can hold.

- Access modifiers are used to specify the visibility of instance variables and methods to objects of other classes.

- You can think of two kinds of thing existing inside an object: its own instance variables and its own methods. All other objects (and their methods) can be considered to be outside a given object. This incorporation of data and behaviour in a single entity is termed encapsulation.

- If you have followed good practice and made all the instance variables `private`, there is no direct access to the state of an object from objects of other classes. The consequence of this is that the only way that an object (or a user) can change the state of another object or make it do something is by sending it a message.

- Object references or values of some primitive data type are returned as values from a method by writing a `return` statement in the method code. Methods that do not return a value declare a return type of `void`.

- A method name is overloaded if there is more than one method with that name in the protocol of a class, with each method of that name having a distinct signature.

- Arguments are used in a message to pass information into methods. The formal argument names in the header of a method are placeholders for the actual arguments. The value of each actual argument is copied into a corresponding formal argument when the method is executed.

Learning outcomes

After studying this unit you should be able to:

- explain the distinction between a method and a message;
- explain what is meant by the term 'method invocation';
- explain the principles of encapsulation, data hiding and reuse of code;
- use an editor to create new methods for a class, and test the methods on a variety of instances of that class;
- add instance variables to a class, initialise them, and write getter and setter methods with appropriate access modifiers;
- write a simple constructor for a class;
- write methods that return values;
- understand the use of arguments in messages, and write code for methods involving arguments;
- explain the meaning of `public` and `private` in relation to both instance variables and methods;
- Explain the meanings of terms such as 'header', 'signature' and 'overloading' in the context of describing methods;
- Explain the distinction between attributes and instance variables.

Unit 5

Selection and iteration

Contents

Introduction

In everyday life you often come across statements such as:

> If it is raining then we go to work by car; otherwise we walk.

This is called conditional selection. It says that *if* something is true *then* we will do one thing *else* we will do another thing. The condition used here is whether or not it is raining.

The need to make similar decisions occurs frequently in computer programs. For instance, you might be prompted for confirmation that you wish to proceed with an action, such as deleting a file. Your response – whether you click the OK button or not – will determine what the program does. Or, as another example, you might wish to withdraw money from a cash machine. The banking system must then decide whether to meet your request or not, based on whether you have enough funds in the account.

You can tell that these kinds of choice will occur in all but the simplest programs and so conditional selection is a fundamental structure in all programming.

In software, choices between one action or another like those described above are decided using conditions that evaluate to Boolean values, either `true` or `false`. Which course of action is followed – that is, what code is executed – will depend on this value.

A second fundamental programming structure is one that results in repetition, also called **iteration** or **looping**. Like conditional selection, repetition is also common in everyday life. For example, we might want to print out 50 copies of a document, or we might want to keep serving customers while there are still people waiting in a queue.

Note that knowing when to stop repeating an action such as printing out a document or serving customers also depends on a condition. In the first case, the condition is whether the number of copies printed has reached 50. In the second case it is whether or not there are any customers in the queue.

The main focus of this unit is to describe how to perform selection and iteration in Java. We will also introduce a new kind of method called a *class method* and a useful graphical component called a **dialogue box**. Dialogue boxes are a common, and familiar, way for a program to interact with a user. Since we will use them throughout *Unit 5* we will begin by looking at dialogue boxes.

2

Dialogue boxes

So far in the module, although you have been able to display output, you have not been able to write Java code that allows true two-way interaction with the user.

The class OUDialog (note the American spelling) provides facilities both for giving information *to* the user (output) and for obtaining information *from* the user (input) using dialogue boxes. In fact, Java provides a much more general form of dialogue box, but the set of dialogue boxes provided by the class OUDialog is designed to be easier for you to use and to cover the most frequently required cases.

Dialogue boxes are not the only way of obtaining input from users – or of displaying output, of course – but they are popular with users and, as you will see, quite friendly for the programmer to work with. Dialogue boxes come in many forms: some just ask the user to click on a button, while others may require the user to enter some text from the keyboard or make a choice, such as 'yes' or 'no'.

You may have seen Java dialogue boxes already. They are used to report some kinds of error that occur when you use the BlueJ environment. Figure 1 shows what we got when we pressed the New Class... button in a BlueJ project window and then deliberately left the class name blank.

Figure 1 A dialogue box produced in BlueJ

The OUDialog class we will be using provides three different flavours of dialogue box:

- alert – displays a message and an OK button;
- confirm – displays a question and asks the user to click Yes or No;
- request – asks the user to type something into the dialogue box and offers an OK or Cancel button.

Each of these types of dialogue box is said to be **modal**. A modal dialogue is one that will not allow you to interact with another part of the program or system until you have responded to it by clicking one of the buttons presented.

These three kinds of dialogue box are found in other programming languages, not just Java.

Using an OUDialog involves using a kind of method we call a *class method*, so we will discuss this kind of method in the next section.

2.1   Class methods

The methods you were introduced to in *Unit 4* are encapsulated by objects along with instance variables. Such methods are always invoked as a result of sending a message to an object and that is why they can use the expression this, which you will remember references the current object when a message is received. These methods (all the ones you have seen so far) are more precisely called **instance methods** because of their relationship with instances of a class (that is, objects).

However, there is another form of method that is invoked without reference to any particular object, which is called a **class method**. Class methods are methods that can be executed irrespective of whether any instances of the class have been created and so they cannot use the expression this. Classes can define class methods as well as instance methods.

A statement that results in a class method being executed looks like a statement that results in an instance method being executed. For example, if SomeClass is a class, we are used to seeing messages being sent as in (a) below:

(a)

```
SomeClass myVar = new SomeClass();
myVar.doSomething();
```

From looking at this code we expect that it ultimately results in the *instance* method doSomething() being executed; that is, it results in the object of type SomeClass referenced by myVar being sent a message.

However, if doSomething is a class method it can perform its work without sending messages to objects and, in this case, the following fragment can be used.

(b)

```
SomeClass.doSomething();
```

This code fragment results in the *class* method doSomething() being executed.

Here is how the execution of instance and class methods differs.

In (a), when the message-send is compiled, the compiler produces bytecode that at run-time passes the receiver and the message to the JVM. It instructs the JVM to find out the class of the receiver and to search for a method that matches the message's signature (starting from the receiver's own class and then searching up the inheritance hierarchy until the method is found). When the method is found, the JVM then invokes that method, with the receiver.

What all this boils down to is that the object referenced by `myVar` gets the message `doSomething()` and the code in the method `doSomething()` is executed. Any references to `this` in the method refer to the receiver.

In (b) however, code such as `SomeClass.doSomething()` is not a message-send, even though it may look like one. `SomeClass` is not a variable that references an object; it is the name of a class (because we followed naming conventions, its name begins with a capital letter). Only objects can be sent messages and classes are not objects.

Class methods are like non-object-oriented functions or procedures. Code such as `SomeClass.doSomething()` is taken by the compiler and translated into much simpler bytecode that instructs the JVM at run-time to go directly to the bytecode for the class `SomeClass` and execute the code inside the body of the method `doSomething()` without reference to a receiver (because it does not involve a message being sent).

To distinguish what happens in the case of execution of a class method from execution of an instance method we describe code such as `SomeClass.doSomething()` as a *method invocation* and we say 'the method `doSomething()` is *invoked* on the class `SomeClass`', whereas we describe code such as `myVar.doSomething()` in terms such as 'the message `doSomething()` is sent to the object referenced by `myVar`'. Likewise, any value returned by a class method is not a message-reply.

So, if we use the term 'method' on its own in M250 we are normally referring to an instance method. When we wish to refer to a class method we will normally be specific.

You will learn much more about class methods in *Unit 7*. For now all you need to remember is that to invoke a class method you simply write the name of the class that defines the method followed by the name of the class method, using the, now familiar, dot notation.

Class methods are quite common in object-oriented languages, such as Java. One of the things they are often used for is providing general utilities, such as mathematical functions. For example, Java has a class (about which you do not need to know any details) called `Math` that provides class methods such as `sin()`, `abs()`, `max()` and `log()`.

In the following sections we will introduce some class methods of the class `OUDialog`. These methods are used to show information to, and obtain information from, a user, using a dialogue box.

2.2   The class `OUDialog`

Table 1 shows the headers of class methods provided by the class `OUDialog`, together with a brief description of each method's purpose. (The access modifier `public` has been omitted.)

Table 1   Class methods in `OUDialog`

Method	Purpose
`static void alert(String prompt)`	Display some information until a user clicks the **OK** button.
`static boolean confirm(String prompt)`	Display some information until a user clicks a **Yes** or **No** button.
`static String request(String prompt)`	Requests some information from the user, which is returned as a string when the user presses **OK**.
`static String request(String prompt, String initialAnswer)`	Requests some information from the user, which is returned as a string when the user presses **OK**. A default response (given by `initialAnswer`) is returned if no response is supplied by the user.

Note the Java keyword `static` in the header of each of these methods, which indicates that a method is a class method. Class methods are also called **static methods**.

Bear in mind while you are reading the examples using these class methods that they do *not* involve sending messages to objects.

2.3   The class method `OUDialog.alert()`

This class method in `OUDialog` has the signature `alert(String)`. It takes a `String` argument, which is displayed in a modal dialogue box. As its name implies, it is often used when alerting the user to something they need to be aware of. For example, executing

`OUDialog.alert("Remember to save your file before exiting");`

results in the dialogue box shown in Figure 2.

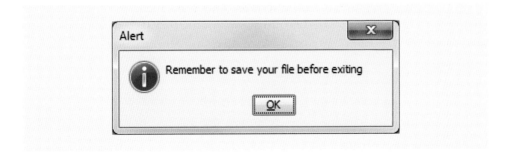

Figure 2 A dialogue box produced using `OUDialog.alert()`

To dismiss the dialogue box, you click the OK button (or close the box using its window control). This method requires nothing else from the user; it does not return a value, and no further action takes place after OK has been clicked.

SAQ 1

Based on the example code that produces Figure 2, write down a statement that when executed displays the dialogue box illustrated in Figure 3.

Figure 3   Another dialogue box produced using OUDialog.alert()

Answer

```
OUDialog.alert("This is my first dialogue box");
```

Note that, although the method alert() may often be used to issue a warning it can be used to display whatever text the programmer chooses.

SAQ 2

Explain how each line of the following sequence of statements is executed, and sketch the dialogue box that results from execution of the complete sequence. (Line numbers are provided for reference.)

This exercise makes use of the message toUpperCase(), which, when sent to a String, returns another String consisting of the letters of the original string all in upper case.

```
String name; //1
name = "Patrick"; //2
name = name.toUpperCase(); //3
OUDialog.alert("The name was " + name); //4
```

Answer

Line 1 declares a variable of type String whose identifier is name.

Line 2 makes the variable name reference the String object "Patrick".

Line 3 makes the variable name reference the new String object returned when the object "Patrick" referenced by name is sent the message toUppercase().

Line 4 uses the method `alert()` of the `OUDialog` class with the argument resulting from concatenating `"The name was "` with the object referenced by `name`, which, from line 3, is now `"PATRICK"`.

The dialogue box produced is shown in Figure 4.

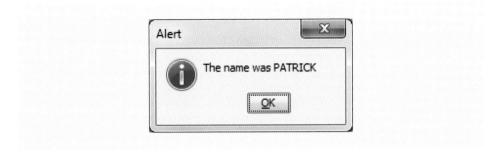

Figure 4   Dialogue box displaying Patrick in upper case

If an empty string (a string containing no characters) had been assigned to `name` in line 2 of the code in SAQ 2, the statement sequence (given below) would have resulted in the dialogue box shown in Figure 5.

```
String name;
name = "";
name = name.toUpperCase();
OUDialog.alert("The name was " + name);
```

Figure 5   The dialogue box that would result if `name` were assigned an empty string

Activity 1

Launch BlueJ and open the OUWorkspace (there is no project for this activity).

In the workspace practise using `OUDialog.alert()` by executing statements with a variety of string arguments.

Some suggestions are given below, but obviously you can make up your own.

```
OUDialog.alert("My name is Bond. James Bond.");
OUDialog.alert("Cannot accept a number larger than 100");
OUDialog.alert("stop".toUpperCase() + "!");
OUDialog.alert("500");
```

Discussion

Note that you were able to display the `String` object `"500"`. Remember that strings can contain a variety of different characters – not just alphabetic characters – and that a string consisting of numeric characters, such as `"500"`, is not the same as the number `500`.

Remember too that a 'warning' produced by the `OUDialog` method `alert()` is just displayed text and has no other effect. For example, it does not actually stop users entering whatever they please. If you wanted to restrict the range of numbers a user could input, you would have to write other code to enforce this.

Activity 2

This activity will give you further practice in using the class method `alert()`. For this and subsequent activities we advise that you write down your answers on paper before launching BlueJ.

In order to test your solutions, open Unit5_Project_1 and the OUWorkspace.

Note that here (as in other parts of the unit) the *single* quotes around some text merely indicate what words the dialogue box should display – the quote marks themselves do *not* form part of the desired display.

1   In the OUWorkspace, write a single statement that, when executed, will display 'My name is Methuselah' in a dialogue box.

2   Write a single statement that, when executed, will display in a dialogue box an upper-case version of the string `"Flood Warning!"`

3   Add a single statement to the end of the code below so that it will display 'I am studying M250' in a dialogue box. Your expression should make use of two string variables, `aMessage` and `moduleCode`.

```
String aMessage;
String moduleCode;
aMessage = "I am studying ";
moduleCode = "M250";
```

4   Modify the two assignment statements in step 3 so that your dialogue box will display information about a module you plan to study next year. (If you have not thought about this yet, just make up something.)

5   In the BlueJ window double-click the `Account` class to open the editor.

Now define two new instance methods for the `Account` class that will display the values of the variables `holder` and `balance` in dialogue boxes.

Here are the method headers and initial comments for the methods.

Make sure to include some explanatory text in your dialogue boxes, using concatenation.

As we saw in *Unit 3*, using the + operator will automatically take care of converting the numerical balance into a suitable string representation.

```
/**
 * Displays the holder of the receiver in a dialogue box.
 */
public void displayHolder()


/**
 * Displays the balance of the receiver in a dialogue
 * box.
 */
public void displayBalance()
```

Once you have successfully recompiled the `Account` class, test your new methods in the workspace by creating an instance of the `Account` class, setting its `holder` and `balance`, then sending it the messages `displayHolder()` and `displayBalance()`.

Discussion

1   To produce the required dialogue box you would need to execute the statement:

```
OUDialog.alert("My name is Methuselah");
```

2   The single statement that will display `"Flood Warning!"` in upper-case letters is:

```
OUDialog.alert("Flood Warning!".toUpperCase());
```

3   You were asked to extend the given statement sequence so that execution would produce a dialogue box with the text 'I am studying M250'. The code you need to add is:

```
OUDialog.alert(aMessage + moduleCode);
```

4   To display information about a module you plan to study next year, you would need to change the two assignment statements to something like:

```
aMessage = "Next year I plan to study ";
moduleCode = "M256";
```

The statement

```
OUDialog.alert(aMessage + moduleCode);
```

will remain the same.

5   This was our solution:

```
/**
 * Displays the holder of the receiver in a dialogue
 * box.
 */
public void displayHolder()
{
    OUDialog.alert("The holder is " + this.getHolder());
}

/**
 * Displays the balance of the receiver in a dialogue
 * box.
 */
public void displayBalance()
{
    OUDialog.alert("The balance is " + this.getBalance());
}
```

Local variables and scope

Often it is helpful to introduce what are called **local variables** into the body of your methods. Using local variables to hold intermediate results in a method can make the code easier to read.

For example, the following alternative `displayHolder` method declares a local variable of type `String` called `theHolder`:

```
/**
 * Displays the holder of the receiver in a dialogue
 * box.
 */
public void displayHolder()
{
    String theHolder = this.getHolder();
    OUDialog.alert("The holder is " + theHolder);
}
```

Variables declared inside a method, like `theHolder` in the code above, are said to be **local** to the method, which means that they cannot be accessed from outside the method's body (which is marked by curly braces).

The region within which a variable can be accessed is called its **scope**. The scope of a local variable is from the point where it is declared to the end of the method's body. By contrast, the scope of an instance variable is anywhere within the class that defines it (between the opening and closing curly braces of the class). The variables you have been declaring in the Code Pane of the OUWorkspace are also local variables; their scope is the Code Pane itself and they exist only while the OUWorkspace is open.

Local variables are created when a method is executed and exist only for as long as the method is being executed. All the code in the method will be executed every time the method is executed, and in each case it will start using newly created local variables.

Access modifiers such as `private` cannot be used when declaring local variables: local variables are automatically visible *only* within their enclosing block and not in any other part of the class's code.

Finally notice that we did *not* write `this.theHolder` in the `displayHolder()` method. If we had used `this`, we would be attempting to access an instance variable of the receiver object called `theHolder`. However, local variables are not instance variables and so cannot be accessed using `this`.

If you consistently use `this` when directly accessing instance variables, it will make it easier for you to identify instance variables and non-instance variables.

Variable hiding

An interesting situation arises when a local variable (or formal argument) has the same name as an instance variable. The local variable is said to *hide* the instance variable and this can lead to bugs which are hard to track down. For example, consider the following class.

```
public class MyClass
{
    private int someVariable; //instance variable
    public MyClass()
    {
        this.someVariable = 99;
    }

    public void hidingExample()
    {
        int someVariable = 10; //local variable
        System.out.println(someVariable); //1
        System.out.println(this.someVariable); //2
    }

    public void regularMethod()
    {
        System.out.println(someVariable); //3
        System.out.println(this.someVariable); //4
    }
}
```

In line `//1` the method `hidingExample()` will display the value 10, since the local variable `someVariable` was initialised to 10 and it *hides* the instance variable of the same name. However, in line `//2` the value of the *instance* variable `someVariable` (i.e. 99) will be displayed.

Lines `//3` and `//4` will *both* display the value of the *instance* variable `someVariable` when the message `regularMethod()` is received. In the case of line `//3`, the only variable with the name `someVariable` that is in scope is the instance variable. (You may remember that we said it is possible to access instance variables and methods without using the expression `this`, as illustrated in line `//3`.)

As you can see, variable hiding can result in confusing code. However this can always be avoided by not giving local variables the same names as instance variables. Consistently using the expression `this` to access instance variables also helps to avoid confusing code.

2.4   The class method `OUDialog.confirm()`

The method `confirm()` takes a string as an argument, usually a question such as 'Do you really want to delete this file?'.

Like `alert()`, the string argument of `confirm()` is displayed in a modal dialogue box, but, instead of OK, there are two buttons, labelled Yes and No.

For example, execution of

```
OUDialog.confirm("Are you over 16?");
```

results in the dialogue box shown in Figure 6.

Figure 6   An example using `OUDialog.confirm()`

To dismiss the dialogue box, you would click either the Yes button or the No button. A confirm dialogue box returns a `boolean` value. Clicking on Yes returns the value `true` and clicking on No returns the value `false`. Depending on what value is returned, the program can choose between alternative courses of action.

As with any other `boolean` value, the result returned by a `confirm` dialogue can be assigned to a `boolean` variable, as in the following example:

```
boolean answer = OUDialog.confirm("Say yes or no");
```

Note that closing the window without clicking on either button also results in an answer of `false`.

Activity 3

If it is not already open, launch BlueJ and open the OUWorkspace (again there is no project associated with this activity).

In the OUWorkspace practise using `confirm()`. Try examples like the following, executing them one at a time:

```
OUDialog.confirm("Ready to start?");
OUDialog.confirm("Have you won the lottery yet?");
OUDialog.confirm("Do you really want to delete the file "
                + "diary.txt?");
```

In each case try both the Yes and No buttons and observe the textual representation of the method's return value shown in the Display Pane.

Discussion

You should have observed that when the Yes button is clicked, `true` is returned as the method's return value, and when the No button is clicked, `false` is returned.

Breaking statements across lines

One of the statements in Activity 3 is longer than the physical line, which raises the question of how you should lay it out. If a statement has to be split across two or more lines, you should aim to make the statement as easy as possible for a reader to understand. It should be made obvious that the line is split.

There are some things you cannot do. One is that you cannot have a break between lines in the middle of a string. For example, this is not permissible:

```
OUDialog.confirm("Do you really want to delete
the file " + "diary.txt?");
```

Also, you cannot break an identifier across lines. For example, this is illegal:

```
OUDialog.confi
rm("Do you really want to delete the file " + "diary.txt?");
```

However, breaks may be placed elsewhere. One common practice is to break a line before an operator such as + and to indent the new line, for example:

```
OUDialog.confirm("Do you really want to delete the file "
                + "diary.txt?");
```

If in doubt, remember that the main criterion is readability, so try to place line breaks at a point that makes the structure of the statement clear.

2.5   The class method `OUDialog.request()`

Whereas the method `alert()` returns no value and `confirm()` returns either `true` or `false`, the method `request()` asks the user for input and, if OK is clicked, returns whatever is in the input box as a `String` object.

For example, executing

```
String inputName = OUDialog.request("Hi! What is your name?");
```

will produce the dialogue box shown in Figure 7.

Figure 7 A dialogue using `OUDialog.request()` with one argument

If you were to type 'Marta Friedman' and click OK, the `String` `"Marta Friedman"` would be returned and assigned to the variable `inputName`. (Remember that single quotes in normal text are just being used to mark the words to be displayed, and do not form part of the display themselves.)

SAQ 3

The dialogue box in Figure 8 is produced as a result of executing the class method `request()` with the argument `"Hi! What is your name?"`. Suppose that the response 'Bina' is entered. What is returned if OK is clicked?

Figure 8 A dialogue using `OUDialog.request()`

Answer

Clicking OK with 'Bina' in the dialogue box shown results in the `String` object `"Bina"` being returned.

Selecting `Cancel` or closing a `request()` dialogue

It is important to understand what happens when the `Cancel` button is clicked in a dialogue box such as the one above, and how this differs from clicking OK with an empty input box.

If `Cancel` is clicked, then the method `request()` will return the value `null`. The value `null` will also be returned if the dialogue is closed without clicking either of its buttons.

On the other hand, if OK is clicked when the input box is empty, an empty string `""` will be returned.

Note that there is a very big difference between `null` and an empty string. An attempt to send any message to `null` is *always* illegal, whereas the empty string has the full protocol of `String` objects. For example, an empty string responds to the message `length()` with the answer 0 as expected.

It is also important not to confuse an empty string with one containing a single space character `" "`. If you send the message `length()` to `" "` the answer will be 1, not 0, so there is no doubt of the difference between the two.

SAQ 4

What would be the value returned from the method `request()` in SAQ 3 if, instead of entering some characters in the input box, the user had left it blank before clicking OK?

Answer

If the input box had been left blank, the method's return value would have been an empty string, `""`.

If you are using the `request()` method it is presumably because you want to get some information from the user of your program; any answer returned by `request()` is therefore important information and you will probably want to assign the returned value to some `String` variable.

Activity 4

By combining different methods from the protocol of `OUDialog` you can code a two-way interaction with the user.

Suppose you want to give the user the option of entering a name that the program will then display in upper case, concatenated to the string `"The name given was "`. The class method `request()` can be used to prompt the user for a name. The string that is returned must then be sent an appropriate message to produce the upper-case version. Then the method `alert()` can be used to display the full string, using concatenation. Open the OUWorkspace in BlueJ and complete the sequence of statements below by replacing the comments with suitable code:

```
//declare name as a String variable
name = //insert code for a request dialogue box
name = name.toUpperCase();
//display name in upper case in a dialogue box
```

Try out your solution in the workspace.

Discussion

Our code is given below:

```
String name;
name = OUDialog.request("Hi! What is your name?");
name = name.toUpperCase();
OUDialog.alert("The name given was " + name);
```

Note how the variable `name` is used first to refer to the string returned by the method `request()`, and then to the string of upper-case characters that is returned from the message `toUpperCase()`. The identifier you choose for a variable does not affect the way in which the code is executed, although you should try to use something informative. An equally good identifier in this case would have been `input`. The following code would have resulted in exactly the same actions:

```
String input;
input = OUDialog.request("Hi! What is your name?");
input = input.toUpperCase();
OUDialog.alert("The name given was " + input);
```

The code could also be written without a variable, but it is often clearer to break up a single complex statement into a number of simpler statements.

Request dialogue boxes with an initial answer

Another version of the `request()` class method has the signature `request(String, String)`. This method is similar to the method with the signature `request(String)`. It returns a `String` as before and the first argument provides the text to display; however, this version has a second argument that lets the programmer provide a default input value by giving an 'initial answer' that will be returned if the user simply clicks OK without typing something into the input box.

For example, executing

```
OUDialog.request("What is your name, Elvis or Buddy?",
                 "Elvis");
```

would result in the dialogue box shown in Figure 9.

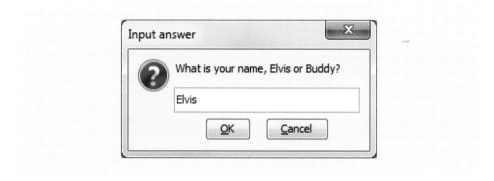

Figure 9 An example using `OUDialog.request(String, String)`

The dialogue box suggests that you type Elvis or Buddy (and provides a default input, Elvis, for you). Anything you type in response to the question – and it could be neither Elvis nor Buddy but something entirely different – will be the answer. If you click OK straight away the answer will be `"Elvis"`.

As with the `request(String)` method, if **Cancel** is clicked or the window is closed the value returned is `null`.

SAQ 5

Write down a statement that produces a dialogue box asking users whether they are using a PC or a Mac, and offers the default answer 'Mac'.

Answer

```
OUDialog.request("What type of computer are you using, PC or Mac?", "Mac");
```

2.6   Converting between strings and numbers

The `OUDialog` class methods introduced above all take `String` objects as arguments, and both `request()` methods return a string (more formally, they return a reference to a `String` object). You may be wondering if `OUDialog` methods can be used only with strings or whether, for instance, numeric data types can also be used with dialogue boxes. They can, but before you can do this we need to explain about conversion between string and numeric types.

SAQ 6

What do you think would happen if you tried to execute the following statement in the OUWorkspace **Code Pane**?

```
OUDialog.alert(100);
```

Answer

If you tried to execute `OUDialog.alert(100)` it would generate an error message as the method `alert()` expects an argument of type `String`, not of type `int`. (In fact, the code will not compile, so it cannot be executed.)

Converting primitive values to strings

The first problem we will solve is how numerical data can be displayed in a dialogue box. You saw in *Unit 3*, and in Activity 4 above, that the concatenation operator + for String has the convenient property that if only one of its operands is a String, then the other operand will be automatically converted into its String representation, whatever its type.

For example:

```
int num;
num = 10;
OUDialog.alert(num + " green bottles");
```

puts up the expected dialogue box shown in Figure 10.

Figure 10 An int is converted to its String equivalent

This works equally well with other numerical types, for example:

```
OUDialog.alert("Pi is approximately " + 3.141592653589793);
```

But what if there is no explanatory text to concatenate and we want to display a number on its own? Well, we might concatenate it to an empty string:

```
OUDialog.alert("" + 42);
```

This does what is wanted, but is not exactly elegant! A better solution is to use the class method valueOf() provided by the class String.

Since valueOf() is a class method, it is invoked on the String class itself with the primitive value to be converted as the argument. The value returned will be the String representation of that value. To display this value the string can then be used as the argument in an OUDialog message. For example, we can do this with an int:

```
int num = 42;
OUDialog.alert(String.valueOf(num));
```

In fact valueOf() works with any primitive data type because the method is overloaded, each version accepting a different type of argument, such as float, double or boolean, and returning an appropriate String representation of the argument.

SAQ 7

What is the result from executing the statement `String.valueOf(100);`?

Answer

The result from executing the statement `String.valueOf(100);` is the string `"100"`.

Building on the solution to SAQ 7, the statement

```
OUDialog.alert(String.valueOf(100));
```

would display the dialogue box of Figure 11.

Figure 11 A dialogue box displaying a number as a string

SAQ 8

Suppose that your age, expressed as a number, is held by the `int` variable `age`. Write down a single statement that displays 'My age is xx' in a dialogue box, where xx is the number held by `age`.

Answer

```
OUDialog.alert("My age is " + age);
```

Converting strings to primitive values

But how about the opposite problem – how to get a primitive value *into* the program via a dialogue box? To be more specific, we consider how to convert the return value from the dialogue box, which will be a `String`, into an `int` value.

There is an `Integer` class that (amongst other things) provides a utility – once again a class method – for exactly this purpose. The method is called `parseInt()`.

Do not confuse the class `Integer` with the primitive data type `int`. There is a close relationship between them, which we will explore later in the module, but they are not the same thing.

As an example of its use, suppose you want to convert the string "1905" to the corresponding `int` value 1905. You use the `parseInt()` method of the `Integer` class, with "1905" as an argument.

```
Integer.parseInt("1905");
```

This will return the `int` value 1905.

So, for example, the following code will prompt the user to enter a string via a dialogue box, convert it to its `int` equivalent and assign the result to the variable `inputNumber`:

```
int inputNumber;
String inputString;
inputString = OUDialog.request("Please enter a number");
inputNumber = Integer.parseInt(inputString);
```

SAQ 9

Complete the following code so that it prompts a user for their age and assigns the response to the variable `age`.

```
String ageString;
int age;
ageString = //add code to display a request dialogue box
age = //convert ageString to an int
```

Answer

```
String ageString;
int age;
ageString = OUDialog.request("Please enter your age");
age = Integer.parseInt(ageString);
```

We can use the method `parseInt` to attempt to produce an `int` value (as we have illustrated here), but the string which is to be converted to an `int` must actually represent an integer. If the user enters something like 'fred' or 'M250' that cannot sensibly be converted to a number, then the method `parseInt()` will be executed with an inappropriate argument and an *exception* will occur. Exceptions, which will be explained in *Unit 8*, are a way programs indicate that something unexpected has occurred and may result in the code ceasing execution.

We have shown an example to convert a string to an `int`, but there are also other classes with class methods to convert strings into other kinds of values; for example, the `Double` class has a method `parseDouble()`.

Exercise 1

Combine the code in SAQ 9 above into a single statement that achieves the same effect.

Activity 5

A common notion in computing is that all computations reduce to the sequence of actions input–process–output. Of course this supposes a broader interpretation of the terms 'input' and 'output' than just interaction with a human user via a keyboard/mouse and a screen, but below are two cases that follow the narrower interpretation.

Open the OUWorkspace in BlueJ.

1   In the **Code Pane** write and test some code which is to be used as part of a survey of how people voted in the last election. Your code should put up a dialogue box displaying the message 'Which party did you vote for?' and assign the answer to a variable called `party`. You can save the researcher time by providing one likely response, say 'Labour', as the initial answer in the input box.

2   Next write code that:

   ○   prompts the user for their year of birth

   ○   calculates the user's age simply as the difference between the year now and the year of birth

   ○   outputs the age in another dialogue box.

   You will need to use one or more variables and appropriate `OUDialog` class methods to perform the input and output. You will also need to use `Integer.parseInt()` to convert the string input to an integer because you need to do arithmetic with it. Conversion of the integer age to a string representation will happen automatically if you include suitable text in the output and use the + operator.

Discussion

1   Possible code to read in the voting survey data is:

```
String party;
party = OUDialog.request("Which party did you vote for?", "Labour");
```

2   Here is some code for calculating someone's age from their year of birth (many different solutions would work equally well).

```
int yearOfBirth;
int age;
//use an appropriate current year here
int currentYear = 2013;
String input;

input = OUDialog.request("What year were you born?");
yearOfBirth = Integer.parseInt(input);
age = currentYear - yearOfBirth;
OUDialog.alert("You are " + age + " years old!");
```

3

Conditions and selection

As we have seen, dialogue boxes allow input to be acquired from a user. This is one example of how a program may obtain input, and for any such input we may need to perform one action or another, depending on the precise value the program received. For example, we may want to ask one set of questions to users of our program who voted for the Labour party, and another set of questions to those who voted for the Green party. Alternatively, we may wish to show a video only to users who are aged 18 or over. In both cases we have to make a decision about what the program code does based on some value the program 'knows'.

This 'branching' of program behaviour into alternate routes, termed **selection** (or **conditional selection**), is a very common requirement. Almost all programming languages provide special keywords and constructs to deal with this case, and Java is no exception.

3.1   `if` statements with simple conditions

In Java (and many other languages) the keyword used to implement selection is `if`; thus `if` statements are statements that allow a program to perform either one or another action depending on some condition.

Imagine we are conducting a survey and we are asked to keep a count of how many persons were of age 40 and over. To do this we will need to query each user about their age, and then count how many users said they were aged 40 or more. This is a branching situation – in one case we count users, and in another we don't, depending on whether each user said they were over 40 or not. Figure 12 represents this branching in the form of a flow chart.

The branch is shown in a flow chart using a diamond symbol – but don't worry about that; the diagram is just a visual aid and you don't have to know how to draw it. What you need to remember is that you implement the branch using an `if` statement.

If the age is high enough, we increment a counter; if not, we just carry on. Notice that both paths the program can follow are reunited after the branch.

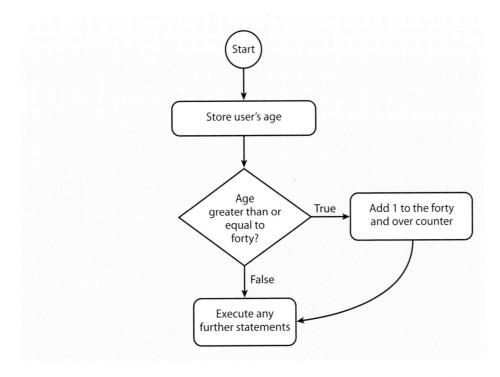

Figure 12 A flow chart for an `if` statement that counts users aged forty and over

Now we can implement each part of this diagram in code. You have already seen how to get a result from a user and store it. In this case we want to get the user's age. We will also require a variable that we can add 1 to each time we find a user of the right age. Finally we require an `if` statement that will increment our counter only when the user is of an appropriate age.

The following code does the job:

```
//initial count of users 40 and over
int fortyAndOver = 0;
String ageString;
int age;

//get a user's age
ageString = OUDialog.request("What is your age?");

//convert string to int
age = Integer.parseInt(ageString);

//increment counter selectively
if (age >= 40) //true or false?
{
    fortyAndOver = fortyAndOver + 1;
}
```

The `if` statement consists of all the code from the word `if` up to the closing curly brace. This statement ensures that

```
fortyAndOver = fortyAndOver + 1;
```

will be executed only *if* the value of `age` is `40` or greater, in other words, if the expression `age >= 40` evaluates to `true`. There could have been more than one statement executed as a result of testing the condition `age >= 40`, but in this case there was just one thing we wanted to do.

If the expression `age >= 40` evaluates to `false` then the code underneath the `if` between the curly braces will *not* be performed. This gives us the branching behaviour we have been looking for.

An `if` statement always works this way: the expression in the parentheses after the word `if` must evaluate to `true` or `false` and so there are just two paths the code may follow:

- into the code in curly braces after the word `if` and then on to any code that follows that, or
- straight to any code after the closing curly brace of the `if`.

After the `if` statement the program flow continues as normal – it just goes on to whatever comes next, which we called 'further statements' in the flow chart. At this point the two possible paths of execution have been reunited.

We ignored the possibility that the user might have pressed `Cancel` in response to the `request()` dialogue, to keep things simple. You will see a way of handling that case later in the unit. We also have not dealt with how we might use this code to query the ages of more than one user: in practice we would need to execute the code after the comment `//get a user's age` repeatedly for a number of users, but we would not reset the counter `fortyAndOver` to `0` each time.

If-then statements

There is more than one kind of `if` statement. The form of `if` statement illustrated above is called an *if-then* or just an `if` statement. Its general form is:

```
if (condition)
{
    //then statements
}
//any further statements
```

Although the word *then* is not used in Java, you may find it helpful to read the statement in your head using the word *'then'*; for example, you might read the above code as 'if the condition is `true` *then* execute the statements in the block of code'.

The *condition* must be a **Boolean expression** so that it evaluates to `true` or `false`. A Boolean expression used in this way is termed a **Boolean condition**, or simply a **condition**.

The condition must be enclosed between parentheses, (and) – if these are left out then the compiler will report an error.

The braces { and } and any code between them are called a **statement block** or just a **block**. A statement block can enclose several statements. Bundling statements together in a block makes them into a unit that will be selected, or not selected, as a whole, so the *if-then* statement can control whether a whole section of code is executed or not. This block can also be referred to as an if statement's **body** (although, as we will see later, an if statement's body doesn't necessarily have to be a block).

Notice also that the if statement does not end in a semicolon, because it has a statement block, and its closing curly brace shows the end of the if statement (we return to this topic shortly).

If-then-else statements

Suppose we also need to keep a separate count of users aged under 40. Figure 13 illustrates this type of branching behaviour.

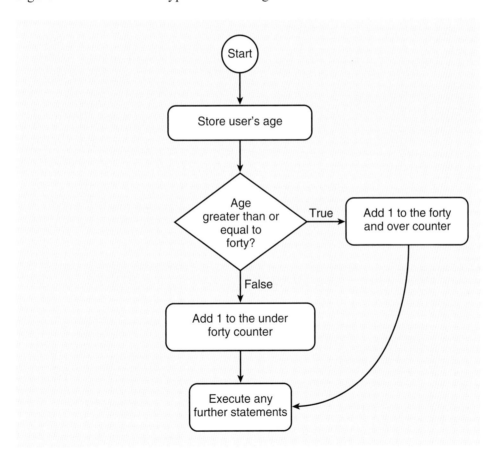

Figure 13 A flow chart for an if statement that counts users aged forty and over, and users aged under forty

This time we need a different form of if statement in which a certain block of code is executed in one case and a different block of code is executed in another case. In both branches there is some work to be done before the paths are joined again. For this scenario we require a second form of `if` statement, which uses the additional keyword `else`.

Here is some code that will perform the new counting task:

```
//initial count of users 40 and over
int fortyAndOver = 0;

//initial count of users aged under 40
int underForty = 0;
String ageString;
int age;

//get a user's age
ageString = OUDialog.request("What is your age?");

//convert string to int
age = Integer.parseInt(ageString);

//increment the appropriate counter selectively
if (age >= 40) //true or false?
{
    fortyAndOver = fortyAndOver + 1;
}
else //age >= 40 was false
{
    underForty = underForty + 1;
}
```

Once again, there could have been several statements in each block, but in this case we just wanted to increment a counter in each case. We have again ignored the case where a user cancels the dialogue box so that we can concentrate on the simple use of the `if` statement.

This second example illustrates the second form of `if`, which we call the *if-then-else* statement. Again the word '*then*' is implied and is never used in Java, but it may help you to read the statement using the word 'then'.

The *if-then-else* statement has the form:

```
if (condition)
{
    //then statements
}
else
{
    //else statements
}
//any further statements
```

If the `condition` evaluates to `true`, *then* the first statement block is executed *else* the condition evaluates to `false` and the second statement block is executed.

When either the *then* or the *else* statement block has been executed, the flow of program control will pass on to any code that follows the *if-then-else* statement. At that point the two possible paths are reunited.

Another *if-then-else* example

This example uses an *if-then-else* statement in combination with both input from the user and output to the user. We give two versions: the only difference is that the first version makes use of local variables to store intermediate results, whereas the second version does not.

In this example we ask a user if 'two and two makes four' using a `confirm()` dialogue. The `confirm()` dialogue returns a `boolean` value, which, in the case of the first version, is stored in the variable `yesClicked`. If the user clicks Yes then `yesClicked` will be set to `true`, and if the user clicks No then `yesClicked` will be set to `false`.

We then use the value of `yesClicked` to perform one action or another and give some feedback to the user using an `alert()` dialogue that tells them whether they are right or wrong. The variable `yesClicked` is already of an appropriate type for use in an `if` statement as it is a (simple) Boolean expression.

First version (local variables store intermediate values)

```
boolean yesClicked;
String output;

yesClicked = OUDialog.confirm("Does two and two make four?");
if (yesClicked)
{
   output = "right.";
}
else
{
   output = "wrong.";
}
OUDialog.alert("You are " + output);
```

In the second version of the code the condition is supplied directly by the value returned by the `confirm()` dialogue.

Second version (no local variables used)

```
if (OUDialog.confirm("Does two and two make four?"))
{
   OUDialog.alert("You are right.");
}
else
{
   OUDialog.alert("You are wrong.");
}
```

Exercise 2

Taking the above example as a guide, write code that uses `OUDialog.confirm()` to produce a dialogue box containing the text 'Click a button' and then reports to the user which button they selected. (You may find it useful to introduce local variables to store intermediate results as shown above.)

3.2   Pitfalls with `if` statements

It is easy to make minor errors in `if` statements that lead to confusing results, but if you are aware of these pitfalls, you can avoid them.

Not using a statement block

In the examples so far we have always used a statement block to write an `if` statement's body. In fact, it is permissible to leave the braces out in cases where there is just one statement to select for execution. However, failing to use a block can lead to program bugs that are hard to detect.

For example, assuming the following local variable declaration and initialisation:

```
int fortyAndOver = 0;
```

suppose that the following *if-then* statement was written, without a statement block:

```
if (OUDialog.confirm("Are you 40 or over?"))
    fortyAndOver = fortyAndOver + 1;
```

Since no statement block was used, the body of the `if` statement is simply the line of code

```
fortyAndOver = fortyAndOver + 1;
```

This all compiles correctly and achieves the same effect as the following code:

```
if (OUDialog.confirm("Are you 40 or over?"))
{
    fortyAndOver = fortyAndOver + 1;
}
```

Now imagine that, having used the original code fragment that does not use a statement block, at some time later the programmer decides that it would be a nice gesture to display the string `"Life begins at forty"` whenever the person concerned is forty or over. So an extra line of code is added:

```
if (OUDialog.confirm("Are you 40 or over?"))
    fortyAndOver = fortyAndOver + 1;
    OUDialog.alert("Life begins at forty");
```

To the programmer's surprise, when the code is run, the message 'Life begins at forty' is displayed for *everyone*, regardless of which button is pushed in the `confirm()` dialogue. This has happened because, in the absence of braces, only the statement immediately following `if (OUDialog.confirm("Are you 40 or over?"))` is controlled by the `if` statement. The next statement after that – `OUDialog.alert("Life begins at forty");` – is executed irrespective of whether the condition is satisfied or not because it is outside the `if` statement.

Once the two statements are written within a statement block, the code will perform as intended, as shown below:

```
if (OUDialog.confirm("Are you 40 or over?"))
{
    fortyAndOver = fortyAndOver + 1;
    OUDialog.alert("Life begins at forty");
}
```

Now the string `"Life begins at forty"` is displayed only when the `confirm()` dialogue returns the value `true`.

For this reason, we suggest that you *always* use a statement block – it is easy to add or remove statements from a statement block, and it is clear which statements belong to the `if` statement's body when you use one. In fact, it is probably a good idea when writing an `if` statement to add the braces in first, and then fill in the statements between them afterwards – that way you don't forget to use braces.

Misplacing a semicolon

Earlier in the module we suggested that every Java statement ends in a semicolon. This was a simplification because, as you have seen we have been writing `if` statements including a block of code, and have not terminated that block of code with a semicolon.

It's an easy mistake to make to use a semicolon after the condition:

```
//what's that at the end of the line?
if (OUDialog.confirm("Are you 40 or over?"));
{
    fortyAndOver = fortyAndOver + 1;
}
```

This time `fortyAndOver` gets incremented whatever the age of the user! The reason is that Java reads the semicolon as the end of an `if` statement that has an empty body like this:

```
if (OUDialog.confirm("Are you 40 or over?"))
    ; //do nothing (empty statement)
{
    fortyAndOver = fortyAndOver + 1;
}
```

Now it does not matter whether the condition is `true` or not. All the condition holds sway over is whether or not the empty statement represented by the semicolon is 'executed'. Either way, after the `if` statement program control moves on normally and executes whatever comes next, which happens to be the statement block containing

```
fortyAndOver = fortyAndOver + 1.
```

A related error is to insert a semicolon between the *then* and *else* parts of an *if-then-else* statement:

```
if (someCondition)
{
    //statements
}; //rogue semicolon!
else
{
    //statements
}
```

If you do this, you will see an 'else without if' compilation error.

3.3   More about selection conditions

Note that it is generally not possible to determine the value of a Boolean condition (which will be either `true` or `false`) simply by reading the program code. In other words, you cannot determine it *statically*. The result can only be determined *dynamically – by executing the code.*

For example, you cannot tell what the answer returned as a result of executing `OUDialog.confirm("Click a button")` will be until the dialogue box has been produced and a button has been clicked. Indeed, if the answer were known in advance there would be no need to include the dialogue box in the first place!

The `OUDialog` method `confirm()` conveniently returns either `true` or `false` and, as we've seen, you can make direct use of this value in an `if` statement. However, things are generally less straightforward. Usually you want to make a selection which depends on a comparison between values – whether one variable has the same value as another, is different, is larger, is smaller, or some combination of these.

Suppose, for example, that you wanted to password protect some sensitive online information. Users would have to enter their password into a dialogue box, and the input string would be compared with the stored password. Suppose that the user input is assigned to the `String` variable `passwordEntered` and that the stored password is `"FirstOfMay"`. The condition to verify the password can be written as the Java expression:

```
passwordEntered.equals("FirstOfMay")
```

If the `String` object referenced by `passwordEntered` has exactly the same sequence of characters in the same order as the message argument `"FirstOfMay"` the message answer is `true`, otherwise it is `false`. (The message `equals()` for the class `String` was introduced in Section 3 of *Unit 3*.)

We might write code similar to the following to interact with a user.

```
String passwordEntered = OUDialog.request("Enter your password.");
if (passwordEntered.equals("FirstOfMay"))
{
    OUDialog.alert("Welcome.");
}
else
{
    OUDialog.alert("Access denied.");
}
```

SAQ 10

Rewrite the example above without using the local variable `passwordEntered`.

Answer

```
if (OUDialog.request("Enter your password.").equals("FirstOfMay"))
{
    OUDialog.alert("Welcome.");
}
else
{
    OUDialog.alert("Access denied.");
}
```

The rest of this section asks you to work on some more examples using `if` statements whose conditions require the use of some different comparison operators.

Exercise 3

Suppose that a new message, called `simplyRed()`, is required in the protocol of the `Frog` class. Here are the initial comment and method heading.

```
/**
 * If the colour of the receiver is red, send the
 * right message twice; if not, send the right message
 * once.
 */
public void simplyRed()
```

Write down (on paper) the code for the method.

Exercise 4

In this exercise you will look in detail at the method `debit()` of the `Account` class. In the code for this method you can see an example of the use of an `if` statement. Examine the code and write down an explanation of the way in which the method achieves the effect desired (imagine that you will post your explanation to a forum in response to another student's query).

```
/**
 * If the balance of the receiver is equal to or
 * greater than the argument anAmount, the
 * balance of the receiver is debited by the
 * argument anAmount and the method returns true.
 *
 * If the balance of the receiver is less than the
 * argument anAmount the method simply returns false.
 */
public boolean debit(double anAmount)
{
    if (this.getBalance() >= anAmount)
    {
        this.setBalance(this.getBalance() - anAmount);
        return true;
    }
    else
    {
        return false;
    }
}
```

Notice in this example how there are two `return` statements used to return a value. There is no need for any further processing as soon as an answer has been determined, so we can 'return' straight away. We said in *Unit 4* that a compilation error results if there is unreachable code after a `return` statement and the code here still obeys the rule, because each `return` statement has no code after it within its branch. It is still the case that when a `return` statement is executed, it is the last statement executed in the method.

Some authors and programmers object to these so-called 'early returns', but you will often see examples of this technique, and you should feel free to use it if it helps to make the logic of your code clear.

In the next activity you will need to test whether an integer is odd or even. You can test whether an integer `x` is odd using an expression such as

`x % 2 != 0,`

where `%` is Java's remainder operator (arithmetic operators were covered in *Unit 3*). This expression evaluates to `true` if `x` is odd and `false` otherwise.

Activity 6

Launch BlueJ and open Unit5_Project_2. Double-click on the `Frog` class to open the BlueJ editor. Write a method `oddRightTwo()` for the `Frog` class that moves a frog right twice if it is currently in an odd-numbered position. If the current position is even, then the frog should not be moved but a suitable message should be displayed in a dialogue box.

When you have written your method, compile the `Frog` class, open the OUWorkspace and from the `Graphical Display` menu select `Open` to make the `Amphibians` window visible.

Then create an instance of `Frog` in the workspace and send it the message `oddRightTwo()`, observing what happens in the **Amphibians** window. Then change the frog's position so that it is at an even-numbered position and re-send the message, checking that the behaviour is as intended.

Discussion

Here is our solution:

```
/**
 * Sends right() twice to the receiver
 * if the position of the receiver is odd;
 * otherwise produces a warning dialogue box.
 */
public void oddRightTwo()
{
   int currentPos;

   currentPos = this.getPosition();
   if (currentPos % 2 != 0)
   {
      this.right();
      this.right();
   }
   else
   {
      OUDialog.alert("Position is not odd.");
   }
}
```

Alternatively you can do without the local variable `currentPos` holding the current position:

```
public void oddRightTwo()
{
   if (this.getPosition() % 2 != 0)
   {
      this.right();
      this.right();
   }
   else
   {
      OUDialog.alert("Position is not odd.");
   }
}
```

To check that the method works as intended the following code could be used in the OUWorkspace.

```
Frog sam = new Frog();
sam.oddRightTwo();
sam.setPosition(2);
sam.oddRightTwo();
```

Activity 7

Open Unit5_Project_2. Double-click on the `Frog` class to open the BlueJ editor.

1   Write a method `rightIfGreen()` in the `Frog` class that works as follows:

   ○   if the receiver frog is green then it should be sent the `right()` message three times;

   ○   if the receiver frog is another colour it should be sent the `left()` message three times.

   When you have written your method compile the `Frog` class.

2   Now open the OUWorkspace. From the **Graphical Display** menu select **Open** to make the **Amphibians** window visible.

   Create an instance of `Frog` in the workspace and send it the message `rightIfGreen()`, observing what happens in the **Amphibians** window. Then change the frog's colour and re-send the message, checking that the behaviour is as intended.

Discussion

1   Here is our solution:

```
/**
 * Sends the right() message three times if the
 * receiver is green, else sends left() three times.
 */
public void rightIfGreen()
{
    if (this.getColour().equals(OUColour.GREEN))
    {
        this.right();
        this.right();
        this.right();
    }
    else
    {
        this.left();
        this.left();
        this.left();
    }
}
```

2   We used the following code in the OUWorkspace to check that `rightIfGreen()` works as intended:

```
Frog sam = new Frog();
sam.rightIfGreen();
sam.brown();
sam.rightIfGreen();
```

Activity 8

Open Unit5_Project_2. Double-click on the Frog class to open the BlueJ editor.

1   Write a method extremeLeft() which returns true if the position of a Frog object is 1 and false otherwise. When you have written your method compile the Frog class.

2   Now open the OUWorkspace, making sure that Show Results is ticked. Create an instance of Frog in the workspace and send it the message extremeLeft(), observing what appears in the Display Pane. Then move the frog one step to the right and re-send the message, checking that the message answer has changed appropriately.

3   So far you have tested your Frog methods on Frog objects, but of course the methods are inherited by HoverFrog and so should work equally well with HoverFrog objects. To check that this is the case, create an instance of HoverFrog and carry out some tests with it as you did with the Frog object.

Discussion

1   Here is our solution:

```
/**
 * Returns true if the position of the receiver is 1;
 * otherwise returns false.
 */
public boolean extremeLeft()
{
    return (this.getPosition() == 1);
}
```

You may have been surprised to see that our solution didn't make use of an if statement, however an if statement is not necessary, all we have to do is return the result of evaluating the Boolean expression (this.getPosition() == 1).

The following also works, but is less elegant:

```
public boolean extremeLeft()
{
    boolean answer = false;

    if (this.getPosition() == 1)
    {
        answer = true;
    }
    return answer;
}
```

You could also have used an *if-then-else* statement here.

It may take you a little while to feel confident that the first version is correct. The longer solution is acceptable, although we would encourage you to move towards the more compact approach.

2   We used the following code, executing it line by line:

```
Frog les = new Frog();
les.extremeLeft(); //Display Pane displays 'true'
les.right();
les.extremeLeft(); //Display Pane displays 'false'
```

3   We used the following, with the same results as in part 2 of the activity.

```
HoverFrog hf = new HoverFrog();
hf.extremeLeft();
hf.right();
hf.extremeLeft();
```

Activity 9

In this activity you are asked to write code using dialogue boxes to allow a user to input a name and then create a version of the name in all upper-case or all lower-case letters, and display the new version. Here is the specification for the code.

- First the user is prompted to input their name. This name is then displayed and the user is asked to confirm that they want the name displayed in all upper-case letters.
- If Yes is clicked, the name is displayed in upper-case letters.
- If No is clicked, the user is next asked to confirm that they want the name displayed in all lower-case letters.
  - If Yes is clicked at this stage, the name is displayed in lower-case letters.
  - If NO is clicked, no further action is taken.

In BlueJ open the OUWorkspace, copy the partial solution below into the **Code Pane** and complete the code where indicated. You will need to use the message toLowerCase(), which can be sent to a String object in order to create a lower-case version of it. (toUpperCase() and toLowerCase() were introduced in Subsection 3.4 of *Unit 3*.)

Execute your code to test that it works correctly.

```
String input;
input = OUDialog.request("Please type in your name.");
if (OUDialog.confirm("Your name is " + input
                        + ". Display it in upper case?"))
{
   OUDialog.alert("Your name in upper case is "
                     + input.toUpperCase());
}
else
{
   //insert code here to handle the case where the
   //user clicks No.
}
```

Discussion

Here is our solution:

```
String input;
input = OUDialog.request("Please type in your name.");
if (OUDialog.confirm("Your name is " + input
                        + ". Display it in upper case?"))
{
   OUDialog.alert("Your name in upper case is "
                    + input.toUpperCase());
}
else
{
   if (OUDialog.confirm("Display it in lower case?"))
   {
      OUDialog.alert("Your name in lower case is "
                       + input.toLowerCase());
   }
}
```

In this example, the `if` statements are said to be *nested*; that is, one `if` statement is written inside another. This is one way of allowing more than one condition to be checked.

if-then-else-if

Strictly speaking there is no Java keyword `else if`. However, an `else` immediately followed by an `if` is often written in that way, because it saves space and tends to be easier to understand.

The solution to Activity 9, written using this alternative style, would be as follows:

```
String input;
input = OUDialog.request("Please type in your name.");
if (OUDialog.confirm("Your name is " + input
                        + ". Display it in upper case?"))
{
   OUDialog.alert("Your name in upper case is "
                    + input.toUpperCase());
}
else if (OUDialog.confirm("Display it in lower case?"))
{
      OUDialog.alert("Your name in lower case is "
                       + input.toLowerCase());
}
```

It is perfectly acceptable to use the *else-if* style if you prefer.

3.4   Handling the output of the Cancel button

The OUDialog class methods with the signatures request(String) and request(String, String) produce dialogue boxes containing two buttons – an OK button and a Cancel button. You may recall that clicking the Cancel button results in null being returned. The dialogue also returns null if the user closes the window without pressing a button. Before going on we will look briefly at how to handle the null value.

Consider the following scenario: a user of a word-processing program has requested a file save, and request(String, String) is used to prompt for the file name. The existing file name is given as the initial answer (the second argument). The user has various courses of action to choose from. They can click OK and save the file under its existing name or they can replace the default name by a new one and click OK.

On the other hand, they may decide not to save the file after all, and click Cancel. This will return null, as you have seen.

What ought to happen if Cancel is clicked? There are various possibilities, but one is to not save the file and to notify the user that the file was not saved. To do this you need some code that will detect if a user pressed Cancel (or closed the window) and that will take the appropriate action in that case.

Here is some Java code that achieves this.

```
String filename;
filename = OUDialog.request("Please specify file name",
                             "currentName");
if (filename == null)
{
   OUDialog.alert("File not saved.");
}
else
{
   //code to save the file would go here
}
```

You are not in a position to write the last part of the code yet, since you have not learnt about files, so for now we have just written a comment showing that something still needs to be done.

The important thing to note here is that you can compare any reference to the value null using the == operator and so provide a branch in your program code to handle a null value. A null value often indicates an exceptional condition that requires some separate code to handle it and so this is quite a common thing to see.

A review of Boolean operators

So far all our conditions have either taken a Boolean value returned by a dialogue box and used it directly, or involved a limited range of comparisons, such as whether two things were equal, or whether one number was greater than another.

To write more complex conditions you also need to be able to combine two or more Boolean expressions into a single condition that can be evaluated to `true` or `false`. For example, you might want to provide a user with a login and password on a website only if they have provided all the required personal data *and* ticked a box that says they agree to some terms and conditions.

In this section we will be reviewing the equality, relational and logical operators you met in *Unit 3* and will also explain a bit more about how logical operators work.

You will recall that Java has a number of comparison operators that can be applied to primitive data types (see Table 2).

Table 2   Comparison operators

Equality operators	`==`	equal to
	`!=`	not equal to
Relational operators	`<`	less than
	`<=`	less than or equal to
	`>`	greater than
	`>=`	greater than or equal to

Remember that the operators `==` and `!=` can also be applied to reference variables, in which case they test whether the two variables reference the same object or not. We have seen that you can also use the literal `null` with these operators to see whether a reference variable is actually referencing an object.

We have also mentioned the use of `equals()` messages with `String` objects. This gives a way of testing if two strings are 'the same' in the sense of representing an identical sequence of characters in the same order, even though the `String` objects concerned may be stored in different locations in memory and so be different objects.

SAQ 11

If `count` and `total` have the values `12` and `14` respectively and `item` has the value `"xyz"`, what are the results of evaluating the following expressions? That is, what do they evaluate to, `true` or `false`?

(a) `count > 12`
(b) `count + 2 != total`
(c) `item.equals("xyz")`
(d) `count + 2 <= 14`

Answer

(a) Evaluates to `false`.
(b) Evaluates to `false`; `count + 2` has the value `14`, and it is false that this *does not* equal the value of `total`.
(c) Evaluates to `true`; the two strings have the same characters in the same order.
(d) Evaluates to `true`; `count + 2` has the value `14`, which is less than *or equal to* `14`.

Recall from *Unit 3* that Java also has logical operators (sometimes termed **Boolean operators**). The operands must be Boolean expressions (see Table 3, in which `a` and `b` are assumed to be `boolean` valued expressions). By using the logical operators you can build up compound expressions that test if some combination of conditions is satisfied. Compound expressions are simply ones that involve more than one Boolean condition.

Table 3   Some logical operators

Kind	Java symbol	Operation	Effect
Unary	`!`	not	`!a` evaluates to `true` if `a` is `false`, and `false` if `a` is `true`.
Binary	`&&`	and	`a && b` evaluates to `true` if `a` is `true` *and* `b` is `true`. Otherwise it is `false`.
	`||`	or	`a || b` evaluates to `true` if either `a` or `b`, or both of them, are `true`. Otherwise it is `false`.

Short-circuit evaluation

We know that `a && b` is `true` only if *both* `a` and `b` are `true`. The way this works in practice is that when `a && b` is evaluated, the value of `a` is determined first. If `a` evaluates to `false`, the JVM deduces immediately that `a && b` is `false` and skips the evaluation of `b`. This is efficient in the sense that no more work is done by this operator than is necessary. Only when `a` is `true` will `b` also be evaluated.

Similarly, `a || b` is `true` if *either* or both of `a` and `b` are `true`. When `a || b` is evaluated, the value of `a` is determined first. If `a` evaluates to `true`, the

JVM deduces immediately that a || b is `true` and skips the evaluation of b. Only when a is `false` will b also be evaluated.

This economical scheme – evaluating only as much as necessary – is called **lazy evaluation** or **short-circuit evaluation**.

It is possible to use short-circuit evaluation to your advantage; however, we would advise against reliance on this behaviour because whilst the logical 'and' and 'or' operators exist in most languages whether or not they use short-circuit evaluation varies from one language to another. Nevertheless, you should know that Java uses short-circuit evaluation so that you can understand code like the following:

```
if (x != null && x.equals("hello"))
{
   //do something
}
```

If x were to be `null`, evaluating the expression x.equals("hello") would cause an exception. However, the programmer knows that the `equals` message will be sent to x only if x is not `null`, thanks to the short-circuit behaviour of `&&`, so there is no danger of this code failing due to x storing a `null` value.

An alternative structure that achieves the same effect and is safe from one language to another is shown next:

```
if (x != null)
{
   if (x.equals("hello"))
   {
      //do something
   }
}
```

Similarly in the following code

```
if (x == null || x.equals(""))
{
   //do something
}
```

there will be no attempt to send the `equals()` message if x evaluates to `null` and the same effect could be achieved using a nested `if` or or an *else-if* structure.

The & and | operators

There are two other operators you may encounter written & and |. When these operators are used with Boolean operands they evaluate to the same results as would be achieved using && and ||. The difference is that these operators always evaluate *both* of their operands, whereas the && and || operators may not. Technically, && and || are called *conditional* operators because they do not always evaluate both of their operands.

The & and | operators have a further use to perform bitwise Boolean operations when their operands are of types that can be converted to integers. This usage is beyond the scope of this module. In this module we use the conditional operators.

4.1   More practice with Boolean operators

When you are writing complex compound expressions it can be useful to use a table to write down a value for each part of an expression. The following exercise asks you to do this.

Exercise 5

Complete the following table with appropriate values in each column to work out the value of the compound expressions in the last two columns. We have done the first row for you.

count	sum	count < 10	sum <= 100	count < 10 && sum <= 100	count < 10 || sum <= 100
10	50	false	true	false	true
20	200				
4	40				
9	110				

Exercise 6

(a) Suppose a variable called `number` of type `int` already exists and has been given some value. Write code to do the following:

- declare three `boolean` variables, called `positive`, `zero` and `negative`

- set `positive` to `true` if `number` is greater than `0` (otherwise set `positive` to `false`)

- set `zero` to `true` if `number` is equal to `0` (otherwise set `zero` to `false`)

- set `negative` to `true` if `number` is less than `0` (otherwise set `negative` to `false`).

(b) Suppose `day` and `month` are variables of type `int` that already exist and have been given values. Write down a single statement that will declare a `boolean` variable `dateValid` and set it to `true` if `month` is equal to `1` and `day` is in the range `1` to `31` inclusive, and set it to `false` otherwise.

Exercise 7

(a) Suppose the date of my birthday is the 16 November and the `int` variables `day` and `month` hold values that specify the current day of the month and the current month respectively. (For example, for 12 May, `day` would have the value `12` and `month` the value `5`.)

Write a single statement that will cause the appropriate value to be assigned to the `boolean` variable `isMyBirthday` according to the values of `day` and `month`. (Assume `isMyBirthday` has been declared already.)

(b) A pharmaceutical research organisation is seeking volunteers to take part in a new drug study. Eligible volunteers must be aged between 25 and 35 inclusive and be non-smokers.

Suppose that the variables `age` of type `int` and `isSmoker` of type `boolean` already exist and have been assigned values that specify a particular volunteer's age and whether or not the volunteer is a smoker. Write down a single statement that will result in the `boolean` variable `isEligible` being assigned a value that reflects whether or not the volunteer is eligible to take part in the study. (Assume `isEligible` has already been declared.)

Activity 10

Open Unit5_Project_2 and the OUWorkspace. From the `Graphical Display` menu select `Open` to make the `Amphibians` window visible.

1   In the workspace create an instance of the `HoverFrog` class and send it some `setHeight()` messages with different arguments, including negative numbers and numbers greater than 6. Observe the effect of each message on the graphical representation of the hoverfrog in the `Amphibians` window. Inspect the hoverfrog to check that the value of the instance variable `height` is consistent with the height of the hoverfrog icon in the window in each case.

2   The following code (which is incomplete) should read in a number from a user, test whether it is in the range 0 to 6 inclusive, and inform the user whether or not it is in range. Without looking at the code for the method `setHeight()`, complete the code by writing the condition we have described in the comment.

```
String inputString;
int number;

inputString = OUDialog.request("Input a number");
number = Integer.parseInt(inputString);
//write a condition to test if number is in the
//range 0-6 inclusive.
if
{
    OUDialog.alert("Number is in range.");
}
else
{
    OUDialog.alert("Number is out of range.");
}
```

Test your code in the workspace with a variety of numbers, both within and outside the range. Test at the boundaries; that is, make sure it works correctly when the user inputs 0 or 6.

Discussion

1   The code for the method `setHeight()` is written so that it sets the `height` to values only in the range 0 to 6 inclusive. If the method argument is outside this range, no action is taken.

2   Our solution was this:

```
String inputString;
int number;

inputString = OUDialog.request("Input a number");
number = Integer.parseInt(inputString);
if ((number >= 0) && (number <= 6))
{
   OUDialog.alert("Number is in range.");
}
else
{
   OUDialog.alert("Number is out of range.");
}
```

Activity 11

Open Unit5_Project_2. Double-click on the HoverFrog class to open it in the BlueJ editor.

Write a method called inTheCorner() for the HoverFrog class that returns true if the receiver has any of the following combinations of values for its instance variables height and position:

   height is 0 and position is 1

   height is 0 and position is 11

   height is 6 and position is 1

   height is 6 and position is 11

For any other combinations, the method returns false.

Compile HoverFrog and close the editor window.

Now open the OUWorkspace. From the Graphical Display menu select Open to make the Amphibians window visible.

Create an instance of HoverFrog. Send it the message inTheCorner() and verify that the result shown in the Display Pane is true.

Now use the messages setPosition() and setHeight() to move the hoverfrog to a range of different locations, and send it the message inTheCorner() at each one, checking that the results are as expected.

Discussion

There are many possible solutions. Here are a few variations:

```
/**
 * Returns true if the receiver is 'in the corner'
 * otherwise returns false.
 * The corners are the following locations:
 * height 0 and position 1;
 * height 0 and position 11;
 * height 6 and position 1;
 * height 6 and position 11.
 */
public boolean inTheCorner()
{
    return
    ((this.getHeight() == 0) && (this.getPosition() == 1))
     || ((this.getHeight() == 0) && (this.getPosition() == 11))
     || ((this.getHeight() == 6) && (this.getPosition() == 1))
     || ((this.getHeight() == 6) && (this.getPosition() == 11));
}
```

A much neater solution would be:

```
public boolean inTheCorner()
{
    return
        ((this.getHeight() == 0)
        || (this.getHeight() == 6))
        && ((this.getPosition() == 1)
        || (this.getPosition()== 11));
}
```

The next possible solution uses nested combinations of if statements instead of using the && operator.

```
public boolean inTheCorner()
{
    if (this.getHeight() == 0)
    {
        if ((this.getPosition() == 1) || (this.getPosition() == 11))
        {
            return true;
        }
    }
    if (this.getHeight() == 6)
    {
        if ((this.getPosition() == 1) || (this.getPosition() == 11))
        {
            return true;
        }
    }
    return false;
}
```

Note that, very occasionally, we will deliberately position code samples to start within the left-hand margin to avoid the introduction of unnecessary line breaks.

It is always possible to use nested combinations of `if` statements to replace an `&&` operator. The solution you choose will depend on factors such as the clarity and efficiency of your code.

Finally, here is a solution that uses a 'helper' method:

```
public boolean inTheCorner()
{
    return this.isAt(0,1) || this.isAt(0,11) || this.isAt(6,1) || this.isAt(6,11);
}


/**
 * Helper method for inTheCorner().
 */
private boolean isAt(int height, int position)
{
    return (this.getHeight() == height) && (this.getPosition() == position);
}
```

We tested our code by creating a hoverfrog and 'walking it round the box' with the sequence of statements given below.

```
HoverFrog hf = new HoverFrog();
hf.right();
hf.setPosition(11);
hf.up();
hf.setHeight(6);
hf.left();
hf.setPosition(1);
hf.down();
hf.setHeight(0);
```

After each statement we executed `hf.inTheCorner();` to check the result. These tests should give alternately `true` and `false` answers!

Finally, we tested in the middle position with:

```
hf.setPosition(6);
hf.setHeight(3);
```

5 Iteration

A very common requirement when you are solving a programming problem is a way of causing an action, or group of actions, to be executed repeatedly. The term for this is *iteration*. For example, you may want to:

- query a user for a filename repeatedly until a valid name has been supplied
- print out each item on some kind of list
- repeatedly add costs of individual purchases to find a total bill.

Most programming languages include mechanisms to repeat actions in this way, and in this section we will be discussing the two main approaches in Java, *for loops* and *while loops*, which use the keywords `for` and `while`.

5.1   Increment and decrement operators

A common requirement in situations where loops are used is to increment or decrement a variable. For example, you might want to write (assuming an `int` variable `x`).

```
x = x + 1;
```

However, because this is such a common requirement, Java provides a special operator to write this in a shorthand way:

```
x++;
```

Similarly, the statement `x = x - 1;` can be written as:

```
x--;
```

Notice that `++` and `--` are being used as **postfix operators**, as in each case the operator appears after the operand `x`.

SAQ 12

What is the value of `myNumber` after the following statements have been executed?

```
int myNumber = 17;
myNumber = myNumber - 11;
myNumber++;
```

Answer

`myNumber` holds the value `7`.

The expression `myNumber++` is not the same as the expression `(myNumber + 1)` because `myNumber++` evaluates to the value `myNumber` has *before* it has the `1` added to it; whereas the expression `(myNumber + 1)` evaluates to the addition of `myNumber` and `1`, leaving `myNumber` unchanged. For example, if we execute the following code:

```
int myNumber, result;
myNumber = 17;
result = myNumber++;
```

`result` is assigned the value 17 *and* `myNumber` is incremented to `18`.

We used a shortcut here in declaring `myNumber` *and* `result` *on one line, separated by a comma. They both will have the type* `int`. *Usually you should declare one variable at a time.*

Compare that with this code:

```
int myNumber, result;
myNumber = 17;
result = myNumber + 1;
```

`result` is assigned the value `18` and `myNumber` still holds the value `17`.

You may like to try executing the code in SAQ 12 in the OUWorkspace to observe the results displayed and confirm the discussion above.

5.2   Examples of loops

Before we describe the syntax of the loop structures, here are some short example snippets of code. These examples are simply meant to give a flavour of how `for` and `while` loops can be used: we will explain more in Subsections 5.2 and 5.3 below. While you are looking at these you will notice that both `for` and `while` loops are examples of statements that include a statement block and they don't end in semicolons. The statement is the whole of the structure from the word `for` or `while` up to the end of the closing brace.

Example `for` loop

The following loop displays the integers 0 to 10 inclusive on the same line, separated by spaces:

```
for (int value = 0; value < 11; value++)
{
    System.out.print(value + " ");
}
```

The output looks like this:

```
0 1 2 3 4 5 6 7 8 9 10
```

Example `while` loop

Next we show an example `while` loop in which a user is repeatedly invited to enter a number. While the number they enter is less than 100, an alert dialogue box is displayed informing them of the fact. As soon as the number entered is 100 or more, the condition becomes `false` and the loop terminates.

```
while (Integer.parseInt(OUDialog.request("Number?")) < 100)
{
    OUDialog.alert("Your number was less than 100.");
}
```

Notice that there is no way of predicting in advance what numbers the user will actually enter. You cannot know how many numbers there will be, nor can these numbers be expected to run neatly in some particular sequence. The execution just has to keep looping round as long as the number the user inputs is less than 100 and will not stop looping until the first value of 100 or more actually materialises.

A `for` loop is suitable when you want to repeat an action a known number of times or when you want to run through a known range of values performing some action for each value in the range. After the specified number of iterations has been completed, the iteration stops.

A `while` loop is suitable when you cannot tell in advance when the iteration should end. The iteration will continue while some particular condition is `true`. As soon as the condition becomes `false` the iteration stops.

In fact it turns out that anything that can be done with a `while` loop can also be achieved with a `for` loop and vice versa. However, in most applications you are likely to find one form of loop is better than the other, in that it is more convenient and natural. In the following subsections we look in detail at the structure of `for` and `while` loops, and put them to use.

SAQ 13

For each of the following scenarios, would you be likely to use a `for` loop or a `while` loop?
(a) Querying a user for a filename repeatedly until a valid name has been supplied.
(b) Printing out each item on some kind of list.
(c) Repeatedly adding costs of individual purchases to find a total bill.

Answer

(a) You will not know how many times you need to ask the user for a filename before a valid filename is provided, so you will need a `while` loop.
(b) In this case since a list of items already exists, and the number of items in the list can probably be easily determined, a `for` loop is the most likely solution.
(c) This could be done using either a `for` or a `while` loop, depending on whether the list of purchases is already available or is being

entered one at a time. For example, at a supermarket till the number of purchases is not known in advance and so a `while` loop is more appropriate. On the other hand, at a restaurant, when the final bill is added up, the number of purchases will already be known and a `for` loop is most suitable.

5.3 `for` loops

First consider the following diagram, which illustrates the operation of a `for` loop.

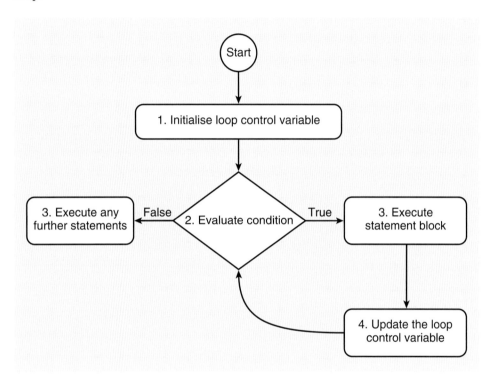

Figure 14 The typical operation of a `for` loop.

The flow of execution depicted in Figure 14 is written in Java using a `for` loop with the following structure:

```
for  (initialise; condition; update)
{
    //statements
}
//any further statements
```

The statement begins with the keyword `for`. This is followed by a structure within parentheses that controls the operation of the loop, and then a statement block that is potentially executed repeatedly.

We have represented the three parts of the code that control the operation of the loop using the words *initialise*, *condition* and *update*, which are not keywords, but rather sections of code that have specific purposes.

- The *initialise* section typically declares and initialises a variable, which we will call the **loop control variable**.
- The *condition* section contains a Boolean expression; that is, something that can be evaluated to `true` or `false`. It is also called the *termination condition*, since when it evaluates to `false`, the loop terminates.
- The *update* section normally updates the variable declared in the initialisation section; typically it increments or decrements the loop control variable.

The sequence *initialise; condition; update* must be enclosed between parentheses, otherwise the compiler will report an error. Notice also that there must be semicolons separating the three parts of the loop control section. The `for` statement block – often called the *body* of the loop – contains any statements that may be executed by the loop.

When the loop is executed the following steps occur, in the following order.

Step 1   The *initialise* section is executed.

Step 2   The expression in the *condition* section is evaluated.

Step 3

- If the *condition* evaluates to `false`, the program flow moves on to the code after the loop body (any further statements)
- If the *condition* evaluates to `true`, the *statement block* is executed, and then

Step 4   The *update* section is executed, and the flow returns to step 2.

The statement block will be executed as many times as the *condition* evaluates to `true`. Of course, it is possible that in some cases the *condition* will be `false` when step 2 is reached for the first time; if so, the loop will stop immediately and the statement block will never be executed. When the iteration terminates, the flow of program execution will pass on to whatever code follows the statement block.

Tracing a `for` loop

Let us see how the steps above work out for the following example, in which we want to send the messages `right()` and `croak()` to the `Frog` object referenced by `bart` three times.

```
for (int move = 0; move < 3; move++)
{
    bart.right();
    bart.croak();
}
```

- The *initialise* section is `int move = 0`.
- The *condition* section is `move < 3`.
- The *update* section is `move++`.

Table 4 is a trace showing the order of statements executed when this loop is run.

Table 4   A trace of the `for` loop's execution

Code executed	Value of `move`	Value of `move < 3`	Comments
`int move = 0;`	0		The *initialise* section is always executed first.
`move < 3`	0	true	Next the *condition* is tested and in this case is found to be `true` …
`bart.right();` `bart.croak();`	0		so the statement block is executed.
`move++`	1		The *update* section is executed after the loop body.
`move < 3`	1	true	The *condition* evaluates to `true` …
`bart.right();` `bart.croak();`	1		so the statement block is executed a second time.
`move++`	2		The *update* section is executed again.
`move < 3`	2	true	The *condition* is tested again.
`bart.right();` `bart.croak();`	2		The statement block is executed a third time.
`move++`	3		The *update* section is executed again.
`move < 3`	3	false	The *condition* is evaluated again and found to be `false`, so the loop ends.

Some notes on the loop

In the example above the variable `move` acts as the loop control variable. Notice that the variable `move` was actually declared *and* initialised as part of the loop structure itself:

```
for (int move = 0;  ...
```

This has the effect of making the variable `move` local to the loop: its scope is the loop header and body, and, once the loop terminates, `move` will be undefined. (The OUWorkspace's `Variables` pane does not display loop control variables, as they are not in the workspace's scope, so `move` will not be shown there.)

We used the name `move` for our loop control variable because it helped to describe the purpose we had in mind. However, it is very common to have loop control variables with short names, sometimes just one letter, because they are only valid from the start of a loop until its end and there is little danger of misunderstanding how they are being used.

You may have wondered why we initialised `move` to 0 and used the condition `move < 3`. Why not initialise the counter to 1 and test `move <= 3`, which would produce the same number of iterations? The reason is that it is a common convention (although not essential) in Java to start loop counters from 0 rather than 1.

Note too the use of the postfix operator ++ to increment move by 1 in the *update* section. An alternative would be move = move + 1. Similarly, if you wanted to decrement by 1, you could use move-- or move = move - 1. The form you use is up to you; we suggest you adopt whichever you feel most comfortable with, and you will see both styles in the rest of the module.

Using a variable in the loop condition

The next code fragment accepts a number from the user and produces a string consisting of that number of 'x's. This demonstrates that the number of iterations can be determined by the value of a variable.

```
int numberOfX;
String result;
result = ""; //empty string to start with
numberOfX = Integer.parseInt
            (OUDialog.request("Please enter a number"));
for (int num = 0; num < numberOfX; num++)
{
    result = result + "x";
}
System.out.println(result);
```

Exercise 8

In this pen-and-paper exercise you should assume that lulu references a Frog object and aNumber has been declared as an int and assigned some value.

(a) Using the example above as a guide, write a for loop that will send lulu the left() message aNumber times. (You will need to use aNumber in the *condition* part of the loop.)

(b) Write a new method for the Frog class, with the method header public void leftBy(int aNumber), which uses a for loop to send the receiver the left() message the number of times specified by the actual argument's value.

Dances with frogs

In the next activity you will use for loops to organise some frogs in the Amphibians window to perform a set of simple 'dances', called the 'frogulika', which mainly consist of two dance sequences: the right-frogulika and the left-frogulika, both of which are repeated some number of times to complete the dance.

Let us suppose that the sequence of moves called the 'right-frogulika' is *right, right, jump, left*, and that we want to repeat this four times. We will need to send the messages required for the 'right-frogulika' repeatedly to the same Frog object. One way to do this is write the sequence out as many times as we require. If, for example, four repetitions were required for the dance, then we could make the `Frog` object referenced by `sam` do the dance using the following set of statements:

```
//right-frogulika
sam.right(); sam.right(); sam.jump(); sam.left();
sam.right(); sam.right(); sam.jump(); sam.left();
sam.right(); sam.right(); sam.jump(); sam.left();
//fourth time!
sam.right(); sam.right(); sam.jump(); sam.left();
```

Clearly, writing out code like this is mightily inconvenient! And what if we wanted the number of repetitions to be large, or to depend on the value of a variable?

Activity 12

From BlueJ, open Unit5_Project_2 and the OUWorkspace, then make the `Amphibians` window visible by selecting `Open` from the `Graphical Display` menu.

To start, create an instance of the `Frog` class in the OUWorkspace by executing:

```
Frog sam = new Frog();
```

Now execute the following group of statements in the OUWorkspace and observe the effect in the `Amphibians` window:

```
sam.right(); sam.right(); sam.jump(); sam.left();
```

Now try the following code, which moves `sam` to his home position before using a `for` loop to execute the right-frogulika four times:

```
sam.home();
for (int count = 0; count < 4; count++)
{
    sam.right(); sam.right(); sam.jump(); sam.left();
}
```

Execute this code and observe that `sam` performs a dance!

Activity 13

Again using Unit5_Project_2, and using the previous examples to guide you, write code in the OUWorkspace that will complete the following objectives using two frogs referenced by `sam` and `lew`.

1   Make the frog `sam` jump five times.

2   Make `sam` jump five times, using the value 5 stored in a variable `numberOfJumps`.

3   Move `sam` directly to the central stone (stone 6). Make `sam` perform the 'right-frogulika' dance (*right, right, jump, left*) three times, followed by a 'left-frogulika' (*left, left, jump, right*) three times.

4   Move the two frogs directly to their central stones (stone 6).

The frogs should then each perform the right-frogulika sequence (*right, right, jump, left*) alternately, three times. Sam gets to go first.

Sam and Lew should then alternately (Sam goes first again), perform the left-frogulika dance (*left, left, jump, right*) again repeating this three times in all.

Observe the `Amphibians` window to test that the frogs move as expected.

Discussion

1   The following loop will make `sam` jump five times:

```
for (int count = 0; count < 5; count++)
{
    sam.jump();
}
```

2   The following loop will make `sam` jump `numberOfJumps` times (which evaluates to 5):

```
int numberOfJumps = 5;
for (int count = 0; count < numberOfJumps; count++)
{
    sam.jump();
}
```

Of course, if the value held in `numberOfJumps` were changed from 5, the number of iterations would be different.

3   The following code will make `sam` move to the centre stone, then do three right-frogulikas followed by three left-frogulikas.

```
sam.setPosition(6);

//right-frogulika three times
for (int count = 0; count < 3 ; count++)
{
    sam.right(); sam.right(); sam.jump(); sam.left();
}

//left-frogulika three times
for (int count = 0; count < 3 ; count++)
{
    sam.left(); sam.left(); sam.jump(); sam.right();
}
```

4   The following code will make `sam` and `lew` alternately do three right-frogulikas followed by three left-frogulikas.

```
sam.setPosition(6);
lew.setPosition(6);
for (int count = 0; count < 3; count++)
{
    sam.right(); sam.right(); sam.jump(); sam.left();
    lew.right(); lew.right(); lew.jump(); lew.left();
}
for (int count = 0; count < 3; count++)
{
    sam.left(); sam.left(); sam.jump(); sam.right();
    lew.left(); lew.left(); lew.jump(); lew.right();
}
```

Java programming style

Good Java style normally dictates that we keep to one statement per line. However, the dance examples contain large numbers of short statements and in many cases we have felt it preferable to put several of these on one line. Our reasoning is that

```
sam.right(); sam.right(); sam.jump(); sam.left();
```

is much more compact than

```
sam.right();
sam.right();
sam.jump();
sam.left();
```

Putting the movements that form a 'frogulika' on the same line may also make it easier to understand the steps.

If you thought that we should really have introduced methods such as `rightFrogulika()` and `leftFrogulika()`, you are thinking like a programmer! We would need to do that in the `Frog` class itself.

Activity 14

1   In the OUWorkspace write a `for` loop that will output the 9 times table, using `System.out.println()`. The output should appear like this:

```
1 times 9 is 9
2 times 9 is 18
```

and so on, until

```
12 times 9 is 108
```

2   Write code that will prompt the user for a number using a request dialogue box, then output, to the `Display Pane`, the chosen number's times table for all multiples from 1 to 12.

Discussion

1   Here is our solution:

```
for (int num = 1; num <= 12; num++)
{
    System.out.println(num + " times 9 is " + num * 9);
}
```

2   Here is our solution:

```
int tableNum;
tableNum =
    Integer.parseInt(OUDialog.request("Which table?"));
for (int num = 1; num <= 12; num++)
{
    System.out.println(num + " times " + tableNum
                        + " is " + num * tableNum);
}
```

In the next activity you will consolidate your knowledge of `for` loops by writing code that requires two `for` loops, one nested inside the other.

Activity 15

In this activity using the OUWorkspace you will write code that will print to the `Display Pane` the well-known song '10 men went to mow', missing out the first verse (which starts 'One man went to mow' because it's different from the others and we want to keep things simple).

In *our version*, the first verse is:

> 2 men went to mow, went to mow a meadow,
> 2 men, one man and his dog,
> Went to mow a meadow.

The second verse is:

> 3 men went to mow, went to mow a meadow,
> 3 men, 2 men, one man and his dog,
> Went to mow a meadow.

Then we have 4 men and so on. This goes on until the last verse:

> 10 men went to mow, went to mow a meadow,
> 10 men, 9 men, 8 men, …, 2 men, one man and his dog,
> Went to mow a meadow.

To display the whole song you will need two `for` loops, one inside the other. The outer loop will control the verse number and the inner loop will help to display the current verse.

The outer loop should declare a variable `verseNumber` that is incremented from 2 to 10. In this outer `for` loop you should first print the first line of the current verse:

> *x* men went to mow, went to mow a meadow,

where *x* is the current value of `verseNumber`.

Then the inner loop should display the second line of the current verse. The inner loop will need to declare a variable `numberOfMen` that will be intialised to the current value of `verseNumber` and decremented down to 2. (The text after each comma requires a change to the value of *x* and the last value of *x* should be 2):

> *x* men, *x – 1* men, *x – 2* men, ..., 2 men,

Next you will need to end the inner `for` loop and print the last part of the current verse, which is always the same:

> ... one man and his dog,
> Went to mow a meadow.

Then finally end the outer loop.

We will use *pseudocode* to draft our solution. Think of pseudocode as something halfway between English and Java. There are no strict rules about how you write it: it's just a way of helping you to get closer to a solution – you can develop your own intermediate language that helps you to visualise the final solution in Java:

```
for verseNumber from 2 up to 10
{
    print first line of verse
    for the numberOfMen from verseNumber down to 2
    {
        print the parts of the second line of the verse
    }
    print "one man and his dog,"
    print "Went to mow a meadow."
}
```

Write a solution using Java and `for` loops. You will need to use both `System.out.println()` and `System.out.print()` to create the appropriate output.

Discussion

Here is our version of the code:

```
for (int verseNumber = 2; verseNumber <= 10; verseNumber++)
{
    System.out.println(verseNumber + " men went to mow, went to mow a meadow,");
    for (int numberOfMen = verseNumber; numberOfMen > 1; numberOfMen--)
    {
        System.out.print(numberOfMen + " men, ");
    }
    System.out.println("one man and his dog,");
    System.out.println("Went to mow a meadow.");
}
```

5.4 while loops

A second form of loop provided in Java and many other languages is called the while loop.

As we saw at the start of Section 5, when the number of iterations required for a loop body is not known in advance, but depends on achieving some condition, a while loop is the appropriate structure.

A while loop is actually simpler than a for loop, as Figure 15 illustrates.

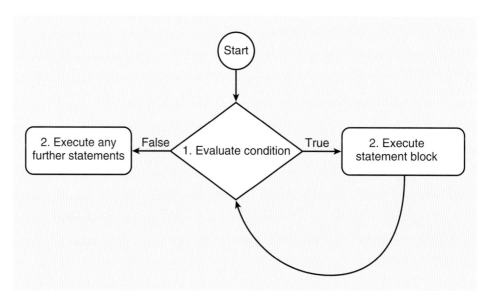

Figure 15 A diagram of a while loop

A Java `while` loop has the following structure:

```
while (condition)
{
    //statements
}
//any further statements
```

A `while` loop begins with the keyword `while` which is followed by a *condition* in parentheses. As usual, the *condition* is some Boolean expression; something that can be evaluated to `true` or `false`.

Like a `for` loop, a `while` loop has a statement block enclosing any statements that might be repeated a number of times. If the *condition* is `false` the first time it is tested then the statement block is never executed and program flow goes on to any code that follows the loop.

When the loop is executed the following steps take place.

Step 1 The *condition* is evaluated;

Step 2

- If the *condition* evaluates to `false`, the program flow moves on to the code after the loop body.
- If the *condition* evaluates to `true`, the *statement block* is executed and the flow returns to step 1.

So the statement block is executed as many times as the condition evaluates to `true`. As it stands, this does not explain how the loop can ever terminate. Something has to happen to make *condition* go from `true` to `false`. Very commonly the value of the *condition* will depend on something declared and initialised prior to the loop, which gets changed each time the body of the loop is executed, so that eventually the *condition* becomes `false`. Another possibility is that the value of the *condition* may depend on input from a user, or from some other source such as a file. You saw an example of this in Subsection 5.1, where a loop was terminated as soon as the user entered a number that was `100` or more.

Here is another example of a `while` loop: it displays odd numbers in the sequence 1, 3, 5, ... while the current odd number is less than 30:

```
int number = 1; //a starting odd number
while (number < 30)
{
    System.out.println(number);
    number = number + 2; //next odd number
}
```

Once each number has been displayed the code adds `2` to it to generate the number that will be used next time round the loop.

In this example we did not have to use a `while` loop, because the range of values we wanted to iterate through was known. We could have used a `for` loop:

```
for (int number = 1; number < 30; number = number + 2)
{
    System.out.println(number);
}
```

Tracing a `while` loop

Our next example shows how to move a frog – whose position is assumed to be somewhere to the left of the central stone – to the central position in the `Amphibians` window (stone 6) by repeatedly executing the statement `fifi.right();` while the frog's position is less than 6.

```
while (fifi.getPosition() < 6)
{
    fifi.right();
}
```

Table 5 shows a trace of what happens if the frog is initially at position 2.

Table 5 A trace of the `while` loop's execution

Code executed	Value of `fifi.getPosition()`	Condition value	Comments
`fifi.getPosition() < 6`	2	true	When the `while` loop starts, the condition is always tested first. 2 < 6 is true.
`fifi.right();`	3		The statement block is executed, making the frog's position increase by 1.
`fifi.getPosition() < 6`	3	true	Test the condition: 3 < 6.
`fifi.right();`	4		The statement block is executed.
`fifi.getPosition() < 6`	4	true	Test the condition: 4 < 6.
`fifi.right();`	5		The statement block is executed.
`fifi.getPosition() < 6`	5	true	Test the condition: 5 < 6.
`fifi.right();`	6		The statement block is executed.
`fifi.getPosition() < 6`	6	false	Test the condition: as 6 < 6 is false; the loop terminates immediately.

Exercise 9

By long tradition, a dance in the Amphibian Worlds begins with all the participants in the central position (position 6) dressed in a red costume. Before the dance can commence, the frogs participating must move to the central stones and put on their red clothing in readiness.

Rather than moving directly to their stone 6, however, they hop towards the centre stone by stone. That is, they jump then move one step left or right, as appropriate, repeating this sequence until they reach the central stone. How many hops a given frog takes to reach the centre will, of course, depend on its starting position.

First consider the situation where a frog is to the *left* of the centre position when it starts. The following `while` statement when executed will cause the frog referenced by `sam` to hop right until it reaches the central stone.

```
while (sam.getPosition() < 6)
{
    sam.jump(); sam.right();
}
```

When the loop is executed, first the Boolean expression `sam.getPosition() < 6` is evaluated to see if the frog is at a position to the left of (less than) stone `6`. If the condition evaluates to `true`, the body of the loop is executed to make the frog jump and move one stone to the right. This is carried out as often as the condition evaluates to `true`.

When `sam` has made the required number of hops and reached the centre stone, the condition `(sam.getPosition() < 6)` will become `false` and the loop will terminate.

(a) The code above assumes that at the start the frog is positioned to the left of the centre. Suppose that on the contrary the frog is initially positioned to the *right* of the central stone. Write the code that is now needed to make the frog hop to the centre.

(b) How can the code that you have just written be combined with the code we gave earlier so that the frog will hop to the central stone from any starting position? (Hint: do not think too hard. The answer is quite straightforward.)

(c) Write (on paper) a method `takeUpYourPosition()` for the `Frog` class. When `takeUpYourPosition()` is sent to a `Frog` object it will make the frog hop to the centre and put on its red costume (remember the red costume?).

Activity 16

Instead of using a `while` loop as in Exercise 9, you could move the frog to the central stone by working out how far to move and in what direction, and then use a `for` loop. On paper, rewrite the solution given above in part (b) of Exercise 9 using this different approach. There is no need to write an actual method; assume the code will be executed in the workspace, so that instead of `this` you should use a specific instance of `Frog` such as `sam`.

Then open Unit5_Project_2 and the OUWorkspace. From the **Graphical Display** menu select **Open** to make the **Amphibians** window visible. Enter your code into the workspace. Create an instance of `Frog` referenced by `sam` and test your code on it.

Discussion

We first set an initial position with:

```
Frog sam = new Frog();
sam.setPosition(4);
```

You can then move `sam` to the central stone as follows:

```
if (sam.getPosition() < 6)
{
    int jumps = 6 - sam.getPosition();
    for (int count = 0; count < jumps; count++)
    {
        sam.jump(); sam.right();
    }
}
```

Similar code can be written to cope with the case that `sam`'s starting position is to the right of the centre stone.

```
if (sam.getPosition() > 6)
{
    int jumps = sam.getPosition() - 6;
    for (int count = 0; count < jumps; count++)
    {
        sam.jump(); sam.left();
    }
}
```

Repeat the test with different values for the variable `initial`.

Exercise 10

A frog is taking part in a sponsored hop with the following rules. Beginning from whatever position the frog happens to be at when the sponsored hopping starts, it repeatedly hops one stone to the right. For each hop it makes, 10 pounds is credited to a bank account, which starts with a balance of 0. The frog continues hopping until either (a) it reaches stone 11, or (b) 80 pounds has accumulated in the account. (Of course, if the frog is already at stone 11 or beyond no money will be earned.)

Assume that the frog and the bank account have already been created, using the following statements:

```
Frog tanya = new Frog();
Account acc = new Account();
```

You need not worry about the attributes `holder` and `number` of the account; in this exercise you are concerned only with the `balance`.

Write down the code that will cause the frog to hop rightwards according to the sponsorship rules given above.

Exercise 11

A well-known puzzle goes like this: a snail starts at the bottom of a well 10 metres deep. (Presumably it fell down!) Each night the snail climbs up 3 metres towards the mouth of the well, but each day it slips back again by 2 metres, if it hasn't escaped. How many days will it take the snail to escape from the well?

Write a `while` loop to simulate this problem. You will need two variables, one to keep track of the snail's height and the other to record the number of days in the well. You will also need to check inside the body of the `while` loop to see if the snail is out of the well yet. If so, it will not slip back 2 metres during the next day, because it has escaped.

5.5   Pitfalls with loops

Just as with `if` statements, looping structures have a statement block that may be executed according to the value of some Boolean condition. Some of the comments we made about `if` statements apply to loops as well.

Leaving out the braces

If there is only a single statement within the body of a `for` or `while` loop, then code that leaves out the statement block is legal; that is, you can have a single statement in the body of a loop without braces around it. We advise against this because if you later decide to add extra statements to the loop body it is very easy to forget to insert the necessary braces.

Misplaced semicolons

If you put a semicolon at the end of the looping structure, before the body you want executed, nothing happens in the loop body! For example, if you write

```
while (condition); //semicolon on end!
//anything here is not in the loop!
```

or

```
for (initialise; condition; update);
//semicolon on end!
//anything here is not in the loop!
```

These examples are equivalent to having a loop whose body is a single, empty statement that does nothing.

Endless loops

With loops there is a further danger, which is writing incorrect conditions, or failing to update any loop control variables correctly. This may result in loops operating for an incorrect number of times or executing endlessly!

Particularly with `while` loops you can easily write code that repeats endlessly if you forget to change the variable that the loop condition is testing, or change it in the wrong way. The condition may always be `true` and, if so, the loop will carry on repeating forever. Here is an example:

```
while (kermit.getPosition() != 6 )
{
   kermit.right();
   kermit.right();
}
```

But what will happen if `kermit` sets off from stone 1? Since it is moved two steps right at a time, after the loop body is executed it will be on stone 3, then on stone 5, then 7 and so on. `kermit` will never be on stone 6! The expression (`kermit.getPosition() != 6`) will therefore *always* be true, and the frog will continue moving two steps right forever. This is not what was intended.

If you encounter this situation in the OUWorkspace, you can choose `Reset OUWorkspace` from the `Action` menu to terminate the loop.

On the other hand there can be situations where we actually *require* a program to run forever. In Java a common way of coding this is:

```
while (true)
```

When the test expression `true` is evaluated the result is invariably `true`, so the loop will run endlessly. For instance, an airline reservation system might be intended to run for 24 hours a day without stopping and so use a `true` condition.

Note that the OUWorkspace will not allow you to use the condition `true` *in a loop.*

SAQ 14

What would happen if you set the position of `kermit` to 3 before executing the following expression?

```
while (kermit.getPosition() != 6)
{
   kermit.left();
}
```

Answer

The statement forming the body of the loop would continue to decrease the position of `kermit` (that is, to 2, 1, 0, –1, –2, …). Hence the position would never equal 6, and the Boolean condition would always be `true`. This means that the loop would be executed forever!

Exercise 12

Using pen and paper, write a new method for the `HoverFrog` class with the method signature `moveTo(int)`, which first sets the `height` of the receiver to `0` and then uses a `while` loop to move the receiver to the height specified by the argument, increasing the height in steps of 1.

Note that if you sent the message `moveTo()`, as coded in Exercise 12, with an argument value outside the range `0` to `6` you would find that it never completed. Since it is impossible to move hoverfrogs outside this range, the condition `this.getHeight() != aHeight` will always be `true`. A possible workaround for this problem would be to have the `moveTo()` method check the value of its height argument and only attempt to reach that height if it is within the known range for a hover frog:

```
public void moveTo(int aHeight)
{
    if ((aHeight >= 0) && (aHeight <= 6)) //extra test
    {
        this.setHeight(0);
        while (this.getHeight() != aHeight)
        {
            this.up();
        }
    }
}
```

Activity 17

Open Unit5_Project_1 and the OUWorkspace.

Imagine a customer saving money in their bank account, which we have represented by an instance of the `Account` class referenced by `theAccount`. In the OUWorkspace, create a new instance of `Account` using a statement such as:

```
Account theAccount = new Account();
```

Here is the specification of the code we would like you to write. Do not start coding until you have read the specification *and* the advice that follows.

Suppose that the customer wishes to save 500. You are asked to write code that uses a `while` loop to repeatedly check the balance of `theAccount` to see if 500 has been reached yet. If this target has not yet been achieved, a request dialogue box is to be displayed asking the customer to pay in an amount of their choice. The amount entered (which should be a whole number, not a decimal) is to be added to the balance of `theAccount`.

As soon as the balance of `theAccount` is at least 500, the iteration should cease and the message 'Congratulations, you have met your target!' should be displayed in an alert dialogue box.

We suggest you work as follows. *(If you get stuck look at the module team's solution.)*

1   In the OUWorkspace type an empty block, as follows. Do not include the first line with the `while` in at this point; you will add that in a minute.

```
{
}
```

Now inside this block add code that will prompt the user for the amount of the deposit and add this to the balance of the account (remember to use `Integer.parseInt()` to convert the string returned by the dialogue box into an integer). You should also use `credit()` to increase the balance of `theAccount`.

Once this block of code is written, test it. It should display a dialogue box and then add whatever amount you enter to the balance of `theAccount`. You can check the balance by inspecting `theAccount`.

By doing this test you are making sure that the code in the body of the loop works correctly. You can see that unless this code is right in the first place there is no point in repeating it over and over again in a loop!

If it does not work, then go back and try to correct it.

The beauty of doing things this way is two-fold.

(a) You break the problem into more manageable chunks.

(b) You know before you add the `while` that the account balance is getting updated correctly – so the chances of accidentally writing an endless loop are greatly reduced.

2   Now add the `while` with the appropriate condition in front of the block, to construct the complete `while` statement. Remember the alert dialogue box that was specified; that goes at the end.

Execute your code to verify that it works to specification.

Discussion

1 This is our version of the code that should go inside the block:

```
int inputAmount
    = Integer.parseInt(OUDialog.request("How much do you want to deposit?"));
theAccount.credit(inputAmount);
```

2 This is the whole thing:

```
Account theAccount = new Account();
while (theAccount.getBalance() < 500)
{
    int inputAmount
        = Integer.parseInt(OUDialog.request("How much do you want to deposit?"));
    theAccount.credit(inputAmount);
}
OUDialog.alert("Congratulations, you have met your target!");
```

Your answer may have been different (for example, you might have written the code without a variable to hold the amount input).

6

Summary

After studying this unit you should understand the following ideas.

- Classes can define class (static) methods in addition to instance methods.

- The execution of a class method does not involve a message-send to an object.

- Dialogue boxes are a means of obtaining input from, and displaying output to, a user. In this module dialogue boxes are created using class methods of the OUDialog class.

- The class methods Integer.parseInt() and String.valueOf() can be used to convert a string to a number and vice versa.

- A sequence of statements can be made into a statement block by enclosing it in braces.

- An *if-then* statement is used to determine whether or not to execute a statement block depending on a Boolean condition that evaluates to true or false.

- An *if-then-else* statement is used to select between two alternative statement blocks depending on a Boolean condition. If the condition evaluates to true the *then* statement block is executed, otherwise the else statement block is executed.

- The operators == != < <= > >= are used for comparing values from primitive data types.

- The operator == can also be applied to reference type variables, in which case it tests whether two variables reference the same object. Similarly != tests whether its operands reference different objects. These operators can also be used to compare to the value null, to see whether a reference variable is referencing an object.

- The message equals() can be used to test if two strings contain the same characters in the same order.

- The operators && and || use short-circuit evaluation.

- Java statement blocks can be executed repeatedly using for and while loops as control structures. The number of iterations is controlled by a condition.

Learning outcomes

After studying this unit you should be able to:

- invoke class methods in the class `OUDialog` to create dialogue boxes to display output to the user or to get input from the user;

- write Java statements that convert string values to number values and vice versa;

- use `if` statements to select alternative statement blocks for execution depending on a condition;

- construct more complex conditions using comparison and logical operators;

- use the Java `for` statement to execute a statement block a number of times;

- use the Java `while` statement to execute a statement block a number of times.

Solutions to Exercises

Unit 2

Exercise 1

As `frog1`, you have been asked to change your colour to the same colour as `frog2`. Now, as a human, you can, of course, see the colour of `frog2` by looking at the graphical interface provided. But, as `frog1`, you have no way of 'seeing' such information. The only way that you, as `frog1`, can find out that colour is to send the message `getColour()` to `frog2`. The colour will be provided to you, as `frog1`, as a message answer. Now you are nearly, but not quite, finished.

You, as `frog1`, still need to change your own colour to the colour given by the message answer. So how do you do this? As you know, the only way you can get an object to do anything is to send it a message. This is often the best way to achieve something even when the object in question is you. Hence the answer is to send yourself the message `setColour()` using as the argument the colour you got from `frog2` as a message answer.

Exercise 2

Double-clicking a variable name creates an inspector, which is itself an object. It was the inspector object that sent a message to `myAccount` to find out its state, and then displayed the result. Hence it still holds true that the only way to find out the state of an object is to send it messages.

Exercise 3

For the message-send `myAccount.setNumber("1234")`

- `myAccount` is the receiver,
- `setNumber()` is the message name,
- `"1234"` is the argument,
- `setNumber("1234")` is the message.

For the message-send `myAccount.credit(100)`

- `myAccount` is the receiver,
- `credit()` is the message name,
- `100` is the argument,
- `credit(100)` is the message.

Exercise 4

Just two messages are required. Note that the first message, `debit(400)`, must be sent to yourself in your role as the object `myAccount`.

```
myAccount.debit(400)
herAccount.credit(400)
```

These two messages can be analysed in tabular form as follows.

Receiver	Message	Message answer
myAccount	debit(400)	true
herAccount	credit(400)	none

The following sequence diagram further illustrates how the receiver of a `transfer()` message carries out its responsibility. In Figure 1 the three vertical lines represent the user and the two objects `myAccount` and `herAccount`. Message answers are not shown as they do not play a major role in this case.

Reading from left to right, the user first sends the message `transfer(herAccount, 400)` to `myAccount`. To satisfy this responsibility, `myAccount` first sends the message `debit(400)` to itself. Next, `myAccount` sends the message `credit(400)` to `herAccount`. This is all that `myAccount` has to do to discharge the responsibility it took on by accepting the message `transfer(herAccount, 400)`.

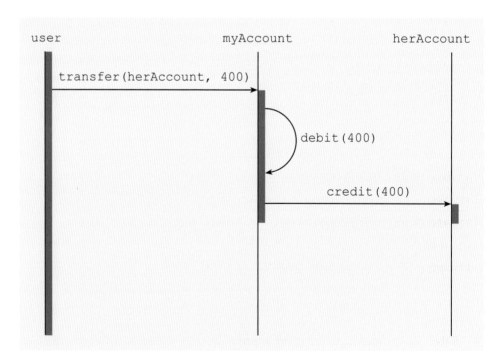

Figure 1 A sequence diagram for the message-send
`myAccount.transfer(herAccount, 400)`

We should emphasise that we are *not* saying that the `transfer()` message is always equivalent to a pair of messages using `debit()` and `credit()`. It will not be equivalent in cases where the receiver of the `transfer()` message has insufficient funds for the transfer. In more detail, what happens when `myAccount.transfer(herAccount, 400)` is executed is that `myAccount` sends itself a `debit(400)` message and only if the message answer is `true` does it then send `herAccount` the message `credit(400)`.

Contrast this with the message `frog1.sameColourAs(frog2)`, where the receiver (`frog1`) *always* sends itself a message using `setColour()` after getting the `colour` of `frog2` by sending `frog2` a `getColour()` message. You will be able to see how this is done at the level of code once you move on to later units, where methods (*Unit 4*) and conditions (*Unit 5*) are introduced.

Exercise 5

This is an open-ended question. Many answers are possible. Some possible answers are noted below. Your answers may be different, but nevertheless correct.

Similarities

- Both involve collaboration between two objects.
- Both involve an object sending a message to itself.
- Both original responsibilities are discharged by the receiver by using exactly two messages.

Differences

- In the frog example, a message answer becomes a message argument.
- In the account example, the message arguments in both of the messages used to discharge the responsibility are taken directly from the message requesting the transfer.

Exercise 6

Receiver	`herAccount`
Message	`transfer(myAccount, 200)`
Message name	`transfer()`
Argument(s)	`myAccount, 200`
Message-send	`herAccount.transfer(myAccount, 200)`

Exercise 7

(a) False. Some messages have no arguments, some have more than one argument.

(b) True.

(c) False. Messages are not objects, and so they are not instances of a class.

Unit 3

Exercise 1

```
char letter;
letter = 'D';
```

Exercise 2

(a) 2

(b) 85

(c) 3

(d) false

(e) true

Exercise 3

(a) The expression (7 + 2) is evaluated first and then multiplied by 3 to give the value 27.

(b) The expression (3 * 7) is evaluated first and then added to 2 to give the value 23.

(c) The expression (5 - 2) is evaluated first to give the value 3. This value is then subtracted from 7 to give a final value for the left-hand operand of 4. Next (8/2) is evaluated to give a value for the right-hand operand as 4. So the operator > has final values of 4 on both the left- and right-hand sides and (4 > 4) evaluates to false.

(d) The expression (3 <= 7) is evaluated first (3 less than or equal to 7) which evaluates to true. Then (7 < 9) is evaluated which also evaluates to true. As the final values of the operands of the && operator both evaluate to true, the result of the operation is also true.

(e) The expression (6 + 4) is evaluated first to give the value 10. Next (6 - 4) is evaluated to give the value 2. The operand / then works with the value 10 on the left-hand side and 2 on the right-hand side to return the value 5.

Exercise 4

This assignment is possible when X is of the same class as Y was declared to be, or is a subclass of Y's declared type.

Unit 4

Exercise 1

```
{
    this.setPosition(this.getPosition() - 1);
}
```

Exercise 2

Here is our solution; your comment will probably differ but should provide the same information.

```
/**
 * Causes the receiver to perform its jump, croak, and
 * right behaviours.
 */
public void catchFly()
```

Exercise 3

```
{
    this.jump();
    this.croak();
    this.right();
}
```

Notice how we were able to write the new method body by reusing existing behaviours of the Frog class. You should look out for opportunities to reuse code in this way.

Exercise 4

Ignoring the statement super(); the next statement initialises the instance variable colour to reference the colour OUColour.GREEN, as noted in Activity 8.

The last statement initialises the instance variable position to the value 1. (We call this a frog's home position.)

Note that direct access to the instance variables was used here, via the expression this, and this is typical of code in a constructor.

So the effect of the Frog constructor is to give a new Frog object an initial state.

Exercise 5

```
/**
 * Return how red the receiver is as an int.
 */
public int redness()
{
    return this.getColour().getRed();
}
```

The expression `this.getColour().getRed()` is evaluated from left to right and could be written using parentheses as `(this.getColour()).getRed();`.

The expression `this.getColour()` evaluates to (returns) a reference to an instance of `OUColour`. The `OUColour` reference is then used to send a `getRed()` message to the referenced colour object. As usual, you use the dot separator between the object reference and the message.

You can write similar code in the OU workspace if you like, as follows:

```
Frog kermit = new Frog();
kermit.getColour().getRed();
```

Inspect `kermit`'s colour in the inspector (double-click on it) to see the value of its red component. Try changing the frog's colour to `OUColour.RED` and check the value of the red component again. You should see that `getRed()` returns the same value as you see in the inspector.

Exercise 6

The method `setPosition()` declares that it expects an argument of type `int`, and `OUColour.RED` is not compatible with the type `int`, so a compilation error message will be displayed in the `Display Pane` of the OUWorkspace. In fact, the error message contains the text:

```
method setPosition in class Frog cannot be applied to
given types;
  required: int
  found: ou.OUColour
  reason: actual argument ou.OUColour cannot be
  converted to int by method invocation conversion
```

The important thing to note is that the method required an `int` (this is the type of the formal argument), but found an `OUColour` (this was the type of the actual argument used), and the two types are not compatible.

In some cases, through automatic type conversion (as discussed in *Unit 3*), it will be possible for an actual argument to be converted to an appropriate type to match the formal argument, but this was not one of those cases.

The words '... `cannot be converted ... by method invocation conversion`' tell us this.

The end result is that the code did not compile, so it was not possible to execute it.

Exercise 7

The message-send `kermit.left()` causes the code of the method `left()`, which is shown below, to be executed.

```
public void left()
{
    this.setPosition(this.getPosition() - 1);
}
```

1   The expression `this.getPosition()` is evaluated first. The value of the `position` instance variable of the receiver (`kermit`) is returned as the message answer. (In this example, the expression `this` will evaluate to the same reference as the one held by `kermit`. You can think of `this` as having been replaced by `kermit`, since `kermit` is the receiver.)

2   The value `1` is then subtracted from the value that has just been returned by `getPosition()` and the resulting value is used as the argument for the message `setPosition()`.

3   The final step is that the method `setPosition()` executes. The code for the method is shown below.

```
public void setPosition(int aPosition)
{
    this.position = aPosition;
    this.update("position");
}
```

When this method is executed, the formal argument `aPosition` is first assigned the value calculated at the end of step 2.

In the body of the method, the value in `aPosition` is assigned to the `position` instance variable of the receiver, which is still `kermit`.

4   Finally an `update()` message using the argument `"position"` is sent to the receiver.

To summarise points 1 to 4: the overall effect of `kermit.left()` is to subtract `1` from the `position` instance variable of the frog object referenced by `kermit` (and to inform the graphical display in the OUWorkspace that the frog has changed position).

Exercise 8

Your method should look something like the following.

```
/**
 * Increases the value of the position of the receiver
 * by the value of the argument step.
 */
public void increasePosition(int step)
{
    this.setPosition(this.getPosition() + step);
}
```

The single statement in the method body of increasePosition() includes the two messages getPosition() and setPosition() as well as the arithmetic operator +.

On receiving the message increasePosition(), the receiver causes the method increasePosition() to execute. The method's formal argument, step, is assigned the message's actual argument and in the expression this.getPosition() + step the value of step is added to the answer from the message getPosition(). The integer resulting from this addition becomes the actual argument for the setPosition() message so that setPosition() causes the instance variable position of the receiver to be incremented by step.

Exercise 9

```
/**
 * Tell a toad to go home and return
 * its ending position.
 */
public int toadGoHome(Toad aToad)
{
    aToad.home();
    return aToad.getPosition();
}
```

We required a formal argument of type Toad, which we called aToad. When this method is executed, aToad will reference the particular object that was used as an argument in the message toadGoHome().

In the body of the method the home() message is sent to aToad to tell that toad to go home.

Finally we returned the toad's ending position using the getPosition() method in the protocol of the Toad class.

Notice that the method doesn't use the keyword `this` at any point because `this` refers to the receiver of the message that caused `toadGoHome()` to execute, and that will be the frog that received the `toadGoHome()` message. It is the toad we want to go home, not the frog.

Exercise 10

Remember that by making a method `public` we allow objects of any class to send the corresponding message. Would it be appropriate for objects of any class to be able to set the value of `flyCount`?

We suggest that in order for the instance variable `flyCount` to be meaningful, it should be incremented only each time `catchFly()` is executed and not altered at any other time. So the only method that *needs* access to `setFlyCount()` (to change the value of `flyCount`) is `catchFly()`.

You could, therefore, make `setFlyCount()` `private` – in fact we have done this in Unit4_Project_4. If you wish to, you may want to check that the method `catchFly()` still works for both `Frog` and `HoverFrog` objects.

What about the getter method `getFlyCount()`? We suggest that it is probably fine for this to remain `public`, as this does not alter the instance variable `flyCount` and it allows the value of `flyCount` to be used by instances of other classes (and in the OUWorkspace). However, if we wanted to keep the fly count information for use by `Frog` objects alone, we could make the getter `private`.

Unit 5

Exercise 1

```
int age = Integer.parseInt(OUDialog.request("Please enter your age"));
```

Exercise 2

```
if (OUDialog.confirm("Click a button"))
{
   OUDialog.alert("Yes clicked");
}
else
{
   OUDialog.alert("No clicked");
}
```

Here is another version, which uses variables to store intermediate results:

```
boolean yesClicked;
String buttonClicked;

yesClicked = OUDialog.confirm("Click a button");
if (yesClicked)
{
   buttonClicked = "Yes clicked";
}
else
{
   buttonClicked = "No clicked";
}
OUDialog.alert(buttonClicked);
```

Exercise 3

```
public void simplyRed()
{
   if (this.getColour().equals(OUColour.RED))
   {
      this.right();
      this.right();
   }
   else
   {
      this.right();
   }
}
```

Remember that the `equals()` method is used to compare objects for equality.

Exercise 4

Our explanation of how the method works is as follows.

If the balance of the receiver is greater than or equal to the amount to be withdrawn, `anAmount`, then the expression `this.getBalance() >= anAmount` evaluates to `true`; otherwise it evaluates to `false`. The debit is carried out only if there are sufficient funds, and the method returns `true` if this is the case and `false` otherwise.

Exercise 5

count	sum	count < 10	sum <= 100	count < 10 && sum <= 100	count < 10 || sum <= 100
10	50	false	true	false	true
20	200	false	false	false	false
4	40	true	true	true	true
9	110	true	false	false	true

Exercise 6

(a) A short solution is this:

```
boolean positive = (number > 0);
boolean zero = (number == 0);
boolean negative = (number < 0);
```

The parentheses on the right-hand sides of these assignments are not required. You may well have used a different approach, such as:

```
boolean positive = false;
boolean zero = false;
boolean negative = false;
if (number > 0)
{
   positive = true;
}
else
{
   if (number == 0)
   {
      zero = true;
   }
   else
   {
      negative = true;
   }
}
```

In this second solution all three variables are first initialised to `false`. When the `if` statement is executed the value `true` is assigned to the appropriate variable.

The first solution we gave is more elegant. Although we realise it may not always be easy to see how to write code that assigns Boolean values directly in this way, we would encourage you to try to do so.

(b) One answer is:

```
boolean dateValid = (month == 1) && ((day >= 1)
                        && (day <= 31));
```

The following, which uses fewer parentheses, also works:

```
boolean dateValid = (month == 1) && (day >= 1)
                        && (day <= 31);
```

Exercise 7

(a) `isMyBirthday = (day == 16) && (month == 11);`

(b) `isEligible = (!isSmoker) && (age >= 25) && (age <= 35);`

Exercise 8

(a)

```
for (int move = 0; move < aNumber; move++)
{
   lulu.left();
}
```

(b)

```
/**
 * Moves the receiver to the left aNumber times.
 */
public void leftBy(int aNumber)
{
   for (int move = 0; move < aNumber; move++)
   {
      this.left();
   }
}
```

Exercise 9

(a) The code needed is:

```
while (sam.getPosition() > 6)
{
   sam.jump(); sam.left();
}
```

Note that if the frog starts at the centre stone, neither loop body is executed.

(b) Simply put the two pieces of code one after another, like this:

```
while (sam.getPosition() < 6)
{
    sam.jump(); sam.right();
}
while (sam.getPosition() > 6)
{
    sam.jump(); sam.left();
}
```

(c) First write the initial comment and method header. Write a pair of braces to receive the body of the method.

```
/**
 * Makes the receiver move to the central stone,
 * hopping one stone at a time.
 * Sets its colour to red on arrival.
 */
public void takeUpYourPosition()
{
}
```

Now copy the code written in (b) into the space between the braces. Go through the code and replace sam everywhere by this, the receiver of the message corresponding to the method we are writing. Add the colour change at the end. Hey presto!

Here is the finished method:

```
/**
 * Makes the receiver move to the central stone,
 * hopping one stone at a time.
 * Sets its colour to red on arrival.
 */
public void takeUpYourPosition()
{
    while(this.getPosition() < 6)
    {
        this.jump(); this.right();
    }
    while (this.getPosition() > 6)
    {
        this.jump(); this.left();
    }
    this.setColour(OUColour.RED);
}
```

Exercise 10

```
while (tanya.getPosition() < 11 && acc.getBalance() < 80)
{
    tanya.jump();
    tanya.right();
    acc.credit(10);
}
```

Exercise 11

```
//call the bottom of the well height 0
int heightReached = 0;
int days = 0;
while (heightReached < 10)
{
    //night - climb up.
    heightReached = heightReached + 3;
    //escaped yet?
    if (heightReached < 10)
    {
        //not escaped, so slip back during day.
        heightReached = heightReached - 2;
    }
    days = days + 1;
}
System.out.println(days);
```

There are alternative solutions; for example, you could have used a height of -10 for the bottom of the well and checked to see if the snail had reached height 0, which is ground level.

Exercise 12

```
/**
 * Sets the height of the receiver to 0 and then
 * moves it to the height specified by the argument,
 * increasing the height in steps of 1 to aHeight.
 */
public void moveTo(int aHeight)
{
    this.setHeight(0);
    while (this.getHeight() != aHeight)
    {
        this.up();
    }
}
```

Glossary

The definitions in this glossary are written assuming that you have completed *Units 1–5*.

access modifier
A keyword that controls the visibility of class members to objects of other classes. The modifiers `private` and `public` are the most frequently used access modifiers.

accessor message
Another name for a *getter message*.

accessor method
Another name for a *getter method*.

actual argument
An actual argument is a value used in a message that is copied to a formal argument for use inside the corresponding method. Actual arguments must be of a compatible type with their corresponding formal arguments.

application domain
See *problem domain*.

argument
See *actual argument* and *formal argument*.

assign
See *assignment*.

assignment
Assignment is the process that results in the variable on the left-hand side of the *assignment operator* receiving a copy of the value on the right-hand side of the assignment operator. The value may be a primitive value or a reference to an object. If the right-hand side of the assignment operator is an expression, it is evaluated first.

assignment operator
An operator (=) used to assign a value to a variable in an assignment statement.

assignment statement
A statement that assigns a particular value to a variable (see *assignment*).

attribute
Some property or characteristic of an object that can be accessed using a getter method. Attributes are generally implemented by instance variables. Examples of such attributes are `position` and `colour` for `Frog` objects, and `balance` and `holder` for `Account` objects.

attribute value
The current value of an attribute, often the same as an instance variable value, but possibly computed using instance variables.

automatic type conversion

Where the Java compiler converts a value of some type to another type without the need for any explicit conversion of type on the part of the programmer. Automatic type conversion occurs in certain contexts, such as in an assignment statement when a compatible type on the right-hand side of the assignment is converted to the type of the variable on the left-hand side of the assignment.

behaviour

A term used to describe the way in which an object behaves in response to the messages in its protocol.

binary digit

Either of the two digits 0 and 1 in the binary number system. Binary digits are used for the internal representation of numbers, characters and instructions. The binary digit is the smallest unit of storage.

binary operator

An operator that has two operands.

bit

An abbreviation of *binary digit*.

block

See *statement block*.

body

Another word for a statement block; for example, the body of a `while` loop is a statement block.

Boolean condition

A Boolean expression used to control the conditional execution of a statement block.

Boolean expression

An expression that evaluates to either `true` or `false`.

Boolean operator

An operator used to combine simple Boolean expressions to form more complex Boolean expressions, which in turn can be combined with other Boolean expressions. They are also known as *logical operators*.

bytecode

Bytecode is the intermediate code produced by the Java compiler. In BlueJ, compilation is done when the `Compile` button is pressed. This will create a bytecode file, for example, `Frog.class`, from the source code file `Frog.java`. The bytecode file is portable because each computer that can run Java programs has a Java Virtual Machine that understands bytecode and converts it into the machine code required for that particular computer. Bytecode is so-called because its instructions are a byte in size.

casting

The prefixing of a value with the name of a type in parentheses in order to convert a copy of that value into a different type. For example, `(int) 99.0` casts the value `99.0` into an `int` value.

class

A class is like a blueprint for the creation of objects and ensures that all its instances have the same instance variables and behave in response to messages in an identical manner.

class header

The line of code in a class definition that provides information about a class such as its name and access modifier. A class header must include the keyword `class`. Example simple usage:

```
public class Marionette.
```

class method

Classes, as well as defining instance methods, can also define class methods. These are methods that can be executed irrespective of whether any instances of the class have been created. A class method is executed as the result of an invocation (not by sending a message to an instance of a class). Class methods in Java are specified by including the `static` keyword in the method header.

comment

A comment is a piece of text in program code to assist human readers in understanding the code, and which the compiler ignores. In Java multi-line comments are delimited by `/*` and `*/`. End-of-line comments begin with two forward slashes (`//`) and continue to the end of the line on which they begin. Javadoc comments are placed between the symbols `/**` and `*/` and must appear immediately before a method, constructor or class header.

comparison operators

A set of operators used for comparing values of expressions, including `==`, `>` and `<`.

compiler

A program that first checks that source code written in a high-level language is syntactically correct. If the check is successful the compiler translates the source code into bytecode or machine code. The Java compiler translates source code into bytecode.

component

See *software component*.

compound expression

An expression built up using other sub-expressions, for example, the following is a compound expression: `(3 + 2) * (6 - 3)`.

concatenation

The joining of two strings. In Java the string concatenation operator is `+` (the plus sign). For example, `"Milton " + "Keynes"` evaluates to `"Milton Keynes"`.

condition

See *Boolean condition*.

conditional selection

The use of `if` statements to select and execute alternative statement blocks based upon the value of a Boolean condition.

constructor
A programming construct, similar to a method, used to initialise a newly created object.

convention
A commonly followed rule for implementing some feature of a software system that is not enforced by the language used, compiler, or platform on which the software is used.

data hiding
Where an object is treated as a black box, with access to the encapsulated data (the instance variables) being possible only through a limited set of methods.

declaration
A statement in which memory is reserved for a variable of some type that is formed by writing the type of the variable followed by some name (its identifier).

delimiter
A character used to mark where some part of a program starts or ends. For example, in Java, the character ; marks the end of a statement and the character { marks the beginning of a statement block.

dialogue box
A type of window with buttons through which users can be given information by a program or provide information to a program on request. In M250, dialogue boxes are provided by class methods of the `OUDialog` class.

direct access (of an instance variable)
Accessing an instance variable using its name, rather than using a getter method.

domain
See *problem domain*.

dynamic compilation
A compilation technique (used by the Java environment) generating real machine code from bytecode (intermediate code). A chunk of bytecode is compiled into machine code just prior to being executed. (This is different from, and faster than, the piecemeal operation of an interpreter.) The real machine code is retained so that subsequent execution of that chunk of bytecode does not require the translation to be repeated.

encapsulation
Encapsulation is the parcelling up of information and behaviour into a reusable component. Objects allow you to *encapsulate* data by incorporating into a single entity (the object) both the data (instance variables) and the behaviour (methods) defined for that data.

end-of-line comment
See *comment*.

escape character
A character used to mark the start of an escape sequence in a string. In Java this is the \ (backslash) character.

escape sequence

A sequence of characters beginning with a special escape character, such as a backslash, that allows subsequent characters to take on a different meaning for the compiler.

evaluate

To find the value of something. We say that expressions have a value or evaluate to some value.

expression

Code that evaluates to a single value. Expressions can be formed from literals, variables, operators and messages.

floating-point type

A type capable of representing a decimal number (to a restricted level of accuracy).

`for` **statement**

A statement allowing a statement block to be repeatedly executed according to the value of a loop control variable (typically of type `int`) and a Boolean condition whose value is dependent on the loop control variable. `for` loops are typically used when a fixed number of iterations is required. See also `while` *loop*.

formal argument

A typed identifier used in a method signature between parentheses to stand for a value (an actual argument) that is passed into the method body by a message.

garbage collection

The process of destroying objects that have become unreachable because they are no longer referenced by variables, in order to reclaim their space in memory. In certain programming languages, including Java, this process is automatic.

getter message

A message that returns as its message answer the value of one of the receiver's attributes. See also *setter message*.

getter method

A method whose purpose is to return the value of one of an object's attributes as its message answer. For example, the method `getPosition()` is a getter method that returns the value of the instance variable `position` held by instances of the `Frog` class.

graphical representation

A visible representation of a software object that, by definition, is invisible.

helper method

A method whose purpose is to do some internal work of an object and which therefore should have `private` access so that it cannot be used by objects of other classes.

high-level language

A language (for example, Java) whose structure reflects the requirements of the problem, rather than the facilities actually provided by the hardware. It enables a software solution to a problem, or a simulation of an aspect of reality, to be expressed in a hardware-independent manner.

identifier

The name given to a *variable*, *method* or *formal argument*.

`if` statement

A programming construct whereby one or more statement blocks are conditionally executed, according to whether a Boolean condition evaluates to `true` or `false`.

inheritance

The process by which a subclass can make use of members of its superclass, such as instance variables and methods, without having had to define them itself.

initialisation

See *object initialisation* and *variable initialisation*.

inspector

An inspector is a tool used in M250 to look at the value held (or object referenced) by a variable declared in the OUWorkspace. In the case of a variable referencing an object an inspector will show the internal state of that object, listing its attributes and their current values.

instance

An object that belongs to a given class is described as an instance of that class.

instance method

Code that is executed as the result of a message being sent to an object.

instance variable

A variable whose identifier and type is common to all the instances of a class, but whose value is specific to each instance. Each instance variable either contains a reference to an object or contains a value of some primitive type. For example, `Frog` objects have the instance variables `colour` and `position`. The values of the instance variables of a particular object represent the state of that object.

integrated development environment (IDE)

A software tool that supports the development, compilation and execution of computer programs. BlueJ is an example of an IDE that supports the development of programs in Java.

intermediate code

See *bytecode*.

interpreter

A program that translates statements (rather than translating a whole program) from a high-level language, such as Java, to a machine code language, and executes the machine code.

invocation

Executing code in a method. Class (`static`) methods are invoked directly on a class, whereas instance methods are invoked by sending messages to objects. Also called *method invocation*.

iteration

Also referred to as repetition. The repeated execution of a statement block for as long as some Boolean condition evaluates to `true`. Examples of programming constructs in Java that support iteration are `while` and `for` loops.

Java edition

A category of Java targeted at a particular platform or domain, such as desktop systems or mobile devices.

Java version

A release of an edition of Java.

Javadoc

A programming tool that comes with Java. The Javadoc tool picks up information from specially formatted comments and other parts of the class code such as the constructor and the method headers. These are all used to create an HTML file, which describes the class in a standard way. This description is aimed not at the Java compiler, but at human readers.

Javadoc comment

See *comment*.

just-in-time compilation

See *dynamic compilation*.

keyword

A Java keyword is a word reserved for use in the language. Keywords cannot be used as variable identifiers.

lazy evaluation

A type of evaluation used in compound Boolean expressions involving the `&&` and `||` operators whereby the second operand is evaluated only when it is necessary to do so in order to determine the truth value of the whole expression.

literal

A textual representation of a primitive value or object. For example, `'x'` is a `char` literal, `4.237` is a double literal and `"hello there!"` is a `String` literal.

local variables

A variable that is declared inside a statement block, such as inside a method body, or `for` statement, or, in the case of M250, the OUWorkspace. The scope of such a variable is restricted to the statement block in which it is declared.

logical operator

An operator whose operands are Boolean values and which evaluates to a Boolean value; for example, the operator `&&`.

loop

In programming, a loop is a sequence of statements that is continually repeated until some Boolean condition is reached.

loop control variable

A variable used to regulate the number of times a loop such as a `for` statement or `while` statement is executed; such a variable is typically declared inside a `for` loop's header or before a `while` loop.

low-level language

A language written for direct programming of a computer's hardware. Each type of computer hardware needs its own low-level language.

member

Instance variables, instance methods, class variables and class methods can all be described as being members of a particular class. Class methods and class variables are explained in *Unit 7*.

message

A message is a request for an object to do something. The only way to make an object do something is to send it a message. For example, the position of a `Frog` object changes when it is sent the message `left()` or `right()`; to obtain information on the value of a `Frog` object's `colour` attribute, you send it the message `getColour()`.

message answer

When a message is sent to an object, then, depending on what the message is, a message answer may be returned. A message answer is a value or an object; it is not a message. Sometimes a message answer is used, sometimes it is ignored. A message answer may be used subsequently as the receiver or argument of another message. Getter messages return the value of an attribute, as with the message `getColour()`, which returns a value such as `OUColour.GREEN`.

message expression

A message-send that evaluates to some value, i.e. the message returns a message answer. We also say that it returns a value.

message name

The name of a message, including the following parentheses, but excluding any arguments. For example, the name of the message `left()` is `left()`, and the name of the message `upBy(6)` is `upBy()`.

message-send

The code that sends a message to an object – for example, `frog1.right()`, which consists of the receiver followed by a full stop and then the message.

method

The code that is invoked by the Java Virtual Machine at run-time when an object receives a message.

method body

That part of a method enclosed by braces that follows the method header. The body of a method is an example of a statement block.

method header

A method header consists of an access modifier (e.g. `public`), a return value (e.g. `int` or `void`) and a name (e.g. `setPosition`) followed by any formal argument names enclosed in parentheses (e.g. `(int aNumber)`). For example, the method header for the method of the class `Frog` whose name is `setPosition()` is `public void setPosition(int aNumber)`.

method invocation

At run-time, selecting and executing a method when an object receives a message. See *invocation*.

method signature

The name of the method together with the parentheses and the types of any arguments. For example, the signature for the `setPosition()` method in the `Frog` class is `setPosition(int)`.

microworld

A computer-based simulation with opportunities for manipulation of content and practice of skills.

modal (dialogue box)

A dialogue box that will not allow you to interact with another part of the program until you have responded to it by clicking one of the buttons presented. All the dialogue boxes provided by the class `OUDialog` are modal dialogue boxes.

model (verb)

To simulate an entity in the problem domain using software.

multi-line comment

See *comment*.

mutator message

Another name for a *setter message*.

mutator method

Another name for a *setter method*.

`new`

A keyword used to create an object – used in conjunction with a constructor.

object

An instance of a class. An object has both state, represented by its attributes, and behaviour, its responses to the set of messages it understands (its protocol). An object models a part of a solution to a software problem.

object diagram

An object diagram represents an object. It shows the class of the object, its state in terms of attribute values, and its protocol.

object initialisation

The state of an object when it is first created depends on its initialisation, a process whereby its instance variables are set to known values. This initialisation is usually carried out by the constructor in the object's class.

object technology
A synonym for *object-oriented technology*.

object-oriented programming.
An approach to programming in which a software problem is modelled using classes of objects that can achieve a solution by sending messages to one another.

object-oriented technology
The technology associated with viewing software as being made up of objects.

operand
An expression provided to an operator. A binary operator such as + has a left-hand operand and a right-hand operand.

operating system (OS)
The software that manages the resources of a computer, including controlling the input and output, allocating system resources, managing storage space, maintaining security and detecting equipment failure.

operator
A symbol used as a function, that is, it has one or more values it operates on and returns a value.

overloading
A method is said to be overloaded when there are other methods, defined in the same class, or inherited from some superclass, with the same name but a different method signature, i.e. different types and/or numbers or arguments.

parameter
A synonym for *argument*.

peripheral device
Any part of the computer that is not part of the essential computer (i.e. the CPU and main memory), such as a mouse, keyboard or flash drive.

postfix operator
An operator that appears after its operand(s).

precedence rules
Rules for determining the order in which various operators are evaluated in a complex expression.

primitive data type
A set of values together with operations that can be performed on them. The primitive data types in Java provide a set of basic building blocks from which all of the more complex types of data can be built. Java's primitive data types include `int`, `char` and `boolean`.

primitive type variable
A variable declared to hold a value of the declared or compatible primitive data type. Less formally we refer to a primitive variable.

primitive value
A value of some primitive type; for example, `true`, `-1.3`, `42`, or `'x'` are all primitive values of different primitive types.

`private`
An access modifier that restricts access to a class member to objects of the class to which it belongs.

private protocol
The part of the protocol of a class or object that is inaccessible from a context outside of the class itself.

problem domain
The collection of real-world entities within the application area that exhibit the behaviours that the required system has to model.

procedural programming
An approach to programming in which a problem is broken down into smaller, simpler procedures, often incorporating global data structures.

program
A software solution to a problem, typically on a small scale (compared to larger application software).

protocol
The set of messages an object understands.

`public`
An access modifier applied to a class member that allows all classes of objects to have access.

public protocol
The part of the protocol of a class or object that is accessible from outside of the class itself.

receiver
The object to which a message is sent.

reference type variable
A variable declared to hold a reference to an object of the declared type (or a compatible type). Less formally we refer to a reference variable.

return type
The type of value returned by a method.

scope
The scope of a variable describes the areas of program code from which the variable may be used. The scope of a local variable is from the point where it is declared to the end of its enclosing statement block.

selection
A technique by which a statement or statement block is executed subject to some Boolean condition. An `if` statement is used to perform selection in Java.

sequence diagram
A diagram that depicts the interactions required between objects to carry out a particular task; this collaboration is shown in the form of messages and message answers.

setter message

A message that sets the value of one of a receiver's attributes. See also *getter message*.

setter method

A method whose purpose is to assign a new value to an instance variable. For example, the method `setPosition()` is a setter method for the instance variable `position` held by instances of the `Frog` class.

short-circuit evaluation

See *lazy evaluation*.

signature

See *method signature*.

software

A general term for all programs that can be run on a desktop computer or another hardware platform, such as a mobile phone.

software component

A piece of software that can be readily combined with other components to construct more complex software.

source code

Program text expressed in a high-level programming language.

state

The values of the attributes of an object constitute its state. The state of an object can vary over time as the values of its attributes change.

statement

A statement represents a single instruction for the compiler to translate into bytecode. In Java most statements end with a semicolon.

statement block

A statement or sequence of statements 'bundled together' for use in a particular context. Any sequence of statements can be turned into a block by enclosing it in braces (curly brackets).

`static`

A Java keyword that defines a variable or method as belonging to a class rather than its instances.

static method

See *class method*.

string

A sequence of characters enclosed in quotation marks; an object of type `String`.

strong typing
A programming language feature that requires variables to have a declared type and enforces rules on the ways in which those types can be used, including what types of values can be assigned to variables of those types and what operators values of those types can be used with. Languages (such as Java) that feature strong typing are said to be strongly typed.

subclass
A subclass is a class defined in terms of an existing class (its superclass). Instances of a subclass inherit attributes and protocol from the superclass, but may define additional attributes and messages. For example, `HoverFrog` is a subclass of `Frog`.

superclass
If `B` is a subclass of `A`, then `A` is the superclass of `B`. In the Java programming language a subclass has only one direct superclass.

syntax
The syntax of a programming language is the set of rules governing the structure of the language, including its valid symbols, expressions and structures.

`this`
An expression used within a method or constructor to reference the object executing the method or constructor.

unary operator
An operator that has just one operand; for example, the minus operator.

variable
A named 'chunk' or block of the computer's memory which can hold either a value of some primitive type or a reference to an object.

variable initialisation
The process of assigning a variable a value for the first time.

variable reference diagram
A diagram showing the relationships between reference variables, objects and their instance variables. Object protocol is not included.

virtual machine (VM)
A layer of software that simulates a computer capable of interpreting bytecode.

`void`
A keyword used in Java to indicate that a method does not return a value.

`while` **statement**
A loop that allows a statement block to be repeatedly executed depending on the value of some Boolean condition. `while` loops are typically used to repeat code when the number of iterations cannot be determined in advance. See also *for loop*.

Index